SHELF DISCOVERY

Teen Classics We Never Stopped Reading

By Lizzie Skurnick

SHELF DISCOVERY:
TEEN CLASSICS WE NEVER STOPPED READING

SHELF DISCOVERY

Teen Classics We Never Stopped Reading

By Lizzie Skurnick

With Contributions By
Meg Cabot, Laura Lippman,
Cecily von Ziegesar, Jennifer Weiner,
Margo Rabb, Tayari Jones,
and Anna Holmes

AVON

An Imprint of HarperCollinsPublishers

HarperCollins books may be purchased for educational, business, or sales promotional use. For information please write: Special Markets Department, HarperCollins Publishers, 10 East 53rd Street, New York, NY 10022.

FIRST AVON PAPERBACK EDITION PUBLISHED 2009.

Designed by Diahann Sturge

Library of Congress Cataloging-in-Publication Data
    Skurnick, Lizzie.
      Shelf discovery: teen classics we never stopped reading / by Lizzie Skurnick; with contributions by Meg Cabot . . . [et al.].—1st ed.
        p.   cm.
      ISBN 978-0-06-175635-1 (acid-free paper) 1. Young adult fiction, American—History and criticism. 2. Teenage girls—Books and reading—United States. 3. Heroines in literature. 4. Girls in literature. 5. Characters and characteristics in literature. I. Cabot, Meg. II. Title.
    PS374.Y57S57 2009
    813.009'92837—dc22

                                                              2009002486

09 10 11 12 13   QV/RRD   10 9 8 7 6 5 4 3 2 1

For my mother,
who told me I was a writer.

Acknowledgments

Thanks first to my mother, who always bought me the books I wanted, let me borrow hers, and rarely let people wandering into the house steal mine. Laura, you are a wonderful friend as well as the strange guidelight of my career. (Shine on, bright and dangerous objcct!) Thanks to the spectacular Casey and Barrie and my singular sister Miriam for libraries, loans, and crucial memories. (*Summer. Of. Fear.*) Thanks to my wonderful agent Kate Lee and my editor Carrie Feron, who always listen to me, and to Tessa Woodward for her hard work. Endless thank-yous to cousin Victoria, who supports me, sponsors me, and takes me to dinner. And last, thanks to all the Fine Lines readers whose stunning insights, polite corrections, and constant commentary have made creating this work both a privilege and a delight.

Contents

Chapter 6
Girls Gone Wild: Runaways, Left Behinds, and Ladies Living off the Fat of the Land

Chapter 7
She Comes by It Supernaturally: Girls Who Are Gifted and Talented

Chapter 9
Old-Fashioned Girls: They Wear Bonnets, Don't They?

Chapter 10
Panty Lines: I Can't Believe They Let Us Read This

Flowers in the Attic

Domestic Arrangements

Foreword

You Are What You Read
By Laura Lippman

A few weeks ago, I found myself playing with the idea that some one had grown thin from carrying a grudge. It was clearly a literary allusion—my mind is an ill-organized attic of such stray and fragmented lines—but I wanted to pin down the source before I, well, stole it. The phrase sounded Shakespearean to my ears; perhaps it was part of Cassius's lean and hungry look? Yet a quick Google search on "grudge" "thin" and, belated inspiration, "stoop-shouldered," yielded nothing. Still I *knew* someone else had said this first. *Thin . . . grudge . . . stoop-shouldered. Thin . . . grudge . . . stoop-shouldered.* I finally conjured an image of a young red-headed man, bent over an experiment in a high school chem lab, and then I had it: My bard was no less than Lenora Mattingly Weber, the author of a young adult series that followed Catherine Cecilia "Beany" Malone of Denver from junior high to the early years of her marriage. The grudge-holder with poor posture was Norbett Rhodes, her first real boyfriend. Aficionados of young adult fiction will not be surprised to learn that Beany's devotion helped to straighten Norbett up and out.

And I was ashamed. Not that I confused Weber with Shakespeare, but that I had to grope for the source. I know Weber's work so well that I used to play Beany trivia with my sister, another fan of the series. Between us, we own all of Weber's books and I re-read them regularly. I also re-read Maud Hart Lovelace, Edward Eager, Noel Streatfeild, Beverly Cleary, Betty MacDonald, Anne Emery, Sally Benson—you get the picture. By day, I pretend to seriousness, reading contemporary novels and classics. But at night, mind soft and eyes bleary, I am likely to crawl into bed with a beloved book from my youth, something I know almost by heart. The familiar words soothe and relax far better than any over-the-counter sleep aid.

Some people are baffled by re-reading in general, the re-reading of children's books in particular. What's the point? Why waste time revisiting the books of childhood when there's so much else to read? With these essays, Lizzie Skurnick has answered those questions far more eloquently than I ever could. It's as if a kindly psychiatrist suddenly appeared with a sheaf of missing brain scans. Do you giggle when someone tells you to "sit here for the present"? You are channeling Ramona Quimby, who turned those simple words into a daunting challenge. Does the mere mention of a mink-trimmed coat make you secretly swoon, even though you are rabidly anti-fur? You have "A Little Princess" complex. Do you long to cover your enemies with leeches? You're having a "Little House" flashback.

Lizzie first started writing these pieces as a regular feature, Fine Lines, for Jezebel.com. In a world measured by page views and comments, Fine Lines was an instant success when it debuted in November 2007. It turned out that the world was teeming with women like me, who had been shaped by the reading lists of their youths. And Lizzie—a poet/critic/journalist who once toiled in the Sweet Valley High sweatshop and wrote *Alias* novelizations—was the perfect guide. (In interest of full disclosure, she also is a dear friend.) Funny, smart, and skeptical, she didn't limit herself to the Newbery-ordained, librarian-blessed works, although there are plenty of those to be found here. No, Lizzie understands that, say, *The Grounding of Group 6*, *Flowers in the Attic*, and *Summer of Fear* affected us as profoundly as *Little Women*. We just needed someone else to say it first.

Don't be fooled, however, by the breezy, comic tone and liberal use of CAPITALS. This is serious stuff, difficult to execute. I know, because I substituted for Lizzie twice, and was surprised by the challenges of the form. (I also was taken aback by the vehemence of adult women who do NOT want to rethink their allegiance to certain childhood classics, and please do not trouble them with anything as picayune as *facts*, thank you very much.) Demon re-reader that I was, I learned from Lizzie not to use beloved texts merely as soothing soporifics, but to root around in them for—sorry, it must be said— subtext. Thus retrained, I found even more to love in writers ranging from Beverly Cleary to Sandra Scoppetone. I also have found a few lacking, even a little dangerous in their agendas, although the sins of YA writers are easily eclipsed by the misogynist worlds of Mario Puzo, Harold Robbins, and even Jacqueline Susann. Which, alas, I also read when very young, but at least had the good sense not to re-read. Except for Susann.

Mary Gordon, in her seminal essay on American literature, "Good Boys and Dead Girls," likened certain novelists to untrustworthy tour guides. They might show us great things of beauty, she wrote, but they also might insist that a fetid swamp is a dazzling waterfall. Even our best writers—William Faulkner, Theodore Dreiser—had their lapses, especially in passages about women. Gordon concluded that we can't change the writers, only ourselves. We must stand firm in the face of their lies and decide if some are worth our loyalty at all. In our voyages back to literary landscapes we loved, Lizzie provides a vital reality check. She will not only tell you that the emperor is wearing no clothes, but might note that he needs a discreet wax job as well.

By the time we realize the profound influences of our youthful reading lists, it's too late to undo them. Yes, if I knew then what I know now, I would have read more seriously and critically during those crucial years that my brain was a big, porous sponge. But I didn't and my hunch is that you, dear reader, didn't either. So stretch out on Dr. Lizzie's couch and find out why you think it would be kind of cozy to be locked up in an attic with your brother. Or learn to dissect the subtle class consciousness of Judy Blume's New Jersey. Ponder the way that Lois Duncan's characters come into unexpected powers, natural and supernatural alike, as they enter adolescence. Contemplate the fact that Ramona Quimby may be a fictional creation on a par with Emma Bovary. We should not be ashamed of re-reading our favorite books, only of re-reading them thoughtlessly.

Laura Lippman

Baltimore, MD
November 2008

Introduction

Getting My Period
By Lizzie Skurnick

I can't remember the book that made me into a reader. (God, how much better would this story be if I could!) All I remember is that first I wasn't a reader, and then, suddenly, I was. (*A Taste of Blackberries*? *The Witch of Blackbird Pond*? The novelization of *The Karate Kid*?) I had been a fretful classroom reciter, following along in a desultory manner while my mother read my brother and me *Lad: A Dog* and *The Hobbit* at bedtime. Now, suddenly, I was the kind of girl who felt true physical pain when asked to put down a book at the dinner table, who asked friends over and ignored them to finish *Island of the Blue Dolphins* for the fifth time. (This created a complex tangle of outrage: my parents wanted me to pay attention to my friends; my friends wanted their parents to stop asking them why they didn't read as much as I did.) But I felt ravenous toward each book, like a vampire desperate to clamp my fangs into the foreign body until it was drained in its entirety, slumping lifeless to the floor. (*A Gift of*

Magic! Sport? Superfudge???) I understood we were eating dinner. But after all, did dinner—and the rest of the people sitting around at the table—really require my undivided attention to be eaten? Eating could happen anytime. This book (*Beat the Turtle Drum? Iggie's House? On the Banks of Plum Creek?*) was happening *now*.

Luckily for my parents, who had tucked away half of their books in my room for storage, I was also, in my tastes, completely indiscriminate. No leather-bound, $100 sets of classics for young readers necessary—if it was my brother's *Tales of the Deep*, completely with a many-armed "kraken" on the cover; if it was my mother's old copy of *The Fixer*; if it was my grandmother's *Nicholas and Alexandra*; it didn't matter. It was on the shelf and I could follow at least 35% of the action? I gave a try. By the age of 10, I had developed a taste for Erma Bombeck, William Least Heat Moon, *The Monkey Wrench Gang*, and Sonia Levitan. I had read Lore Segal's *Her First American*, and understood it, a little—ditto *The Assistant*. I was very fond of *Terms of Endearment* and read it dozens of times. (I still think it's under-appreciated.) There was a Richard Bach stage—I'm not ashamed, although, if you must know, *Jonathan Livingston Seagull* is his weakest work—and, pressed by my mother, a dalliance with *Tess of the D'Urbervilles*, which I'm also not ashamed to say, eluded me completely, especially after I'd seen Nastasia Kinski in the movie.

The conventional wisdom is that a precocious reader is a child in possession of a preternatural grasp of both the facts and features of the adult world. This may well be true of some, but it was not true of me. My reading list didn't grant me access to the particulars of adult life, but to its moody interstices, the dark web of complex feeling that apparently suffused life after grade school. Like a child reciting nursery rhymes, I was consumed with the music of the words, not the circumstances surrounding Little Miss Muffet and her actual tuffet. (Well, can you, even now, confidently define "tuffet"?) Let's take *The Good Earth*. (*The Good Earth*???) I knew nothing about rice farming, mistresses, dynasties, or opium—I couldn't have pointed out China on a *map*—but still, I understood Wang Lung in all his lust, kindness, weakness, and rage, and O-Lan in her sorrow and strength. The former slave who, freed, keeps two pearls hanging between her breasts! Which her husband *takes* from her, for his mistress! Which he thinks of still, miserably, after her death! Gah—who cared where exactly China was!

One would also think such precocity would make one's school reading a snap, but in fact, I took a dim view of all of our reading assignments. After all, after a character like *Terms of Endearment*'s Emma, who soaks triumphantly in the tub after she goads her husband into punching her to exorcise her guilt for having an affair, how worked up was I supposed to get about Curley's wife in *Of Mice and Men*? (Anyone who wanted to read seriously scary Steinbeck, I knew, should try that rape scene in *The Wayward Bus*.) All those animals . . . *The Red Pony*, *The Old Man and the Sea*, *Of Mice and Men*, *Watership Down*—was this English class, or 4-H? I still credit those teachers for my categorical refusal to read *Animal Farm*. Books for middle-graders, young adults, and teens, apparently, were moral stories painted in broad strokes, slim texts in large fonts, small plots with big ideas with some furry friends thrown in to keep it bedtime-ready. The pigs are how power corrupts, the fish is God, the pony is innocence, or death, or something. Forget about seducing a realtor in an empty house while your wussy husband toils away on his thesis, then making sure you get socked in the jaw so you don't feel too bad about it.

Still—had I only had my parents' leftovers and my teachers' assignments to go on, I'm sure I would have survived just fine on a diet of *The Counterlife*, occasionally cut with *The Catcher in the Rye*, getting my girl-growth vitamins from works like *Little Women*. (The discerning reader would definitely throw some Trixie Belden in there for seasoning, too.) But, as most of the bookworms born about a hundred years too late for *An Old-Fashioned Girl* and a few decades, give or take, too early for *Gossip Girl* know, there was another option.

The early 60s to the late 80s was a funny time in YA literature. Before, books for young girls were just that—a marvelous work like *The Secret Garden*, say—or simply wholesome and entertaining works centering around a spunky female character, like Nancy Drew, whose mysteries didn't deal with adolescence for girls so much as star a young adolescent girl. (In this vein, I seem to have some memory of a work called *Candy Striper*, one of a workplace-based series— *Ski Instructor?*—which had a lot of tightly pulled bed corners, water pitchers, and stiff starched caps.) In short—we were in the story, but you'd be hard-pressed to say it was *our* story, any more than *Love Boat* was a moving depiction of life at sea.

But, starting with books like Beverly Cleary's *Fifteen* or Lois Duncan's *When the Bough Breaks*, we started to see an entirely new animal—books that dealt with the lives and dramas of adolescent girls on their own terms, in their own worlds. There was, of course, Judy Blume's whole oeuvre, which took us from getting our periods to losing our virginity, and also Lois Duncan's, which put a supernatural twist on the family dynamic. Writers like Katherine Paterson or Robert Cormier had novels with an adult's level of complexity in the inner worlds of the protagonists, and Paul Zindel's mordant, funny books about the lives of the teens of Bayonne and Staten Island were a window into an unusual world, to say the least. (Well, not that unusual for ME. I was raised in Jersey.) There were Scott O'Dell's historical novels of brave girls left alone on islands, Paula Danziger's laser-like dissection of high schools and camps, Norma Klein's blasé, sexually active NY sophisticates, Madeline L'Engle's three stunning heroines—Meg, Vicky, and Polly (you could write an entire book just on L'Engle's heroines!)—girls in the center of their own adventures.

But it wasn't only that the books were about teens living, quote unquote, today. It was that *these* books treated us as adults, capable of understanding complex issues, of appreciating complicated plots, of getting sophisticated jokes—of being funny and smart, ourselves. These weren't classics tailor-made for Cliffs Notes, and they weren't the adult books deemed mild and metaphorical enough to still be safe for children. (Seriously, though—when *will* administrators start noticing that gay sex scene in *The Great Gatsby*?) Whatever complex strains of melancholy, whatever deep reservoirs of mordant humor, whatever sophisticated irony I had found in the books I plucked off my parents' shelves—here they were in books for teens too, in guises both serious and shallow.

When I first started doing reviews of classic young adult literature for Jezebel's Fine Lines column, I was amused and surprised by the odd, visceral details that returned to me with every work: Pa bringing the girls real white sugar wrapped in brown paper in *Little House in the Big Woods*, Sally J. Freeman having a man-o'-war wrapped around her foot (who even knew what a man-o'-war was?), Claudia choosing macaroni at the Automat in *From the Mixed-Up Files of Mrs. Basil E. Frankweiler*. These strong, charged images that have never left me—they're often even stronger than memories I have of my own life. I simply see the cover, and they come back—like fragments of a dream I can't quite remember, Proust's madeleine, but even stranger, since I've never even tasted one.

Some of the lives I read about were very similar to mine (I could see a lot of my own camp life in *There's a Bat in Bunk Five*, minus the cute boyfriend, natch), and some couldn't be more different (despite my best efforts, I have yet to achieve psychic synergy with a dolphin). But it wasn't about finding myself—or not finding myself—in the circumstances of a girl's life, as much as I might be fascinated by it. It was about seeing myself—and my friends and enemies—in the actual *girl*.

It might have begun with the covers. Most were either snapshots or looked like soft paintings of snapshots (whither, whither the painted cover?), with girls who were neither good-looking nor not-good-looking, girls in glasses, with braces, standing in front of the mirror or smiling happily in the arms of a boy, glowering in front of a locker, standing with bonnet and hoop skirt on a lonely plane, girls with head, feet, and body miraculously intact. There they were, waiting like very large dolls for the tug on the string that would start them moving and speaking.

In them I found a window, a scrying glass, into a complex consciousness, a life like my own, but writ large in all of its messy ambiguity. Nothing, as of yet, had happened to me. But there was the world, and everything happening in it, right in the bright row of spines. It was waiting for me to pull out its next chapter, to turn the book over, to open the first page and read.

Chapter 1

Still Checked Out
YA Heroines We'll Never Return

Mom . . . Can Sally J. Sleep Over?

If you ask me, it is truly a symbol of the great injustice of life as we know it today that the only girl heroine's name that can truly be said to have entered the vernacular is "Pollyanna." (I mean, have you even read *Pollyanna*? I may have made it through about 10 minutes of the movie—that is, if I'm not confusing it with *Heidi*.) It's an even greater injustice that the appellative, of course, is a pejorative. It's not only that, out of the 9,000 exciting heroines you could mention, our language reflects only one. It's that the one character elected for immortality, the linguistic ambassador for young women in the world, is a prating goody-goody who spreads her good cheer with the relentless force of a Caterpillar.

If I had my way, we would add some other options to the mix. What, for example, about being a Ramona? (Inquisitive, inspired, unaccountably amusing.) A Meg? (Stubborn, brainy, admirably self-questioning.) A Claudia! (Exquisitely tasteful, stylized, demanding—

the Michael Kors of the under–12 set.) A Wifey! (Sorry, wrong chapter.) A Margaret! (Still Chapter Two.)

But you get my point. Just as there are certain books we drag with us to bed year after year like a beloved, worn blanket, there are certain heroines we find continually in circulation, like especially festive members of a slumber-party circuit. (Ramona! Are you putting *toothpaste* in the sink *again*?)

And why do they continue to receive our coveted Saturday-night invitations? Well, first, they are marvelously fun to be around. (See above: Toothpaste.) They also teach us new things, like what an Automat is, or what's a charming, off-the-beaten-track place you might want to consider when you next run away. (Here's a hint: Admission is only what you can give!) They remind us of ourselves—Meg's glumness over her awkward stage comes to mind—even as they perform galactic feats of travel that challenge our 8-year-old grasp of algebra. (You had me at "square the square.") They have annoying brothers, worried mothers, and affectionate fathers—even doting *bubehs*—and while they see themselves in the mirror, we can see ourselves in their Margaret O'Brien coronet.

And they challenge us, like the best of friends, in general—not only to be ourselves, but to be more interesting, inspired versions of ourselves, girls unafraid to squeeze toothpaste, sleep on a Louis XIV bed or keep important tabs on all the neighbors, even if they're not afraid they're Hitler. (Yes, Sally—but you didn't think I'd forget Harriet, did you?) In search of their constant company, I'm sure the nerdier among us will be happy to cop to the occasional commemorative costume, poem, or diorama or website. This is nonsense; we owe our best friends a durable immortality. Next stop: Let's get them into the lexicon.

A Wrinkle in Time
By Madeleine L'Engle
1962

The Great Brain

It was a dark and stormy night.

If I had my way, none of us would have to read this essay at all. Instead, we'd join hands, hear a great thunderclap, and be whisked off to a rambling house in the country, where we'd view odd things bubbling in a lab with a stone floor, consume hot cocoa, jam on bread, and liverwurst-and-cream-cheese sandwiches at the kitchen table while swinging our legs, and then sidestep for a moment onto a planet inhabited by gentle gray creatures with dents for eyes. We would be inserted into some mitochondria, battle for the soul of Madoc/Maddox, and eat crayfish with our lesbian kind-of aunt who insisted on calling us our full name (Polyhymnia). We'd hop on a freighter and solve a mystery, then go to boarding school in Switzerland. We would make a brief detour on the Upper West Side and the Cathedral of St. John the Divine by way of Portugal, and be concerned with cell regeneration in starfish. We'd be smacked on the ass by a dolphin. We'd try to answer the questions of God, sex, and the galaxy, and if the principal ever tried to get us to come back to school, why, we'd drag him along with us, too.

God, how much it kills me that we can't do those things! (Especially the dolphin part.) But, as A *Wrinkle in Time*'s opaque Mrs. Who would have us recall, Dante said, *Come t'e picciol fallow amaro morso.* ("What grievous pain a little fault doth give thee!") Alas, it will have to be enough for us to spend a bit of time in the company of a most short-fused, half-cocked, bespectacled literary heroine—Meg Murry, the first heroine to endear herself to the reader by way of atom rearrangement.

Meg Murry—brilliant at math, poor at geography, eschewing rumination for action—is the first in a line of L'Engle heroines who flit across the boundaries of space and time, even more flummoxed by adolescence than they are by being whipsawed across the universe. (Which they are, generally, just to complicate things, in the process of saving.) In *A Wrinkle in Time*, Meg, joined by her neighbor Calvin O'Keefe and her quietly remarkable younger brother Charles Wallace, hopstops her way through a number of only occasionally hospitable galaxies, searching for her father in the shadow of the Dark Thing, the shadow of evil threatening to overtake Earth, and all of creation.

And that's it for those of you who haven't read the book. (Just stab me in the eye; it's less painful.) For the rest, first off, I am embarrassed to say that, swooning over memories of red-tinged Sloppy Joe brains and calm, fragrant creatures with dents for eyes (Aunt Beast!), I had entirely forgotten that, when we first come across the studious, brilliant Murry family, they—and Meg in particular—are in somewhat of a crisis. Their father has been missing for some months, a fact that the town's citizens are only too happy to snidely snicker over. Long scorned for their elite, egghead predilections (Dr. Murry, a physicist, is an advisor to the president) the Murry family is finally in a position where the town can feel superior to *them*.

Meg has responded to this with admirable intemperance— namely, slugging a boy who's just called Charles Wallace her "dumb baby brother." Charles Wallace, of course, is anything but—he's a polymath whose exquisite intellect also makes him highly attuned to those around him, particularly Meg, whose fury Charles Wallace sympathizes with, but only because he knows it hurts Meg more than anyone else. This is more than we can say for Mr. Jenkins, the principal, who will be brought down in a later sequel but is now just being kind of an ass:

> "Meg, don't you think you'd make a better adjustment to life if you faced facts?"
>
> "I do face facts," Meg said. "They're lots easier to face than people, I can tell you."
>
> "Then why don't you face facts about your father?"
>
> "You leave my father out of it!" Meg shouted.
>
> "Stop bellowing," Mr. Jenkins said sharply. "Do you want the entire school to hear you?"
>
> "So what?" Meg demanded. "I'm not ashamed of anything I'm saying. Are you?"

Unfortunately for Meg, as in the case of so many of the outwardly belligerent, a propensity for bellowing hides a healthy case of "I hate myself and would like to die." Still outraged by the boys' insults, alone in the bathroom, Meg tells her cat, "Just be glad you're a kitten and not a monster like me."

The problem for Meg is that, while she's well able to see the truth about others, good or bad, she has a miserable lack of insight into herself. Worse yet, she is surrounded by people who know *exactly* who they are. Her younger twin brothers, alone among the Murrys, manage to fit in: "The twins didn't have any problems. . . . They were strong and fast runners and good at games, and when cracks were made about anybody in the Murry family, they weren't made about Sandy and Dennys." Then there's her mother, who's beautiful, kind, and a brilliant scientist. (Meg snorts at the idea that her mother's looks or accomplishments are ordinary, although her mother, also enragingly modest, assures her they are.)

Youngest brother Charles Wallace may have issues on the vast social stage of their country town ("Thinking I'm a moron gives people something to be smug about"), but only because being brilliant, psychic, and self-assured before reaching five feet never plays well on the playground. (FYI, Charles Wallace is the only preternaturally wise child I've ever been able to stand, in literature. Maybe that's why I can't stand the other ones—they're NOT Charles Wallace.) Even their neighbor Calvin O'Keefe, whom Meg thinks of only as a popular, well-adjusted basketball player, only pretends to be standard-issue—he, like Charles, is both bright and highly attuned to unseen currents.

Meg, on the other hand, is all flyaway hair, braces, irritation, and uncertainty—not ordinary enough to be popular in school, but not quite the extraordinary being Charles Wallace is. (As Charles Wallace puts it, "Meg has it tough. She's not really one thing or the other.") When she hears someone say, "The two boys seem to be nice, regular children, but that unattractive girl and the baby boy certainly aren't all there," there's no more coherent rejoinder than her flying fists.

But Calvin O'Keefe, whose unabashed affection for Meg marks the beginning of her transformation, dispatches this whole line of inquiry neatly. "Oh, for crying out loud," Calvin said, "you're Meg, aren't you? Come on and let's go for a walk."

I'm sorry. I'm going to need to just swoon for one second over Calvin:

> Tall he certainly was, and skinny. His bony wrists stuck out of the sleeves of his blue sweater; his worn corduroy trousers were three inches too short. He had orange hair that needed cutting and the appropriate freckles to go with it. His eyes were an oddly bright blue.

Loving. Him. LOVING HIM. (You Poly and Vicky girls can keep your Zachary Grays and Adam Eddingtons.) Anyway, enough backstory. As you know, Calvin has been brought on the scene at the request of Mrs. Who, one of three mysterious old women who have arrived in order to help the Murrys retrieve their father, who, as the family knows perfectly, has not gone on the lam with a beautiful woman, but has, obviously, been stuck in a high-tech jail on a galaxy far, far away.

But in order to spring him loose, they are going to have to perform the act that landed Professor Murry in trouble in the first place—engaging in a tesseract. (Is the tesseract the object or action? Whatever.) As Mrs. Whatsit unhelpfully explains, "Oh, we don't travel at the speed of anything. . . . We *tesser*. Or you might say, we *wrinkle*."

I'm going to need some visuals on that! (Readers who always skipped over the technical points in L'Engle: you might want to commence skipping now.) Okay, imagine an ant crawling on a piece of string. Now, imagine the string is a skirt! Oh, whatever, just listen to Mrs. Whatsit:

> Swiftly Mrs. Who brought her hands, still holding the skirt, together. "Now, you see," Mrs. Whatsit said. "He would be there, without that long trip. That is how we travel."

Exactly! Sort of. I have always been grateful to L'Engle for the next section, which helped me pass fourth-grade geometry. Charles Wallace begins to quiz Meg on dimensions, taking her through the first dimension (a line), the second (a square), the third (a three-dimensional square, in which we live), then what's the fourth:

> "Well, I guess if you want to put it into mathematical terms you'd square the square. But you can't take a pencil and draw it the way you can the first three. I know it's got something to do with Einstein and time. I guess maybe you can call the fourth dimension Time."

That great *whooshing* sound you hear is the noise of 10 million readers deciding to just go ahead and be English majors. In any case, having tesseracted, fourth-dimension style, Meg's father is not simply lost—he is imprisoned by the great brain of the Dark Thing, a shadow stretching over the entire universe that is also starting to creep over Earth, cloaking it in evil and despair.

In order to release him, the children are going to have to travel first to a lovely planet where Aunt Beast, part of a lovely race of eyeless, psychic, agreeably beast-y creatures, serves as their protector, then to Camazotz, where Dr. Murry is being held, a planet where the forces of evil have coalesced into a dreadful reign of conformity:

> Then the doors of all the houses opened simultaneously, and out came women like a row of paper dolls. The print of their dresses was different, but they all gave the appearance of being the same. Each woman stood on the steps of her house. Each clapped. Each child with the ball caught the ball. Each child with the skipping rope folded the rope. Each child turned and walked into the house. The doors clicked shut behind them.

Just as in Meg's small hometown, conformity alone is the face of evil, and *knowledge*—individual, eccentric knowledge—is a force of good.

This is a grand theme in L'Engle overall, but we see it in full force in the first few chapters of the book, where the reader is introduced, in no particular order, to $E=mc^2$, megaparsecs, Peru, Boswell's *Life of Johnson*, Euripides, Delille, and a host of other terms with which your presumably middle-grade reader is rarely familiar. Even as the children watch the Dark Thing encircle their planet, they are comforted when Mrs. Whatsit tells them that there have been heroes fighting against it throughout history—not swashbucklers with laser guns, but saviors such as Leonardo da Vinci, Michelangelo, Shakespeare, Pasteur, and Madame Curie and Einstein, and, for the purists among you, Jesus.

But, if the saviors of Creation are creative thinkers, it's no surprise that the forces of evil are embodied in a large, red-tinged *brain*, IT—one whose droning repetition seeks to draw all comers into its Maoist haze. Meg resists its overwhelming pull first by reciting the periodic table, then the square roots of odd numbers (get it—odd!), and finally, when Charles Wallace is pulled into the great brain, appropriately enough, the Declaration of Independence:

> "We hold these truths to be self-evident!" she shouted, "that all men are created equal, that they are endowed by their creator with certain unalienable rights, that among these are life, liberty, and the pursuit of happiness."
>
> As she cried out the words she felt a mind moving in on her own, felt IT seizing, squeezing her brain. Then she realized that Charles Wallace was speaking, or being spoken through by IT.
>
> "But that's exactly what we have on Camazotz. Complete equality. Everybody exactly alike."
>
> For a moment her brain reeled with confusion. Then came a moment of blazing truth. "No!" she cried triumphantly. "*Like* and *equal* are not the same thing at all!"

How does Meg defeat evil? She, like the great thinkers before her, has an *insight*. That's not her only tool against the big, throbbling blob of jelly, though. Among her peers, Meg also has one matchless strength:

> "My faults!" Meg cried.
> "Your faults."

"But I'm always trying to get rid of my faults!"

What were her greatest faults? Anger, impatience, stubbornness. Yes, it was to her faults that she turned to save herself now.

L'Engle has an interesting twist on the nature of knowledge, which is the weapon of choice in *A Wrinkle in Time*. Charles Wallace thinks his brain power alone can stand against IT, but he's prideful—and easily overpowered. Calvin, who's previously teased Meg for her spotty grasp of basics, is also put out of commission by the mighty IT early. Ensnaring Dr. Murry, who, I might remind you, advises the *president,* is like shooting fish in a barrel. Only Meg, who has been castigated by her math teachers for doing problems *her* way, not theirs; who has no idea where Peru is or who wrote Boswell's *Life of Johnson*, who clings stubbornly to her own vast, spotty store of knowledge, can stand up to IT. Originality, it seems, is its own form of stubbornness— and it's not enough to *know.* One must *think*—for oneself.

And because Meg is able to think, she realizes what she can do that IT can't do—and how she can free Charles Wallace, Calvin, and her father:

> Her own Charles Wallace, the child for whom she had come back to Camazotz, to IT, the baby who was so much more than she was, and who was yet so utterly vulnerable.
>
> She could love Charles Wallace.
>
> Charles. Charles, I love you. My baby brother who always takes care of me. Come back to me, Charles Wallace, come away from IT, come back, come home. I love you, Charles. Oh, Charles Wallace, I love you.

Tears were streaming down her cheeks, but she was unaware of them.

Now she was even able to look at him, at this animated thing that was not her own Charles Wallace at all. She was able to look and love.

I love you. Charles Wallace, you are my darling and my dear and the light of my life and the treasure of my heart. I love you. I love you, I love you.

. . . Then suddenly he was running, pelting, he was in her arms. He was shrieking with sobs. "Meg! Meg! Meg!"

Jeez, now I'M crying. But make no mistake, it's not Meg's love that saves Charles Wallace—it's Meg's bullheadedness, her insistence on doing things her own way, her belief that she is probably right. Meg isn't simply a cute narrative depiction of a spunky girl. She's indubitably, prepubescently *bullheaded*. This fault, because it allows Meg to stand behind her leaps of insight and her outsized love, in *A Wrinkle in Time*, amounts to no less than a kind of courage. Why, Meg, who laments in everyone else's secure self-knowledge, turns out to actually have faith in herself—and it's the kind of faith that can vanquish evil. Reading this book for the 18th time in my pajamas on a Sunday morning, I knew it was unlikely I'd be called upon to save the universe anytime soon. But—despite my glasses, temper, flyaway hair, and constant sense of outrage at our benighted world—it was nice to know I'd still have a shot.

From the Mixed-Up Files of Mrs. Basil E. Frankweiler

By E. L. Konigsburg
1967

Artful Dodgers

Claudia knew that she could never pull off the old-fashioned kind of running away. That is, running away in the heat of anger with a knapsack on her back.

I miss New York. Not the New York currently hugging the edge of the Atlantic. But the New York of my youth, where a trip to the Museum of Natural History to stand agape at a white whale truly was a magical day (one before *The Squid*

& *The Whale* associated it forever with that era's less magical divorce rate); a New York before nannies got groped; a New York before private-school girls intertwined lustily on beds in some benighted plan to rule the school. It was a quieter, less overpopulated, pre-Reagan New York, one that had room for a notepad-toting minor to spy unaccompanied on people through dumbwaiters; a boy to wander Chinatown having adventures with a cricket; teenagers to contend with a genie in a mystery at the Cathedral of St. John the Divine. It's a New York that keeps adults perpetually at shoulder level, briefcases and purses jostling, while the children, front and center in the frame, get up to whatever children get up to.

The children in question are one Claudia and Jamie Kincaid, Greenwich-residing, grammar-school-aged siblings. In *From the Mixed-Up Files of Mrs. Basil E. Frankweiler,* as befits such an august title, these children's getting-up-to entails one very long, unauthorized stay in the Metropolitan Museum of Art, where they come upon a statue of an angel that may or may not have been carved by Michelangelo—which, as they say, changes everything.

Claudia Kincaid, architect of the above scheme, is a child of her own mind in all the best ways, quite unlike the Mini-Me adults passing for precocious nowadays. (When, when will we be free of the preternaturally wise, sophisticated child who wryly keeps adults in line? *Gilmore Girls* notwithstanding, I hate that child.) Forgoing hot-fudge sundaes for weeks to finance the venture, Claudia's choice of hideout is the very reflection of how very particular she is:

> She didn't like discomfort; even picnics were untidy and inconvenient: all those insects and the sun melting the icing on the cupcakes. Therefore, she

decided that her leaving home would not be just running from somewhere but would be running to somewhere. To a large place, a comfortable place, an indoor place, and preferably a beautiful place. And that's why she decided upon the Metropolitan Museum of Art in New York City.

Her choice of her brother Jamie, a third-grader, is equally practical: he is a total tightwad and in possession of a transistor radio. Claudia's practicality, which also includes poking into the family garbage for such useful bits as a train pass with one free ride and scouring the AAA tour guide, extends so far she almost forgets why she is running away in the first place:

> . . . But not entirely. Claudia knew that it had a lot to do with injustice. She was the oldest child and the only girl and was subject to a lot of injustice. Perhaps it was because she had to both empty the dishwasher and set the table on the same night while her brothers got out of everything. And, perhaps, there was another reason more clear to me than to Claudia. A reason that had to do with the sameness of each and every week. She was bored with simply being straight-A's Claudia Kincaid. She was tired of arguing about whose turn it was to choose the Sunday night seven-thirty television show, of injustice, and of the monotony of everything.

Our narrative tour guide is, in fact, Mrs. Basil E. Frankweiler—as the novel in its entirety takes shape in the form of a letter to her lawyer, Saxonberg, also, as it happens, Claudia and Jamie's grandfather. In the grand epistolary-meets-omniscient tradition, Frankweiler is in possession of more knowledge than Claudia, both about the Angel she's sold to the museum, and about Claudia herself.

But more about that later! First, the Met.

It will be generally admitted that the scenes depicting Claudia and Jamie's initial stay at the Met are the most sublime realizations to have ever penetrated the shelves of man. After filling their violin and trumpet cases with clothes, hiding out on the back of their school bus, then sneaking off to ("How can you sneak *off to*?" Claudia asks her brother impatiently) catch the 10:42 to Grand Central, they spend the day at the museum choosing the antique bed upon which to sleep; then they hide in the bathrooms until all the staff have left:

> . . . She lay there in the great quiet of the museum next to the warm quiet of her brother and allowed the soft stillness to settle around them: a comforter of quiet. The silence seeped from their heads to their soles and into their souls. They stretched out and relaxed. Instead of oxygen and stress, Claudia thought now of hushed and quiet words: glide, fur, banana, peace. Even the footsteps of the night watchman added only an accented quarter-note to the silence that had become a hum, a lullaby.

And! The! Automat! And! Bathing! In! The! Fountain! And! Brushing! Your! Teeth! In! The! Quiet! And! Washing! Your! Clothes! Until! They're! Gray! Chock! Full! O! Nuts! Gah!!!!! I could go on for 1,200 words just about the meaning of Claudia's eventually choosing macaroni, baked beans, and coffee over "breakfast food" for breakfast at the Automat, paying with coins picked up off the bottom of the now-gone fountain—

thereby combining two fantasies for which I would still happily give up a weekend at Canyon Ranch.

However, I have to get around to the Angel, the statue of dubious provenance that becomes, in its mysterious beauty, the after-the-fact reason Claudia cites for her escape in the first place. Frankweiler explains why in one of many asides (this one railing) to Saxonberg:

> Are photo albums of your grandchildren the only pictures you look at? Are you altogether uncon- scious of the magic of the name of Michelangelo? I truly believe that his name has magic even now; the best kind of magic, because it comes from true great- ness. Claudia sensed it again as she stood in line. The mystery only intrigued her: the magic trapped her.

Because, as Claudia begins to realize, she has come to the museum not only because she is sick of being the old Claudia, but because she wants—needs!—to return to Greenwich a *dif- ferent* Claudia, a Claudia who has bigger concerns than keeping her whites and colors separated, brushing her teeth, and correct- ing her brother's grammar: "An answer to running away, and to going home again, lay in Angel," she thinks, then attempts to convince Jamie of their need to stay:

> . . . "The statue just gave me a chance . . . almost gave me a chance. We need to make more of a dis- covery."
> "So do the people of the museum. What more of a discovery do you think that you, Claudia Kin- caid, girl runaway, can make? A tape recording of Michelangelo saying, 'I did it?' Well, I'll clue you

in. They didn't have tape recorders 470 years ago."

"I know that. But if we make a real discovery, I'll know how to go back to Greenwich."

"You take the New Haven, silly. Same way we go here." Jamie was losing patience.

"That's not what I mean. I want to know how to go back to Greenwich different."

Jamie shook his head. "If you want to go different, you can take the subway to 125th Street and then take the train."

"I didn't say *differently*, I said *different*. I want to go back different."

. . . "Claudia, I'll tell you one thing you can do different . . ."

"Differently," Claudia interrupted.

"Oh, boloney, Claude. That's exactly it. You can stop ending every single discussion with an argument about grammar."

"I'll try," Claudia said quietly.

Readers, did you catch that "boloney"? (Yes, that's the way it was spelled!) Thankfully, "Bologna" is spelled correctly in the filing system of Frankweiler, where she's hidden the proof that the statue is indeed Michelangelo's—proof that she gives to Claudia, contingent upon her always keeping the secret of the Angel.

It's mildly absurd to place the idea of baptism into a book for children, but I'll use it as a bold excuse for pointing out that, upon her arrival in Mrs. Frankweiler's home, Claudia proceeds to take a bath in her ornate black marble tub, revealing yet again her penchant for the luxurious and surprising:

. . . Claudia's excitement flowed not bubbled. I could see that she was a little surprised. She had known that Angel would have the answer, but she had expected it to be a loud bang, not a quiet soaking in. Of course secrets make a difference. That's why planning the runaway had been such fun; it was a secret. And hiding in the museum had been a secret. But they weren't permanent; they had to come to an end. Angel wouldn't. She could carry the secret of Angel inside her for twenty years just as I had. Now she wouldn't have to be a heroine when she returned home . . . except to herself. And now she knew something about secrets that she hadn't known before.

I'm sorry—I'm going to have to add that unauthorized bath in an ornate claw-foot tub to the experiences I'd choose over a hot-stone rub. Because one of the many great things about Claudia's character is how she takes a perceived girly negative—being picky—and turns it into what we see in our adulthood is a virtue: an appreciation for the sublime, for the very best in everything, and a respect for the mystery inherent in all things beautiful. While, doubtless, a grown-up Claudia would have conceived of a longing for Christian Louboutins, she's a wonderful reminder, in our post-irony era, about how at its very heart, a love for the very best isn't necessarily pretentious, consumerist, or craven.

And in our post-irony age, Claudia's experience is also a wonderful reminder of how children, though they may be precocious, certainly aren't born knowing everything; and that when they do learn about life, it's not always something awful they discover. (Say, the nature of divorce—one so horrible you'd have to find a metaphor for it in the Museum of Natural History.) When our class used to go for our twice-yearly trip to the Museum of Natural History and the Metropolitan Museum of Art, the sense of splendor and possibility found in the quiet displays of histories and treasures was, to my young heart, almost unbearable. (It is still.) Rereading *Mixed-Up Files*, I couldn't help but cheer for the fact that Claudia's childhood isn't some walled-off tomb, and it doesn't end unceremoniously when it's tragically shattered by some awful experience. Indeed, the vision of childhood in *Mixed-Up Files* is that of a museum at night, filled with secrets to uncover, and the freedom to find them unencumbered and alone. When Claudia finds the answer to just one of those secrets, she's not only "different"— she's become, like the Angel, a singular entity with her own history, her own mystery. And when she leaves the museum, she's also leaving her childhood, like some abandoned violin case filled with gray clothes, triumphantly behind.

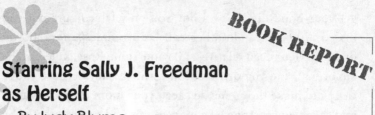

Starring Sally J. Freedman as Herself

By Judy Blume

1977

Florida Orange Jews

"Can I have another jelly sandwich?" Sally asked her grandmother, Ma Fanny.

Okay, everyone, quick poll: raise your hand if, after V-day, you want your brother to get sick with nephritis so your dentist father can send you, your mom, and your *bubeh* from New Jersey down to Miami for the winter to help him get better, and you can go to school in a trailer and bike around being afraid that your neighbor, Mr. Zavodsky, is Hitler while you get your braid tugged by a boy you only later figure out you like, and your grandmother calls you *mumeshana* and you dream of your dead relatives, Lila and Tante Rose, killed in the Holocaust, and you drink cocoa with whiskey because you're trying to make the creme de cacao your mom drank in Cuba, and then you get stung by a man-o'-war and complimented by said brother on being braver than he thought and catch Virus X and eat two bowls of chicken-with-rice soup, then try on some toe shoes.

Blume's wondrous near autobiography is the story of one Sally J. Freedman, whose father (dubbed by our heroine "Doey-bird") moves the rest of the family from New Jersey to Miami after the end of the war for one year when Douglas, the older son, needs to recover from a bout of nephritis. Thus ensconced in the Sun Belt with her mother and Ma Fanny, Sally embarks on a series of adventures that only another girl could understand are truly thus, including getting nits, having a friend fall on a bike, getting stung by a man-o'-war, washing diamonds with a hotsie-totsie in the Ladies Room, having her neighbor get knocked up by a goy, and discovering her neighbor is Hitler.

You might note from that last that Sally is also given to vast flights of fancy, which, given the times, wend to spy missions in Europe and captures of Hitler (who has, in fact, killed her cousin Lila and Tante Rose, her grandmother's sister, both gassed in Auschwitz). A typical, triumphant narrative:

> *Sally F. Meets Adolf H.*
> It is during the war and Sally is caught by Hitler
> in a round-up of Jewish people in Union County,
> New Jersey . . . He orders the Gestapo to bring her
> to his private office. Tell me, you little swine, Hitler

hisses at her. Tell me what you know and I'll cut off your hair.

. . . Sally shakes her head. I'll never tell you anything . . . never!

So Hitler goes to his desk and gets his knife and he slowly slashes each of her fingers. She watches as her blood drips onto his rug, covering the huge swastika in the middle.

Look what you've done, you Jew bastard, Hitler cries hysterically. You've ruined my rug!

Ha ha, Sally says. Ha ha ha on you, Adolf. . . . And then she passes out.

When she comes to, Hitler is asleep and snoring with his head down on the desk. Sally crawls out of his office, then dashes down the hall to the secret passageway of the underground. She gives them valuable information leading to the capture of Adolf Hitler and the end of the war.

Sally's approximations of what is actually going on in her family and the world around her run at roughly the same level of accuracy. After espying the "Love and Other Indoor Sports" sign-off on her babysitter's stationery, she knows it is a fine way to take leave, but not exactly what kind of letter it's for. She knows her father has called her mother's lavender-and-black bathroom a bordello, but not why praising someone else's bathroom as same might not yield a joyous response. She is hazy not only on the concept of Latin Lovers but on the question of whether there is a country, in fact, called "Latin." And while it's possible that Mr. Zavodsky, her next-door neighbor, might in fact be Adolf Hitler, she's not quite old enough to give up on the possibility.

It seems impossible to write about *Starring Sally J.* using a straightforward plot synopsis, because, like some glorious dish of kreplach, its mighty stuffing of detail exists in a symbiotic relationship with the soup of the plot. Instead, you hear about curtains being run up on sewing machines and you can't help but be transported right into Sally's apartment, with its Murphy bed and courtyard fountain with goldfish, and in the kitchen you sit, being spoken to by Ma Fanny entirely in Yiddish, reverse-syntax English and ellipses. There's your grade-school teacher Miss Swetnick over there, with her heart-shaped glasses and chipped tooth, and there's your sundae at Herschel's, with just a little cherry juice on top. That's the ring on your four-party phone (one long ring, followed by two short), and there you are in the grade-school bathroom pulling down your Esther Williams-esque coronet to make Margaret O'Brien braids and stuffing your white socks into the garbage to look more like the girls in Florida and not the ones in NJ. (And hoping God will forgive you this one time, when the starving children in Europe could probably—right?—use those white socks.)

But I wonder if another reason we swoon for Sally J. is that, as readers, we were very much at the same level of detail comprehension—not only in our real-world lives, but in our reading of the book itself. After all, not only did I also have no idea what an "addition" might mean to a family or what "creme de cacao" was (though I too tried to approximate it with Hershey's and whiskey) I was also ignorant of so many of the ready references of Sally J.'s world that she understood perfectly well: Jolly Roger, dog tags, "Swells," Esther Williams, Margaret O'Brien, open-sided pinafores, Admiral Halsey. (To be perfectly honest, I still have no idea who Admiral Halsey is.) Given Ma Fanny's frequent lapses into Yiddish, I can only assume that goyishe readers must have been even more *ferblondzet*!

Of course, by twenty years later or so I had realized who Esther Williams was. (I confess it was a recent reread that allowed me to realize that Ma Fanny borrowed Sally's English book to practice English and THAT'S why it was in the pantry). But even as an eight-year-old, I understood that Sally realizing Peter Hornstein liked her, or that she was more adventurous than her mother, was a great leap forward for my beloved character. And though, at age 8, I may not have known yet who Eva Braun was, or where Union Woods could be found, I knew when Sally made peace with the fact that, probably, Hitler was not running amok in them, I too could set aside this childish dream.

Still longing for a finished basement, though!

Harriet the Spy
By Louise Fitzhugh
1964

Diary Land
By Anna Holmes

That night at dinner everything was going along as usual, that is, Mr. And Mrs. Welsch were having an interminable, rambling conversation about nothing in particular while Harriet watched it all like a tennis match, when suddenly Harriet leaped to her feet as though she had just remembered, and screamed, "I'll be damned if I'll go to dancing school."

It's hard for me to imagine that anyone who loved—or still loves—Louise Fitzhugh's 1964 classic *Harriet the Spy* does not love that passage, for it perfectly encapsulates everything I love about young Harriet, namely her powers of observation, her tendency toward impulsiveness, her wealth of opinion, and her unapologetic outspokenness.

Although she's been compared to the most famous female sleuth of children's literature, Nancy Drew, Harriet, in fact, has long reminded me of another precocious young tomboy of classic literature who goes through a loss of innocence: Scout Finch. Like Scout, she is scrappy, primarily male-identified (Harriet's father seems to play a more influential role in her life than her mother, who is neither career woman nor home-maker), obsessed with spying on her neighbors (birdcage designer Harrison Withers is Harriet's Boo Radley), and, is among other things, the recipient of a role as a foodstuff in a school holiday pageant (Harriet is an onion to Scout's ham).

I've often wondered if Ms. Fitzhugh—like Harper Lee, a Southern "belle" transplanted to New York—took inspiration from her contemporary's book, which was published just four years prior. For what it's worth, the illustrations provided by Ms. Fitzhugh imply that, like Ms. Lee's Scout, Harriet is a brunett with a utilitarian, androgynous hairstyle, and a love of denim and sneakers.

In short, Harriet is no young lady.

Eleven-year-old Harriet Welsch—excuse me, Harriet *M.* Welsch—is a precocious, bossy, privileged 6th grader on Manhattan's Upper East Side with a beloved, strangely named nanny, Ole Golly, a preference for sneakers over Mary Janes, an appetite for both the culinary (cake, and tomato sandwiches), and an after-school "spy route" that takes her from the city's leisure class in her upper East 80s street to the working poor who live just a few blocks away.

As the story begins, Ole Golly (can someone explain to me exactly how "Ole" sounds —*IS IT "OLD" OR RHYMES-WITH-OLAY?*) takes Harriet and her best friend, Sport (In Fitzhugh's world, boys and girls on the cusp of puberty maintain close friendships without a hint of sexual tension) on a long subway ride to Far Rockaway, where the two children meet Golly's obese simpleton of a mother—and, to borrow a phrase from Jacob Riis, catch a glimpse of how the other half lives.

The trip, although short, is the first clue as to the dichotomy between Harriet's privileged, cloistered existence—Manhattan townhouse, full-time cook, exclusive all-girls private school—and the ugly reality of the world outside, where street urchins beg for handouts from the stockroom boys at local grocery stores. Harriet's privilege does not mean that she is unprepared to face the many New Yorks in which she lives. As the book's title suggests, she is a young girl of limitless curiosity. But it is a curiosity tempered by a distinct lack of empathy. Before she even gets home to scribble her thoughts in a notebook, she describes Ole Golly's mother as "fat," "stupid," and resembling a "balloon." She continues:

I THINK THAT LOOKING AT MRS. GOLLY MUST MAKE OLE GOLLY SAD. MY MOTHER ISN'T AS SMART AS OLE GOLLY BUT SHE'S NOT AS DUMB AS MRS. GOLLY. I WOULDN'T LIKE TO HAVE A DUMB MOTHER. IT MUST MAKE YOU FEEL VERY UNPOPULAR. I THINK I WOULD LIKE TO WRITE A STORY ABOUT MRS. GOLLY GETTING RUN OVER BY A TRUCK EXCEPT SHE'S SO FAT I WONDER

WHAT WOULD HAPPEN TO THE TRUCK. I
HAD BETTER CHECK ON THAT.

As comedy, Harriet's scribblings in her notebook—at just
11 years of age she has already filled a baker's dozen of them
with her observations—are pure gold: brash, honest, and
often deliciously nasty and judgmental. Another gem about
her school's dean:

MISS WHITEHEAD'S FEET LOOK LARGER
THIS YEAR. MISS WHITEHEAD HAS BUCK
TEETH, THIN HAIR, FEET LIKE SKIS, AND
A VERY LONG HANGING STOMACH. OLE
GOLLY SAYS DESCRIPTION IS GOOD FOR
THE SOUL AND CLEARS THE BRAIN LIKE A
LAXATIVE. THAT SHOULD TAKE CARE OF
MISS WHITEHEAD.

Unlike most girls' scribblings, Harriet's notebook is less
diary than dossier, more concerned with the exterior than the
interior. It is also what, a little over halfway through the book,
gets her in a heap of trouble. When her group of friends—
including Robert Oppenheimer-in-training Janie Gibbs—get
ahold of her notebook, they turn on her, having discovered
that even they are not immune to Harriet's critical eye.

Up to this point, Harriet has lived her life confidently and
unapologetically: there is no sense that she feels any sort of dis-
comfort over the fact that she is an opinionated soap-adverse
tomboy who, as she explains to Janie's flummoxed, harried
mother Mrs. Gibbs, moves "fast." (As fans of the book will remember, Harriet has a tendency to run pell-mell into her family's cook.)

Narratively speaking, a crisis is understandable—especially as the beloved Ole Golly has moved onto Montreal and marriage. But it is also lamentable, because part of what makes *Harriet The Spy* such an amazing, groundbreaking book is that it presents a young female protagonist who is *damned if she will conform.*

After the notebook scandal, Harriet suffers a crisis of confidence and social banishment for which I am not sure I ever forgave Ms. Fitzhugh. Certainly, growing up can be a painful reality, both in life and in books, but does Harriet have to suffer the consequences of her actions so quickly and so harshly?

In the end, of course, Harriet is both able to hold onto her sense of self ("I LOVE MYSELF" she writes in her notebook) while adding a new skill to her already formidable repertoire: empathy. And in doing so, she becomes not only one of the most well-rounded female characters in the book, but one of the most well-rounded female characters in children's literature—less interested in dance classes, attracting boys or playing bridge or mahjong than sating her own appetite for curiosity about the world around her.

But back to that notebook, the driving engine of Fitzhugh's plot. It is to Fitzhugh's credit that her young charge does not give it up altogether, even after it has brought her to her lowest point. Three pages before the book's conclusion Harriet is still practicing, still observing, still writing . . . albeit with a more compassionate, inward-directed eye. Perhaps the end of a dossier and the beginning of a diary? Maybe it's the end of spying and the beginning of writing:

I HAVE THOUGHT A LOT ABOUT BEING THINGS SINCE TRYING TO BE AN ONION. I HAVE TRIED TO BE A BENCH IN THE PARK,

AN OLD SWEATER, A CAT, AND MY MUG IN
THE BATHROOM. I THINK I DID THE MUG
BEST BECAUSE WHEN I WAS LOOKING AT IT
I FELT IT LOOKING BACK AT ME AND I FELT
LIKE WE WERE TWO MUGS LOOKING AT
EACH OTHER. I WONDER IF GRASS TALKS.

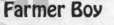

Farmer Boy
By Laura Ingalls Wilder
1933

Thrashing, Threshing, Whitewash, Blacking

Had I not already known from my older brother's perennial head-in-the-fridge pose that the two major activities of prepubescent boys are eating and getting into trouble, *Farmer Boy* would have driven home the point forever. Rerun junkies may forever envision a sun-kissed Dean Butler as Almanzo James Wilder (a.k.a. Laura Ingalls Wilder's First Dude), but those in the know understand the pre-Half Pint schoolboy depicted in the second book of the Little House series, *Farmer Boy*, is truly the one to watch. Nearly 9 years old, clad in fullcloth underwear woven by his mother, able to "tuck away" a piece of pie on top of pretty much any meal, in-print Almanzo is the young exemplar and guide to all that the rich earth can offer to its most hardworking, prosperous citizens.

Which is to say—have you EVER read a book that contains so much cropland transmuted into so much good to eat? Thick stacks of pancakes! Apples 'n' onions! Piping hot potatoes! Baked beans with crispy bits of pork meat! Cream rising from milk pans! Plump brown sausage cakes and fluffly chicken pie and cold beets—Good God! I'm even sold on headcheese!

And besides all this bringing-in-the-sheaving, there are Almanzo's many, many adventures—*not* licking a tempting frozen water pump, letting his oxen run away, secreting an unsheared sheep (mmm . . . *sheep*), feeding candy to a piglet (candy!), winning with a milk-fed pumpkin (*milk* . . . !), saving the crop from an early frost; and, in a most touching (retouching?) scene, being saved by his sister Eliza from a fit of pique involving some blacking and white-and-gold wallpaper.

Lost in all the succulent food and house porn, I'm not sure I noticed as a girl what's truly wonderful about this book— that, as an adult, Laura Ingalls Wilder felt close enough to her husband to write *his* childhood with as vivid an eye as she wrote her own. Okay, most of that relates to food, too. But, as my worn edition's back-cover copy submits, "Was there ever a boy with a bigger appetite?" Reader: I humbly submit—was there ever a work, outside Proust, in which every single meal was as affectionately and brilliantly depicted? I'm not particularly romantic, but something of that old affection for one's husband must transfer, like osmosis, to the reader—because, of my old boxed set, *Farmer Boy* is the only one whose too-oft-turned-front cover, oxen-illustration and all, is long gone.

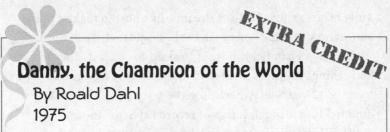

Danny, the Champion of the World
By Roald Dahl
1975

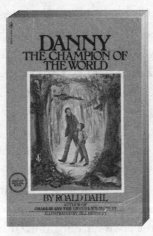

Raisin D'etre

Somewhere between Roald Dahl's wicked writing for children and far wickeder writing for adults (try *Switch Bitch*—not a golden ticket to be found!) lies *Danny, Champion of the World*, the only unexpurgated paean to an adult in all of Roald's work. (And likely one of the few in young-adult literature.) A book about, of all things, a father's teaching his son how to properly poach a pheasant, it's also a book about a father's secrets. But refreshingly, these aren't the kinds of dark family secrets that tend to hound the under–10 set. Instead, they're the wonderfully bizarre stuff of a boy's dreams, like how to make a pheasant stand still using horsehair, the best way to drive in the dark, and that you can tickle a trout to sleep to catch it. They're not only things Danny is thrilled to know. They're things that your average 12-year-old American girl—say, me—was not likely to find tickling through stacks of records at Sam Goody.

Tickling one's way through an act less-skilled mortals would achieve by force, in fact, could well serve as the book's overarching theme. The view of Danny's father—and of the town's other unregenerate poachers: the vicar, policeman, and doctor—is that stealing is an act of style, ideally carried off with wit, panache, and most important, cleverness. Danny, who hatches (*ba-dump!*) the greatest pheasant-poaching plan of all time, takes the raisins that pheasants, as his father puts it, are "mad for" and stuffs each with a bit of sleeping-pill mixture, to stupendous success, at least temporarily. That's also, apparently, how one justifies stealing from wealthy landowners resting on their fat, greedy haunches. "It never pays," comments the doctor, gazing on Danny's avian victims, completely ko'd by their raisin booty, "to eat more than your fair share."

Ludell
By Brenda Wilkinson
1975

The Peach State

I found a copy of this book in the nurse's office of my middle school, and I still, all these years later, don't feel at all guilty that I filched it immediately. (Especially as, twenty years later, someone filched it from me from my college dorm room and never gave it back—library karma's a bitch.) The story of Ludell, a young dreamer who's being raised in rural Georgia in the 50s by a strict churchgoing grandmother, it was one of the few books of its era to depict young black characters—and definitely one of the only ones also written by a black author. (The only other one that comes to mind is Ernest J. Gaines's wonderful *A Long Day in November*, a book-length story of a difficult day in the life of a boy whose parents aren't getting along, all taking place on a sugarcane farm in rural Louisiana.)

Ludell—which continues with *Ludell and Willie*, the story of her not-particularly-approved-of-by-grandma boyfriend, and with *Ludell in New York*, when Ludell goes to live with her mother, Dessa—is one of those portraits of a time so detailed, from everything from snack foods (peanut patties) to dialect (working "from caine see to caine see," which took me a few months to puzzle out, confused as I was by Gaines's sugarcane) that it would make an admirable addition to any time capsule. But it's also wonderful because Ludell, like Meg Murry, is both smart and too smart for her own good; both easily angered and filled with a sense of righteous justice; and both awkward and hopeful for the day when she can finally get beyond it, though her strict upbringing makes her a little dubious that that day will ever come. And, like the Little House books, it's also a wonderful portrait of a time—filled with alternately funny, sour, and surprising insights about segregation and poverty and the roles of young women in the 1950s. Unlike some of the more conscientious books of today, these insights have nothing explictly uplifting or educational about them—but because they're so interesting and true, are all the more so.

Now, who took my goddamn first edition, and give it back!

The Great Brain
By John D. Fitzgerald
1967

Brain Food

Should I be ashamed that most of what I remember about this series about a Beave-like troublemaker from a large Mormon family at the turn of the century is the food? Homemade ice cream, fried chicken, pickles, and Aunt Bertha's apple pie. Oh, yes, the first indoor water closet. Also, endless mayhem. Well, that pretty much covers anything your average turn-of-the-century boy would be interested in, anyway.

Chapter 2

She's at That Age
Girls on the Verge

Driving Force

Can you pinpoint the day when you looked at your family and realized soon, strangely soon, all of this would end? (I'm not speaking of the many days you looked around the dinner table and *wished* it would end.) If childhood is a long, leisurely car ride during which one has all the time in the world to take in sights and pester parents about when you will get there, puberty comes with the brute force of a Driver's Ed instructor who places you behind the wheel and gazes sourly at your attempts to park. Like signs on the highway mapping a distant destination, intimations of the future pop up at regular intervals (Breasts, Exit 12. For Menarche, Take Route 48), but no one, least of all you, really has any idea where you are going.

Enter the heroines below, much-welcomed fellow travelers on a very long road with a car that's suddenly making weird noises.

Keeping us company, first of all, is Margaret Simon, easily the most famous pubescent heroine of all time, confessional in matters both corporeal and divine. We have Beverly Cleary's Barbara McLane, struggling with the nature of personal liberty alongside whether a short or long veil is appropriate for a spring bride. Vicky Austin has gone from using a potato to stop a dripping radiator to debating how much joyful love is appropriate in the face of death, while *Tiger Eyes'* Davey Wexler, after the murder of her father, needs to know if growing up means always being afraid.

Make no mistake, the changes wrought by puberty—on both the mind and the pysche—are paramount to these novels, but to miss each character's simultaneous examination of larger philosophical issues of humankind is to do them discredit. Alongside chanting "We must increase our bust," Margaret is struggling with the issue of dual religious identity. *The Long Secret's* Mouse, alongside her period, has acquired an interest in adults' capacity for self-deception, and Vicky, when given a chance to ask the universe a question, has a far more powerful one than whether Adam Eddington likes her.

It's always assumed that puberty draws children inward, into a newly intimate relationship with their visible hormonal eruptions, consequent mortification, and not much else. But a new need for privacy shouldn't be mistaken for narcissism. In these novels, puberty, like a moon's gravitational pull dragging a body of water into motion from light-years away, stirs up powerfully universal considerations as well. It's a charged period on a personal level, sure. But these heroines remind us a very large part of the charge is becoming acquainted with the world outside themselves.

Are You There, God? It's Me, Margaret.

By Judy Blume
1970

A Real Girl Loved By Girls Everywhere
By Meg Cabot

"What book are you reading right now?" a girl named Boitumelo asks me.

I'm standing in front of 200 girls, 12 to 16 years old, and we're all many, many miles from home, in the auditorium of the Oprah Winfrey Leadership Academy for Girls, which helps underprivileged girls from all over South Africa (a nation with 11 official languages) achieve academic excellence.

I'm hesitant to answer the question. I'm there to talk about writing to girls who come from families so impoverished that Oprah has to send prepackaged meals home with many of them during school holidays just to make sure they get enough to eat. I'm worried that not many of them are going to have heard of the book that I'm reading, which was published in America in 1970 (when I was 3 years old), and that I'm actually rereading in preparation for writing this essay.

But what the hell. It's one of my favorites. And I'm there to talk about writing, right?

"I'm reading *Are You There, God? It's Me, Margaret,* by Judy Blume," I tell them.

I actually jump as the walls of the auditorium reverberate with the thunderous roar of the girls' approval.

They've heard of it, all right. And read it.

And like all girls who've read *Margaret,* they *love* it.

Never mind that South Africa is about 8,000 miles from New Jersey, where *Margaret* is set, or that the book was written nearly thirty years before these girls were born.

Seriously—how can the universal (truly, it expands the globe) appeal of Judy Blume be explained?

I can only explain why *I've* always loved Judy Blume's books: It's the likableness of her heroines; her raw, spare narrative style; her sarcastic sense of humor; the fact that she'd never *dream* of talking down to her readers; and the relatability of her themes.

Okay, sure, there was *Forever,* which a few (well, me) much-too-young-to-"get-it" readers smuggled into their elementary schools and giggled over (need I mention page 96 and Ralph?). Maybe we couldn't all relate to *Forever* in the fourth grade. But later we could. And sadly, smarting from our own breakups, we did.

And maybe for some of us, *Deenie,* with her model good

looks and her "special spot," went over our heads the first time around (I remember at age eleven wishing *I* had a "special spot" like Deenie that I could rub and make myself feel better. It took me a while to catch up in that area, but thanks to later readings of *Forever*, I eventually put two and two together).

But then there was Margaret. Everyone can relate to Margaret. Margaret's parents moved her to a new place, against her will, and away from her beloved grandmother Sylvia. Who couldn't relate to that—and especially to being forced to make all new friends?

And Judy Blume makes a special point to remind us of those certain *kinds* of friends peculiar to childhood—friends you only hang out with because they live close to you. Yes, Nancy was *that* kind of friend. Why else would anyone, particularly Margaret, have liked someone as bossy and unkind in the first place? It was only because Nancy happened to live so close.

But that's what Judy Blume does so well—remembers those tiny details from childhood . . . like friends you only had because they Lived Nearby . . . as well as create characters as fully fleshed out and recognizable as Nancy, whose insistence on being the Leader in Follow the Leader (and later, of the girls' secret club) is never questioned—and what makes Blume such a master at her genre. Nancy isn't the villain in *Margaret*. She's Margaret's friend . . . until she isn't. And even then, she still sort of is. Blume pretty much invented—or at least was one of the first to depict, in contemporary YA lit, anyway—the "frenemy."

Then there's the PTS, the club Margaret and her friends form. Who didn't relate to—or at least long to be in—a club like that? The glamour of belonging to a secret club is what childhood is all about, and Judy Blume captures that . . . along with the petty squabbles that accompany membership in such a club.

Couple that with Margaret's interest in and confusion over boys—and even her own body—and suddenly, *Margaret* becomes the blueprint for almost every girl's adolescence experience, no matter where she's grown up. Although not every girl may have been longing for breasts and her period the way Margaret and her friends were (I certainly wasn't), all girls are highly aware of one another's rate of development at that age, and wondering what's going on with her own.

And finally, there's Margaret's relationship with God and the spiritual quest on which she embarks to find the religion that's right for her. This is surely the most polarizing issue in the book for many readers, and the one responsible for the book's being pulled from so many school library shelves (along with Margaret's frank—and frankly realistic— discussions with her friends of menstruation, bras, breast-growth exercises, boys, possible student-teacher romances, sex behind the A&P, the makeout game Two Minutes in Heaven, and the possibility of being felt up while wearing a training bra stuffed with cotton balls).

Upon the book's censoring in the Reagan-era 80s, horrified parents exclaimed, "This is not how eleven-year-olds talk!" while their 11-year-olds were not only talking that way, but doing far, far worse.

Some refer to *Margaret* as Judy Blume's "period" book, but to me it was always actually her "spiritual crisis" book, in which a girl without religion—Margaret's parents have raised her with the thought that she'll choose her own faith when the time is right—struggles to find her place in a community where "everyone" except Margaret goes either to Sunday school or Hebrew school. With a loving Jewish grandmother and a set of distant but fairly well-meaning Christian grandparents, each pressuring Margaret to choose their own faith, Margaret suffers an eventual spiritual crisis, declaring her lack of belief in the existence of God, and refusing to speak to him anymore.

A typical tween, Margaret is as much upset over the hypocrisy of the adults around her as she is over the fact that all of her friends have gotten their periods—everyone, it seems, except for her. Even her own body is betraying her.

It's all delicious stuff, deftly and humorously handled. The novel ends with Margaret realizing Nancy is a liar, finally getting her own period, and thus reopening the lines of communication with God—but Judy Blume, as always, avoids a tidy denouement: Margaret doesn't choose one religion over the other. She still hasn't decided where she fits in, Sunday school or Hebrew school, and there is more than a slightly cynical suggestion that she may never choose.

The most delightful thing to me about Judy Blume books is that unlike so many other children's books, they never feature a sage adult offering the younger characters wise counsel in their time of need (at the most, during the height of her spiritual crisis, Margaret's mother suggests Margaret go to the movies with a friend. Margaret uses the opportunity to buy feminine products she doesn't need to see what it "feels like"); Judy Blume's books aren't "issue" driven, never offering readers a "message" or "lesson"; and they don't have pat, sugarcoated Hollywood endings to leave readers feeling satisfied.

Instead, Judy Blume's heroines, like Margaret, simply go on living. Just like the rest of us.

Which is why we loved Margaret when we were younger. And why new generations of girls the wide world over—as I found out at Oprah's school in South Africa—are discovering her today, and loving her as well. Margaret is, simply, real.

Sister of the Bride
By Beverly Cleary
1963

Veiled Messages

I guess this is just one of those days, thought Barbara MacLane on her way home from school one bright afternoon late in April. She was not alone. She was walking beside a boy, a very tall boy, but their thoughts were like those famous parallel lines that lie in the same plane but never meet.

Is it possible to write a feminist novel featuring a cunning lace jacket and the baking of many batches of Snickerdoodles?

I hope so, because I have always been so obsessed both with the cover's little lace jacket and the seaspray-green organza bridesmaid gown that primly reveals our heroine's trim arms (so much so that I have unconsciously bought its clone two or three times) that I'd like to think all my purchases have also been politically uplifting. In any case, giving it the old college try is Beverly Cleary, best known for the unsinkable Ramona Quimby, not her many novels of young love—though many of them put as profound a spin on adolescent girldom as Ramona does on a girl's childhood.

When we meet Barbara MacLane, she is a junior in high school, a scant—in her optimistic view—two years behind her sister Rosemary, who's just announced she's marrying her college beau, Greg. Barbara, painfully stuck at home spatting with her younger brother Gordy, is at that mutable age where one's personality seems as up for debate as health-care reform, and Rosemary—a chilly, eminently more sophisticated moon—is currently the tidal draw toward which Barbara is pulled.

While Barbara toils along, hounded by the family Siamese, teased by her father, and seemingly only tolerated by her busy mother, Rosemary is newly slim, getting exposed to Plato and psychology, beloved by a former Air Force captain, and otherwise enjoying all the intellectual and emotional fruits available to a liberated woman of the early 1960s.

Barbara is desperate to be similarly liberated, but her own prospects for the future, school- and boy-wise, seem dim. Not only are her grades endangering her future at Cal, Barbara's current swains are only the moody neighbor Tootie Bodger, a trombonist with a desperate crush on her, and Bill Cunningham, who appears, dashingly, on his Vespa to flirt with her and gobble up all the cookies, then departs before asking her out.

But when Rosemary announces her impending wedding,

she pounces. "Maybe at last she had found what she wanted to do . . . get married in two years like Rosemary." If she can't live Rosemary's new, sophisticated life, she can at least, for one day, live her wedding.

As befits a dreamer casting about for a dream, Barbara's idea of a wedding is born from the bright pages of magazines she studies busily, involving flowing veils, handsome groomsmen, exquisite flowers, and other celebratory perks. In her world, a wedding is less an event than spiritual Kabuki, aesthetics and accoutrement reflecting the purity and poetry of true love.

But Rosemary, newly practical and modern, is irritatingly unwilling to invest in this fantasy. Her post-pillbox view of marriage involves a small wedding, a suit, brown towels, and, ideally, hand-thrown pottery. Engagement rings are "middle class"; presents mean she and Greg will be plagued by "things"; and she's going to finish school, not drop out to be a better wife—because Greg thinks school will make her "a better wife and mother." Rosemary and Barbara's mother is bemused, their grandmother aghast, but Barbara deeply crushed:

> She's overdoing it all the way, thought Barbara. No pretty dishes, no pastel linens, that practical suit. The whole thing, from Barbara's point of view, was beginning to sound just plain dreary. If this went on, she and Greg would probably spend their honeymoon picketing something.

But if Rosemary's view of marriage leaves much to be desired, Barbara thinks the vision offered by her mother's generation is even worse. A member of a happy-housewife group called the Amys (Rosemary's college-educated verdict, much to the amusement of her parents, is that the Amys "don't use their minds"), Barbara's mother seems unduly concerned with the price of flowers and the length of the veil, practical matters Barbara thinks should be divorced from the altar's joys. When the Amys give Rosemary a shower complete with dish towels, sequined oven mitts, and endless fish molds, Barbara internally grouses, "There was no poetry in their soul. Just recipes."

But now Rosemary, who has finally accepted the idea of an engagement ring and veil, is starting to display a dismal household-drudge streak, too. She and Greg secure an apartment where they can exchange rent for being landlords, and Barbara, picturing a sleek, modern building or, alternatively, charming old place crawling with plants, is dismayed about the actual digs: a gray, junky apartment with a taxi-yellow bathroom and a Murphy bed in a building where Rosemary will be stuck lining the garbage cans with newspaper and cooking in the teeny kitchen. "And bragging about how she would clean those halls to pay the rent! What was the matter with her anyway? Had the poetry gone out of her soul, too?"

But the absolute nadir occurs when Rosemary, who, in her new sophistication, is usually a dependable co-snickerer at the Amys and her mother's generation, starts, appallingly, to soften:

" . . . but next semester I think I'll join the Dames."

"And what are the Dames?" demanded Barbara, beginning to undress.

"A club for wives of students," answered Rosemary.

"What do they do?" Barbara was always curious about university life.

"Oh—things like having someone talk on nutrition and how to get the most out of the food dollar," said Rosemary.

At least this was on a higher plane than the Amys, who were inclined to exchange cooky recipes. It was evidence that the Dames used their minds.

"And at the end of the semester there is a party," continued Rosemary with a mischievous smile. "That is when the girls who work while their husbands go to school are awarded their Ph.T. degree."

Barbara had heard of a Ph.D. degree, but never of a Ph.T. This was a new one. "What does that stand for?" she asked, pulling on her nightgown.

"Putting Hubby through," answered Rosemary, laughing.

Barbara groaned. "They sound every bit as bad as the Amys. Worse, even."

"Maybe," agreed Rosemary, "but they have fun." She thought a moment before she said, "And so do the Amys."

It's interesting that, on the cusp of the feminist movement, with its cowl-neck-sporting support groups, Cleary chose to offer a defense of the women's support groups that already *did* exist. Dispatching with a poison pen the psychobabble-spouting coeds in muumus who think women should "use their minds" but can't themselves finish a dress, Cleary, through Barbara, emphasizes that the Amys are capable of doing both:

There was actually a variety of women in the room— the Amy who wore leather sandals and wove her own skirts, another who was active in the League of Women Voters, the mother whose calm was never disturbed by her six children, a mother who wanted to write but could not find time, an Amy whose rough hands and deep tan were the results of hours spent in her hillside garden.

There might be something silly about sequin-trimmed oven mitts—but it's not clear it's any less silly than only wanting hand-thrown pottery and brown towels. Cleary's housewives, and Rosemary, aren't just housewives—Barbara's mother works, both for money and enjoyment, and if Rosemary rolls her hair, she rolls it while studying Plato. Even Barbara has to admit that the Amys, who take on the flowers, food, and sewing needs of the wedding, have impressive and useful skills: "The Amys had many talents . . . Barbara and her mother were most grateful of all to the Amy who dropped in to admire the wedding presents, and watched Millie stolidly sewing her way through the sea-spray organza, and simply took the whole thing away from her and that morning had returned it, complete and pressed."

This may explain why Barbara, who's been seduced by wifely fantasies into playing Bill's help meet, begins to chafe. Bill, stuffed to the gills with Snickerdoodles Barbara's already begun buying at the store (she has chemistry class, after all), finally kills his chances with her when he has the audacity to bring her a shirt to mend because she seems so "domestic":

> She discovered she was tired of baking cookies for that—cooky hound. She was tired of trying to win him, and as for her daydreams about getting married someday, she found them so silly she was embarrassed even thinking about them. Imagine living in an apartment like Rosemary's with Bill Cunningham and washing his socks. Never, never, never!

Domesticity, Barbara is learning, is deeply unpoetical. It's a battery of practical skills. But, in its dingy, fond way, it strains toward its own rubber-glove beauty, when there's love:

> Not everything about Rosemary's life was wrong. There was Greg. And marriage was not something out of the slick and colorful pages of a magazine. It was not just parties and new clothes and flowers and a wedding veil. . . . It was a lot of other things, too, like love and trust and living within one's income and, in Rosemary and Greg's case, putting their educations ahead of their immediate comfort. Why, Rosemary was prepared to do all of this cheerfully, even gaily, and it had not even occurred to her that she was being brave or self-sacrificing. She was doing it because she loved Greg and had faith in his future.
>
> And for the first time the thought came to Barbara that Greg was lucky to be marrying her sister.

By the end of the book, Barbara has happily tossed aside her bouquet dreams—as well as her desire to follow in Rosemary's footsteps. She's not going to pin her future on a hazy groomsman, she's going to figure out what kinds of people she likes—and what kind of person she is. Shockingly, both Tootie and Bill ask her out, and she happily accepts. "It was funny, but now that she suddenly had dates with two boys for the same weekend, a lot of things were changed. Life was interesting, something to be explored, and a wedding did not seem nearly so desirable." And, with an irony far greater than a bejeweled oven mitt, a cheery book about an early wedding becomes an argument for anything but.

Blubber
By Judy Blume
1974

Ethnic Flensing
By Jennifer Weiner

For years, I've fondly remembered Judy Blume's *Blubber* as the *ne plus ultra* of fat-girl lit—the uplifting, seminal story of how downtrodden, picked-upon Linda Fischer delivers a righteous comeuppance to the fifth-grade classmates who tripped her, teased her, played keep-away with her coat and her lunch, and called her Blubber.

For years, it turns out, I have been completely and totally wrong.

Blubber is not a story of the big girl triumphant. It does not feature a happy ending for poor picked-upon Linda Fischer, who's crucified by her classmates for the sin of weighing 91 pounds in the fifth grade (and maybe this is a sign of the times, or a result of the 400-pound sixth-grader whom I just read about in the *Times,* in a story about kids who desperately need, and cannot afford, fat camp, but these days, 91 pounds doesn't sound like a weight that would get you noticed, let alone teased to the point of vomit and tears).

Linda may have inspired the book's title, but she's not the main character in *Blubber.* Neither is the fifth grade's queen bee, Wendy, who leads the classwide [**class-wide**, *but either way!*] charge against Linda, after Linda delivers an unfortunate report on the mammal of her choice—the whale.

The star of the show is Jill Brenner, a skinny and conflicted classmate who's just trying to fit in to her privileged Philadelphia suburb . . . and if the rule of the day is making fun of the fat girl, then Jill's eager enough to go along, even though she knows that her best friend Tracy Wu was herself the victim of bullies.

Blume doesn't pull punches in describing the realities of fifth-grade pecking orders, or the girls who end up at the bottom of the pyramid. Linda Fischer isn't the kind of friendly, funny fat girl that other, less-edgy YA authors might have offered. She receives neither of the consolation prizes typically offered to fat girls in fiction: the pretty face or the great personality. Instead, poor Linda's got a head shaped like a potato, which sits on her shoulders without the benefit of an intervening neck, and a gray tooth. She responds to the teasing not with stoic silence or slashing wit, but with tattling and tears. She's a whiner, a martyr, babyish, a bit of a drip (and, Blume takes pains to point out, she's not even the fattest kid in fifth grade. It's her personality, not her pounds, that make her a target).

In *Blubber*'s bleak world, there are no heroes and a surplus of villains. There is no redemption for Linda, or for Jill, and no happy ending. Blubber never stands up to the bullies; she just gets briefly co-opted by them, and then dumped once more. The book ends with Linda just as isolated and pathetic as when the story began.

Returning to *Blubber* as an adult, I'm amazed, once more, at the unflinching verisimilitude with which Blume describes what preteen girls are really like (monsters in training bras). But part of me was a little heartbroken: Why couldn't Blubber have actually been Blubber's story? Why is the story Jill's and not Linda's to tell? Why didn't, or couldn't, Judy Blume write a book about a fat girl?

The afterword (which I don't remember reading as a ten-year-old) offers a clue. In it, Blume writes that she was inspired by her own daughter Randy's experiences, and that Blume wanted to tell a story about bullying, not from the perspective of the victim but from the point of view of one of the faces in the crowd, a girl struggling to balance morality with self-preservation in the Lord-of-the-Flies world that is fifth grade. In *Blubber*'s classroom, the adults are absent or clueless or cruel, or too busy struggling with their own vices to offer more than mealymouthed platitudes in a crisis—and that's when they're not lighting up a cigarette or turning a blind eye.

But I wonder whether there's not a bigger issue here. Blume's heroines, from well-meaning Winnie in *Iggie's House* to flat-chested, religiously conflicted Margaret in *Are You There, God? It's Me, Margaret,* to Deenie, the so-pretty-she-could-model fourteen-year-old afflicted with scoliosis, are all smart and spirited, reasonably introspective and interested in doing what's fair and what's right. They are also all, to a one, thin, pretty girls . . . or at least thin girls who are well on their way to becoming pretty. You just knew that once Margaret's breasts arrived and Deenie's brace came off, they'd grow up to be beautiful, just like Catherine in *Forever*, who effortlessly caught the eyes of not one but two hunky teenage boys (and who also had vaginal orgasms during her second attempt at intercourse, the lucky bitch).

I wonder if, deep down, Judy Blume found Linda just as repellent, just as icky, as Jill and her friends did . . . or if she didn't want to write about a fat girl because she suspected that, unlike Margaret and Deenie and Winnie and Sally, Linda would not emerge from the chrysalis of a back brace or belated puberty as a beautiful butterfly, and that her life wouldn't necessarily have a happy ending.

Whatever the reason, I'm grateful. I imagine there's a bunch of young women writers who are grateful, too. Had Judy Blume taken on the story of a young Jewish woman from a Philadelphia suburb who grew up overweight and found her way to her own happy ending in spite of it . . . well, for starters, I would have had to find something else to cover in *Good in Bed*.

In many ways, my first novel answered the questions I had when reading *Blubber* as an adult. What was Linda's story? What was going on behind the doors of the house that Jill and Wendy dashed past, laughing, on Halloween night? Did Linda's parents love her, or were they ashamed, or did they feel love and shame in equal measure? Could Linda find a best friend and a first love? Would she end up with a career and a husband and a baby and a life that, minus her extra pounds and her unhappy history, wasn't that different from the one her classmates would have?

I remember *Blubber* as a big girl's story, but, in retrospect, I'm glad it wasn't . . . because what Judy Blume gave us was a big fat tempting blank just waiting for a generation of writers who grew up on Judy Blume to fill in with our own experiences, our own stories, our own hard-won truths.

The Cat Ate My Gymsuit
By Paula Danziger
1974

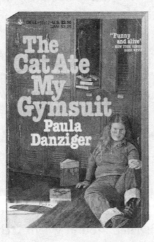

Teach for America

I hate my father. I hate school. I hate being fat. I hate
the principal because he wanted to fire Ms. Finney,
my English teacher.

I feel bad for teens today. Their parents listen to them. Teachers
are invested in their intellectual development and well-being.
Books are published on their optimal care and feeding; vio-
lins brandished for their edification; trips abroad marshaled
so they may broaden their horizons and spread their wealth to

others, eventually spearheading their own microloan organizations and so forth. What the hell! How are they ever going to learn about the world?

Marcy Lewis is no rarefied hothouse flower from the West, ruthlessly cultivated to within an inch of her stamen. She is, by her own admission, a "baby blimp with wire frame glasses and mousy brown hair" who fears impending acne and hands her gym teacher a creative reason every day to not be forced to put on her gymsuit in front of everyone.

She is not the only one on board. Her friend Nancy gives her this practical assessment: "Marcy. Come on. You're not ugly. You are too fat, but you have good points too. It's just that kids think you're stuck up because you won't play and you're smart." Her tepidly supportive mother tells her that she should really "lose some weight and look like everyone else." Her 4-year-old brother, Stuart, wants her to be his best friend so that, as she says, " . . . I can help him put orange pits in the hole in his teddy bear's head." And her father, yet another in the line of apoplectic dads obviated around when Archie Bunker transmuted to Steven Keaton, renders this judicious opinion, not infrequently: "I don't care if you get good grades. You do stupid things. Why do I have to have a daughter who is stupid and fat? I'll never get you married off."

Enter Diane Finney, un-teachery teacher, wearer of turtlenecks, jean skirts, and macrame necklaces. Ms. Finney, in her 1970s way, reins in the unruly students by some Psych-101 method of staring at them unnervingly, then exposes them to an eye-opening battery of novel teaching methods while actually teaching them English—including but not limited to making a commercial to "sell" a book, using Monopoly to learn vocabulary, and drawing from the works of Marshall McLuhan.

Drunk on this genuine engagement, both with their intellect and with their psyches, the students ask if they can form an after-school club to "do more about how we felt inside." That is where Marcy finally meets Joel Anderson, unconventional love interest, when they are paired off to learn about each other:

> I didn't know. Was I supposed to tell him I was a blimp trying to disguise myself as a real person; or that I probably had a horrible case of contagious impending pimples; or that I had this weird brother with a teddy bear filled with orange pits; or that I thought that he was cute and brave and probably thinking about how suicide would be better than talking to me?

Joel—who is the type of boy to answer, in my favorite answer ever, "Joel Anderson," to the question of what he wants to be when he grows up—actually tells the class: "This is Marcy Lewis. She says she doesn't like lots of things, but I bet she really does . . . and she has a nice smile."

All this, of course, cannot stand. Despite Ms.—Ms!—Finney's demonstrable skill as a teacher, her refusal to say the pledge while she salutes the flag provides a ready hook for the ire of Principal Stone, who, we are meant to understand, is not interested in the teachings of Marshall McLuhan. Ms. Finney, who is really only guilty of occasionally forgetting she's holding a piece of chalk and trying to smoke it, is suspended, and the only good thing about this is that it provides Marcy with the opportunity to come into her own, both in love, life, and her family.

After sticking it to the man by telling Principal Stone, "You have not converted a man because you have silenced him," Marcy shocks herself by spearheading the movement to save

Ms. Finney, joined along the way, surprisingly, not only by the quietly supportive Joel, but also by her mother, who graduates from capitulating to her husband's sullen abuse to defending Ms. Finney at the school-board meeting to decide her fate.

The Cat Ate My Gymsuit is not only a snapshot of Marcy's psyche, but also of a family and an entire country in transition. The war in Vietnam and the feminist movement are rarely mentioned explicitly, but their looming presence underpins Mr. Stone, Mr. Lewis, and all the other old-guard parents' wholesale rejection of Ms. Finney, whose teachings, they think, are divesting their children of a crucial conformity. Ms. Finney, who will salute the flag but won't say the pledge because "I am sorry to have to say that I don't believe this country offers liberty and justice for all" signals peacenik touchy-feelyness to the powers that be. But in an atmosphere of divorce, unrest, and uncertainty, she's not a handholder—she's trying to start a movement to create adults worthy of holding hands with.

But it doesn't work. It doesn't work! It *stubbornly refuses to end happily.* Instead, we have a semi-progression into sort-of-slightly better circumstances. Ms. Finney wins the case but declines to return, because she knows she'd be too divisive. Joel and Marcy remain close friends. ("You have to start somewhere.") Marcy's mother registers for night courses at the local university and stops plying her daughter with ice cream. But her father, Marcy says, "hardly ever says anything to me anymore. He and my mother talk a lot, but he just looks at me and shakes his head." As the book ends, Marcy informs us: "Yesterday I looked in the mirror and saw a pimple. Its name is Agnes."

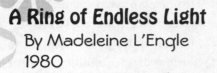

A Ring of Endless Light
By Madeleine L'Engle
1980

Deep Thoughts

I saw him for the first time at the funeral.

Dolphins. Do I even need to write another word? Oh, I know I do, but ... *dolphins*, I had to write it again! You dog/horse/wolf/ rabbit/mouse/cave lion/alley-cat girls, keep your creatures. I am sticking with the one that can leap entirely out of the water, is psychic, uses over 80 percent of its brain, and symbolizes the timeless mystery and wisdom of the universe!

In *A Ring of Endless Light*, Vicky Austin, seemingly the

most ordinary of the triptych of L'Engle heroines that includes Meg Murry O'Keefe and, in later installations, Meg's daughter Polly, yet again reveals herself to possess unseen depths. Having spent the previous summer on a camping trip across the country (*The Moon by Night*), then a year in New York (*The Young Unicorns*), Vicky returns to her grandfather's house on Seven Bay Island under sad circumstances. Not only is her grandfather, a minister who marries passion with a cool intellect and warm faith, dying of cancer, a dear family friend, Commander Rodney, has just been killed trying to rescue a drowning boy. What has always been a happy summer on the water for Vicky has become a slow march into the sea.

Luckily—it is summer, after all—L'Engle has seen fit to break up all this agony with a passel of love interests for Vicky, though all three boys are wrestling with their own boatmen as well.

First up is the familiar Zachary Gray, Vicky's pale, raven-haired suitor from *The Moon by Night*. While his old death wish used to mainly take shape in driving too fast and getting caught in rock slides in canyons, he's moved on to driving on the wrong side of the road, flying prop planes too close to jetliners, and defending his cryogenically frozen mother. There's also the matter of his recent suicide attempt—in which Commander Rodney lost his life while saving Zach's.

No wonder, after Zach pulls up in his hearse-like black station wagon, he wastes no time telling Vicky she's all that stands between him and chaos. ("You're reason where there isn't any reason. Reason to live—")

Stick a pin in that, Zach! Awkwardly enough for him, Vicky has another ardent pursuer: Leo Rodney, the son of the man Zach has just, though inadvertently, killed. Luckily for Zach,

Vicky can't bring herself to think of Leo romantically, but she's not quite ready to count him out, either:

> Without realizing what I was doing, I put my arms around him. "Cry, Leo, don't hold it back, you need to cry—" I broke up because I was crying, too, for Commander Rodney, for my grandfather, who was dying slowly and gently, for a thousand porpoises who had been clubbed to death. . . .
>
> . . . I held Leo and he held me and we rocked back and forth on the old elm trunk, weeping, and the salt wind brushed against the salt of our tears. And I discovered that there is something almost more intimate about crying that way with someone than there is about kissing. . . .

The French figured out that sex can evoke death; Vicky is learning, at least on the East Coast, it's sex that can evoke death—and at the center of the novel lies this strange exchange.

Complicating the mix even more is the darkly romantic figure of Adam Eddington, who's studying dolphins at the island's marine biology lab with Vicky's older brother, John. Fans of L'Engle's *The Arm of the Starfish* know that, when Adam meets Vicky, he's still grieving over the death of his former mentor and friend, Joshua Archer, agonizing over the role he played in that death.

But where *The Arm of the Starfish* was about how easily innocence can be corrupted by evil, *A Ring of Endless Light* is about the three great mysteries L'Engle always returns to: God, sex, and love. Adam asks Vicky for help with the dolphins, thinking that, in her (relative) youth, she might communicate with them better. But he has no idea what a change it will bring in their relationship to pair her passion with his intellect—or how much it will touch upon those three questions. In an electric, sensual scene, Vicky meets the dolphins (dolphins!!!!!!!!) and turns Adam's heretofore practical project into a kind of spiritual communion:

> "Tell me what he feels like to you," Adam urged.
>
> How can anybody describe the feel of a dolphin? "Something strange, alien," I murmured, "like touching a creature from a different planet—and yet completely familiar, too, as though I've always known what a dolphin feels like. . . ."
>
> Again I lifted my hand from the water, but I couldn't see anything, and this time when I stopped scratching, Basil dove down, his great fluke flicking so that again I was drenched in spray, and appeared far beyond us, leaping up in a great and glorious arc before diving down again . . .
>
> I was still treading water and feeling more exhilarated than I have ever felt in my life.

Yes, that's right, she gets to swim with dolphins. Contain your jealousy. (Actually, just save it for when she has *psychic conversations* with them.) But Vicky's summer is one of absurd juxtapositions and extremes—one moment quietly spent reading philosophy with her grandfather by his bed, the next being taken to a spa and a classical music concert by Zachary, the next eating spaghetti with her family and discussing the nature of death and cellular regeneration, the next skinny-dipping with Leo. It's an overwhelming deluge of physical, philosophical, and psychological stimulae, sex and death, Eros and Thanatos, one in which the dolphins prove a crucial link for Adam—and for her:

> "It's just—it's just—there's death everywhere— Commander Rodney—and watching Grandfather, and now Ynid's baby for no reason—it's just everywhere . . ."
>
> . . . "Are you afraid?" he asked softly . . . "Of what, Vicky?" He picked up another handful of sand, and started trickling it through his fingers. "Dying?" his voice wasn't loud, but the word seemed to explode into the night.

Unlike Zach, who is far too dangerous, and Leo, who is far too tame, Adam is capable of making Vicky feel strongly without making her feel entirely out of control—or making her feel entirely unlike herself:

> . . . I heard every word he said. And I think I understood. At the same time my entire body was conscious of the feel of his fingers stroking my hair. I wondered if he felt as strongly as I did.
>
> At that moment there was a rip in the clouds and an island of star-sparkled sky appeared, its light so brilliant it seemed to reach down beyond the horizon and encircle the earth, a ring of pure and endless light.
>
> I wasn't sure that Adam's words were very comforting. But his arm about me was. He made me feel very real, not replete with me at all, only real, and hopeful. . . . And I knew that if Adam kissed me it

was going to be different from Zachary, with all his experience, or Leo, with all his naivete.

Adam did not kiss me.

Yet I felt as close to him as though he had.

This is a far cry from Leo, whom she can grieve with but not kiss, or Zach, whom she can kiss but not grieve with. But here again, we find that the dolphins have the answer for her. After the baby of the dolphins at the lab dies, she asks the wild dolphins (wouldn't you?) to explain the nature of death to her:

> I thought of Ynid and her grief at her dead baby, and I asked Basil, Is Ynid's baby all right? (Is Commander Rodney all right? Is my grandfather all right? Am I? Is it all right?)
>
> Basil pulled himself out of the water and a series of sounds came from him, singing sounds.
>
> And what it reminded me of was Grandfather standing by Commander Rodney's open grave and saying those terrible words and then crying out, full of joy, *Alleluia, alleluia, alleluia!*

Like Vicky's minister grandfather, the dolphins—as they inform Vicky, telepathically—believe that life and death are intertwined. (Unlike the freeze-dried, death-seeking Zachary.) But when Vicky, on the cusp of womanhood, tries to assert her new psychic powers to get closer to Adam as well, she's slapped back:

> Without consciously realizing what I was doing, I turned my mind toward Adam. Do a cartwheel in the water, like Basil.

I held my breath.

Adam dove down. Up came his legs. Flip. Head and arms were out of the water. Just like Basil.

Adam, do you really think of me as nothing more than a child? I realize I'm naive and backward for my age in lots of ways, but I don't feel about you the way a child feels. I've never felt about anybody else the way I feel about you, touched in every part of me . . . Is it only my feelings? Doesn't it touch you at all?

He broke in, saying sharply, "Vicky, what are you doing?"

I could feel heat suffusing my face. "N—nothing."

Now he was shouting at me. "Don't do that!"

"Why? Why not?"

"Because—because—" He clamped his mouth shut. But he was telling without speaking. *Because it's too intimate.*

But I did it with the dolphins. Why was it all right with the dolphins?

And the answer came lapping gently into my mind like the water lapping about my body. Because this is how the dolphins are, all the time. They're able to live with this kind of intimacy and not be destroyed by it.

I have always loved the part of this book where Leo tells Vicky how his parents made love after his own grandfather's death as an "affirmation of life" (it's not creepy, I swear), and it seems to sum up the entire thesis of this book—that sex and death are both part of joy, which is, as Vicky's grandfather puts it, "the infallible sense of God in the universe." Meg Murry may well get to be consumed by tilting planets and fandolae and the future of the universe, but Vicky is, in her own quiet way, touching on questions just as crucial, however young and awkward she is. Like Meg, Vicky is a conduit for discussing the big questions, but her experiences are also a stand-in for the overwhelming feelings of adolescence, especially for girls. As Adam puts it, "I simply did not expect that John Austin's kid sister would be thunder and lightning and electricity." Ah, to be John Austin's kid sister, and get some dolphins and psychic powers to go with all those hormones.

Tiger Eyes
By Judy Blume
1981

Managed Care

It is the morning of the funeral and I am tearing my room apart, trying to find the right kind of shoes to wear. But all I come up with are my Adidas, which have holes in the toes, and a pair of my flip-flops.

Long ago, in a writing workshop far, far away, I seem to remember a certain teacher informing his charges that one should make sure to tell the entire story in the first sentence. I can't imagine he was speaking of this book in particular, but *Tiger*

Eyes is a shining example of packing a major punch in under 30 words. From a shelf filled with Blume's awkward, not-yet-grown preteens, I always loved this book's heroine, Davey Wexler, the most. With her boyfriend, smart tongue, and moody, independent streak, she was like the older sister to the Margaret Simon in me, pulling on her frayed jeans and scrambling off to a canyon to meet a mysterious stranger while I fumbled with the belt on my sanitary napkin.

As the novel begins, Davey Wexler has just turned 15, and her father has just been killed—shot when two junkies hold up the 7-Eleven he owns, which was filled with the beautiful drawings that were the last remnants of the artistic career he never pursued. Davey, her mother, and her younger brother, Jason, are wholly shattered by his death—Davey most of all. After spending weeks in bed, not eating or washing her hair, she returns to the world of the living when school starts—then succumbs to a series of panic attacks that knock her out (literally) on a daily basis.

Into the breach step her Aunt Bitsy, her father's sister, and her Uncle Walter, who live in Los Alamos, where Walter works in the W (weapons) division at the famed lab that developed the bombs dropped on Hiroshima and Nagasaki. (I thank this book for all Trivial Pursuit tournament "Fat Man and Little Boy" wins.) After the doctor recommends a change of scene for Davey, the family relocates to Los Alamos for an unspecified period, which lengthens into a year-long visit after the store at home is vandalized.

Aunt Bitsy, who gives tours at the Bradbury Science Museum where the remnants of the bomb reside, is the kind of woman who wears a uniform to work because, as she says, "it makes her *feel* official." Walter is the kind of man who hands his niece a bomb-shelter card her first month in the house. The

Kronicks, who allow Davey to ride their (clearly "Kronick" labeled) bikes only as long as she wears a helmet, have strict views on anything Davey wants to do: Climbing in canyons ("You could wind up a vegetable!"), riding in hot-air balloons ("It's beautiful to watch, but only a fool would actually participate"), driving ("Why rush?"), skiing ("You don't want to wind up a vegetable, do you?"), and the aforementioned bomb shelter ("Russians . . . have an outstanding civil defense program. If they're attacked, chances are, they'll survive. I wish I could say the same for us").

But Davey, who has been spending her nights in bed clutching a bread knife for protection and her days smacking her head against the ground each time she faints, has an odd reaction to the sudden onslaught of stability and security: She starts to become her old, adventurous self again. On some level, Davey realizes that her life has weathered its own enormous bomb without a shelter, and she's still here.

After begging off yet another family sightseeing tour ("But we had rest and relaxation scheduled for next week!" Bitsy cries) she goes off on a bike ride, climbs down into a canyon, and meets the very embodiment of mystery and danger—a guy who calls himself Wolf, a tanned, inscrutable fellow hiker who hears her shouting "Daddy" to the empty canyon and thinks she's shouting for help.

Davey, still on the alert for maniacs, is not happy to be caught out in such a vulnerable position:

> "So . . . I'm alone," I say, sounding bitchier by the minute. "Is there a law against that?" I am standing in front of the rock now. All I have to do is bend over, pick it up, and wham. . . .
>
> "No, but there should be," he says.

"Oh yeah . . . why?" I am having trouble following our conversation but I know it is best to keep him talking. The longer he talks the less likely that he'll attack. I read that somewhere.

"Who's going to help you if you need it?" he asks me.

And with that, Davey remembers something important—which is that, while being alone with a stranger can make you vulnerable, so can just being *alone*. This realization is hastened along by her extreme thirst, which has reached epic proportions since her climb down into the canyon at midday with zero provisions:

"You're thirsty."

"A little," I tell him, licking my lips.

"You came into the canyon without a water bottle. . . . Here. . . ." he passes his to me. I am so relieved I feel like crying. I mean to take a quick swig, but once it's to my lips I can't stop. I drink and drink until he takes it from me.

"Easy," he says, "or you'll get sick."

I begin to relax. He's not out to get me after all.

"What's your name?" I ask him.

"You can call me Wolf."

"Is that a first name or a last name?"

"Either," he says.

"Oh." I can't think of anything else to say.

He stands, puts the water bottle back into his knapsack, stretches and says, "Okay, let's go."

"Go?" I should have let down my guard. "Where?"

"Back up," he says. "It's one o'clock. I've got an appointment at two."

"So, go," I tell him.

"You're going with me."

"Really!" I say.

"Yeah . . . really."

"Guess again," I say.

"I'm not about to leave you down here by yourself. I'm not in the mood to be called by Search and Rescue later. I have other things to do."

"Search and Rescue?"

"Right."

I think about the fourteen-year-old boy who was killed by a falling rock and about the woman who broke her leg and went into shock and I wonder if Wolf was called in then. But I don't ask him. Instead I say, "I'm tougher than I look."

"Sure you are. Let's go. I'm in a hurry."

"How do I know I can trust you?"

"You see anybody you can trust more?"

Life in Los Alamos is very different from Davey's life in Atlantic City, a brilliant mix of color and class on the edge of the ocean, where no one needs Search and Rescue any more than they need proper boots to climb down into the canyon. By contrast, Los Alamos is flat and arid, rigidly divided along class lines that mimic those at the lab—meaning the kids whose parents are highest up are the grinds at school, any Hispanic kids are the offspring of the maintenance workers in the lab, and there are barely any black kids at all. (In Atlantic City, Davey's best friend, Lenaya, was black, and a budding scientist.) Davey, whose life with Walter puts her in the grind group but not of it, wishes that there was a group for people like her, called "The Left-Overs."

Even as Davey starts to come back to life, the novel is bracketed by scenes from what happened the night her father died, each snapshot from the past appearing as Davey takes another stop forward, making it that much more excruciating:

> I walked behind the counter to where Dad was sitting at his easel and looked over his shoulder. "Very nice . . ." I said. "Especially the eyes. I wish I could draw like you."
>
> "You can do other things."
>
> "Oh yeah . . . like what?"
>
> My father pretended to think that over. "You're very good at stacking the bread," he said.
>
> "Thanks a lot!"
>
> We both laughed. I hung my arms over his shoulders, from behind, and rested my face against his hair, which was soft and curly and smelled of salt water.
>
> "So, where are you off to?" Dad asked.
>
> "Oh, Hugh and I are going out."
>
> "What time will you be back?"
>
> "I'm not sure."
>
> "An educated guess."
>
> "Ten . . . eleven . . . something like that."
>
> "Stay off the beach. It's not safe at night."
>
> "I've already had that lecture."
>
> "I just don't want you to get carried away and forget."

"I won't. I promise."

. . . Outside the sun was setting.

It's not only physical safety that her father is talking about—it's the fact that she was conceived under Atlantic City's Million Dollar Pier, and her father doesn't want Davey to derail her own life like his. ("A waste of a life," Walter bitterly sneers one night about her father, ridiculing how his lack of planning put Davey and her family in its present circumstances.) But would planning ahead have done anything to help her father stay alive?

This is the question Davey asks after things have come to a boiling point with her and Walter and Bitsy. While Jason has taken on Bitsy and Walter's love of planning ahead, even going so far as to sport an apron while he and Bitsy make endless sheets of cookies, her mother has descended into a cocoon of pain medications, blotting out the entire world:

> I face Mom and say, "Mom, please. I really want to take Drivers Ed. It's very important to me. All you have to do is sign the little green card."
>
> Mom looks at me and we make eye contact for the first time in months. Then, just as she is about to speak, Walter says, "Statistics show that accidents, especially automobile accidents, are the leading cause of death among young people."
>
> "Why go looking for trouble?" Bitsy says. She pours the batter into the cake pan and Jason pulls the oven door open for her.
>
> "Mom . . . say something, will you?"
>
> "Walter and Bitsy know what's best," Mom says.

"Since when . . . since when I'd like to know? . . . I'm sick of hearing how dangerous everything is . . . Dangerous . . . dangerous. . . . dangerous. . . . Stay out of the canyon, Davey . . . you could be hit by a falling rock. Don't forget your bicycle helmet, Davey . . . you could get hit by a car. No, you can't learn to ski, Davey. . . . you might wind up a vegetable!" I am really yelling now.

"Davey, honey . . ." Mom begins and she reaches for me. But I pull away from her.

"Some people have lived up here so long they've forgotten what the real world is like," I shout, "and the idea of it scares the . . ."

"You can just stop it, right now," Walter says, before I have finished. He says it slowly, making every word count.

"You're a good one to talk," I tell him. "You're the one who's making the bombs. You're the one who's figuring out how to blow up the whole world. But you won't let me take Drivers Ed. A person can get killed crossing the street. A person can get killed minding his own store. Did you ever think of that?" I kick the wall and stomp out of the room. I am crying hard and my throat is sore.

Davey may realize that living as irresponsibly as her parents did isn't the best idea, but she also is learning that if your whole life is built around trying to stave off death, taking up arms against unseen forces can make your life arid, a place where responsibility blots out possibility. ("I don't want to go through my life afraid, but I don't want to wind up like my father, either," Davey writes to Wolf. ". . . I think about that a lot, especially in this town, where so many people seem afraid. Does building bombs make them feel afraid . . . ?")

Tiger Eyes must be the only teen novel in which the heroine stars in a production of *Oklahoma!* and the entirety is summed up in a paragraph. But Blume has bigger fish to fry, namely describing, in amazingly adult detail, how Davey comes from being too scared to sleep with anything but a bread knife to a girl who can face her father's death—not because of anything that has happened to her, but because of something that is *in* her. After her mother refuses the proposal of a man at the Lab and decides to take the family home, Davey realizes this is true of her mother, too:

> "It's time for us to leave," Mom says. "It's time for us to start making a life on our own. We're going home. We're going home to Atlantic City."
>
> "No!" Bitsy says. . . . "What about the children. . . . They're secure here. You can't keep moving them around."
>
> "I'm not going to," Mom says. "I'm taking them home."
>
> "But Atlantic City . . . it's not safe . . . you, of all people, should realize that, Gwen."
>
> "I can't let safety and security become the focus of my life," Mom says.
>
> I can't believe how sure of herself my mother sounds. I want to stand up and cheer for her.

Everyone knows that if you worry about how how you'll die, you'll never enjoy being alive. But Davey learns something even more subtle: that although people think preparing for death is being responsible, it's also ducking a greater responsibility: one's responsibility to *live*.

Davey learns that herself the day she meets Wolf, and the day she starts to let her father go:

> "Stop!" I tell myself. Stop thinking about that night. Concentrate on how good it feels to be alive. No matter what. Just to see the color of the sky, to smell the pine trees, to meet a stranger in the canyon.
>
> I go to my room, tear a piece of paper from the yellow pad on my dresser and write one word. *Alive*. Then I tear off another piece and write *Wolf*.

Maybe the answer to the question lies in the shoes Davey finally settles on after teetering on her mother's borrowed heels at the funeral and then slipping down into the canyon where she meets Wolf in her Adidas. She knows she'll never be the kind of person who is so afraid of what can happen to them they'll never go into the canyon at all, but she's also not ready to be like her parents were—stumbling and slipping down, and then caught out without water or shelter when tragedy strikes. She's become the kind of person who keeps around the pair of hiking boots and canteen Wolf tells her to buy after escorting her out of the canyon when they first meet. These are sturdy, long-lasting, and strong, letting Davey take on any situation—alone or not.

The Long Secret
By Louise Fitzhugh
1965

A Note on the Type

The notes were appearing everywhere.

Traditionally, in women's fiction, from *Little Women* to *The Women's Room*, the spotlight has been squarely on what goes down between the, you know, women. (It's in the titles and everything.) But as *The Group* begat *Golden Girls* begat *Gossip Girl*, we've lost the most important font of all drama—*friends*. No, not friends who like the same boy as you do, thereby creating explosive competition. Not friends who turn on you and isolate you among your peers. Not friends who stand behind you come what may all the way; not friends who become anorexic/alcoholic/cutaholic; not friends who offer witty quips when you get pregs and attend your teen-mom birth. In *The Long Secret*, you put away all the drama and simply turn to the side to see *your best friends*—who are difficult simply because you are you and they are they.

The Long Secret, the sequel to *Harriet the Spy*, understands having a BFF is extremely complicated even when no one is blowing the UPS man. (Don't get me wrong. I love Samantha and *Sex and the City* and its ilk in a greasy, 1:00-A.M., fried-chicken-in-a-bag way. I've just never understood how anyone could be friends with Carrie without therapeutic intervention.) But where *Harriet the Spy* introduces us to the remarkable Harriet, *The Long Secret* takes over with Harriet's friend Beth Ellen, her spiritually wispy sidekick for years.

When we catch up with them, the girls have hit adolescence and Beth Ellen, whom Harriet has always called "Mouse," is coming out from under her well-meaning thumb whether she likes it or not. Here's them talking about Beth Ellen's inappropriate crush on the itinerant, pot-bellied, piano-playing Bunny:

"I don't want to write about him; I want to marry him," said Beth Ellen.

"Well!" said Harriet, "that's the most ridiculous thing I ever heard. You're only eleven."

"Twelve."

"How can you be twelve when I'm only eleven?" Harriet looked furious.

Beth Ellen waited.

"Oh, that's right," said Harriet finally. "I always forget that about birthdays. I remember, you just had one."

There you have it: just being older than your friend briefly is sufficient betrayal, at the age of 11. (The opposite becomes true at 28.) Harriet is also enraged that Beth Ellen cannot think of anything more interesting for her future profession than marrying a rich man and moving to Biarritz. But wait a minute, Harriet! Something far more upsetting is coming up!

> "MOUSE!" Harriet gave one great agonized yelp.
> "What?" whispered Beth Ellen.
> "WHAT'S WRONG WITH YOU?"
> "I'm—"
> "WHAT?"
> Beth Ellen's voice suddenly found itself and came out so loud she jumped. "I'm—menstruating!"
> "What's that?" asked Harriet, awed.
> "It's—"
> "I just remembered," yelled Harriet. "How come you're doing that and I'm not?"
> It was an unanswerable question. "I don't know—" began Beth Ellen.
> Harriet hung up on her.

The girls are spending the summer on Montauk, Harriet with her parents and Beth Ellen with her grandmother, whom she's always lived with while her mother, Zeeney, gads about Europe. As Beth Ellen accompanies Harriet biking around on her summer reconnaissance, the sleepy town of Water Mill is being rocked—as rocked as sleepy towns on Montauk can be, that is—by a sneak who is leaving around, for all members of the populace, slightly tweaked quotes that are, as one recipient puts it, like a "nasty fortune cookie" and, as another admits, "kinda hit home sometimes."

Harriet, being Harriet, is, of course, on it:

> NOW THE THING IS WHO WOULD LEAVE NOTES LIKE THIS? SOMEBODY WHO READS THE BIBLE BECAUSE THEY ALL SOUND LIKE THEY'RE RIGHT OUT OF THE BIBLE. WHO DOES READ THE BIBLE? DOES ANYBODY? DOES MY MOTHER? CHECK ON THIS.

NOW I KNOW WHERE I GOT MY HUGE ADDICTION TO CAPPING EVERYTHING. But while Harriet is bursting with questions about what motivates all the adults around her, Beth Ellen is in a similar quandary about herself:

> *Dear Me:*
>
> *Why am I so different? Why am I never happy? Is everybody like this or just me? I am truly a mouse. I have no desire at all to be me.*
>
> *Goodbye,*
> *Mouse*

Beth Ellen and Harriet are still in the roles they played as children—not because one is a sap and one is a bully, but because it still shields them from the complications of the world. But the world, as it does, is not going to let their friendship alone long. Jessie Mae, a deeply religious Southern girl they meet on one of their spying missions, observes their interaction and neatly dissects it, to Harriet's shock and consternation:

> "You the captain and she the lieutenant?" said Jessie
> Mae, beside herself with giggles. "If I may say so,
> you do speak sharply to your friend."
> "She's MY friend," said Harriet, appalled.
> "Well . . ." said Jessie Mae, looking away and fan-
> ning rapidly, "I do feel that, like the Good Book
> says, we should honor our father and mother, but I,
> personally, think we should honor our friends too."
> Harriet was stunned into silence.

It's not that Beth Ellen needs an excuse to start to dislike Harriet—it's just that she needs to stop using her as a security blanket. "Hurrying after Harriet," Beth Ellen tells us, "made her feel curiously liberated, as though she could be a child and it was all right. Harriet always gave her this feeling. It was one of the few things she really liked about Harriet, as a matter of fact, because the principal feeling she felt when with Harriet was one of being continually jarred." But Beth Ellen is jerked out of Harriet's protectorate even further by the announce- ment that Zeeney, whom she does not even remember, is re- turning from Europe to resume her role in Beth Ellen's life:

> Try as she might she could not find one emotion
> connected with this piece of news. She lay back on
> the bed. She felt the bedspread. It was nice to feel
> something with her hands, something solid. Was
> her mother coming to take her away, like some-
> thing she had bought at a dress shop and couldn't

wait to have delivered? Would her grandmother let them take her? Did her grandmother want her to go? Where do I live, she thought, and began to cry. She cried a long time, then fell asleep, her face lying in a white patch of tears.

Actually, the only one who is really excited about this development is Harriet, who is practically beside herself that Beth Ellen has a) A REAL MOTHER, b) A FREAKISHLY BEAUTIFUL MOTHER, and c) A MOTHER WHOM APPARENTLY HER OWN FATHER KNEW IN HIS YOUTH, ALTHOUGH HE WILL NOT TELL HER NEARLY ENOUGH ABOUT IT. There is nothing exciting about Zeeney's arrival for Beth Ellen, however, since she mainly regards her as a vaguely irritating presence to be stifled out of all recognition.

> . . . Beth Ellen lay in the bathtub staring at her body. She and her mother had just gotten back from Elizabeth Arden's in time to bathe and dress before they went to dinner. She lay there with a blank mind. . . . I have straight hair. I am called Beth. She had heard Zeeney and Wallace discussing her that morning at breakfast as if she were a piece of toast. Zeeney had said, "I think her head is too little." Wallace had disagreed but said, "No, I don't think that, but she does have curious knees."

Between her grandmother who wants her to be a lady and her mother who wants her to have straight hair and her body which wants her to grow up and Harriet who cannot stop exploding with frustration at her passivity, Beth Ellen's mysterious activity, when we discover it, is not that surprising.

Yes! Spoiler! Beth Ellen is leaving the notes. Your basic dutiful sleuth of the third-person indirect would probably handily notice that she is present at every instance of note-discovery and never wonders herself who is leaving the notes whatsoever. But perhaps not. Beth is so successfully blank to her herself, she's a little blank to us too.

Maybe because the long secret of the book is not really that Beth Ellen is leaving all the notes, but that Beth Ellen is *angry*.

This becomes monumentally clear when Zeeney declares she will be taking Beth Ellen back to Europe with her, and Beth Ellen, in her first act of rebellion, throws an enormous tantrum in the bathroom:

> They started banging on the bathroom door. Beth Ellen sat on the tub and pretended she was sitting under Niagara Falls. She hugged her knees. I will flood the house, she thought. Then I will begin to grow and be huge. I will get so monstrously big that I will break the bathroom and fill the house, the yard, all of Water Mill. I will tower over the Montauk highway like a collosus. They will all run away like ants.
>
> The cold water ran down on her, on her head, her clothes. It beat around her ears like the safe rain of a summer's day.

And just like that, Beth Ellen exits the *limbo utero* of the bathtub and comes into her own. As the book ends, Harriet has found her out:

> "What ever gave you the idea to do it anyway?" asked Harriet with not a little admiration in her voice.

Beth Ellen smiled and said nothing.

"Well, you could have told me," said Harriet. "I knew it at The Preacher's. I watched your face and I knew. But you could have told me." And flinging the book on the bed, she stomped into the bathroom.

Beth Ellen sat on the bed and looked fondly at the book. I'm a child, she thought happily, and I live somewhere. Nobody can ever take me away.

Beth Ellen laughed, a loud, happy laugh.

"WHAT ARE YOU LAUGHING ABOUT?" yelled Harriet from behind the closed door. "Wait'll you read the story I'm going to write about *you* and those *notes*!"

Beth Ellen laughed again. It didn't matter.

And I assume by the time "Harriet" did actually get around to doing it, they were friends enough that it still didn't.

Then Again, Maybe I Won't
By Judy Blume
1971

Window Undressing

> Who says March is supposed to come in like a lion
> and go out like a lamb? That's a load of bull. All it's
> done this March is rain. I'm sick of it.

It's difficult to say why they keep trying to ban this book by
Judy Blume. Significant anecdotal evidence continues to suggest it's perfectly possible for a young body of either sex to read
it numerous times, understand many of its adult complexities,
yet still have no idea what a wet dream is until told explicitly

many years later under entirely different circumstances. I know that I was, say, a good twenty-two (I'll cop to it) before, sitting around, I finally realized WHY Tony would have wanted to carry a raincoat to school and a stack of books to the front of the room when he wrote on the blackboard. (What can I say? The school play, SATs, and papers on Blake had pretty much eaten up most of my free brain space in the intervening decade.) I certainly understood stained sheets had something to do with sleep, not sex—I'll leave readers to access their own dorm-room memories, here, if you don't mind—but I can't say it made it hard (I'm just not going to be able to get away from puns, at this point) for me to understand Tony.

Written in the years before being working-class was considered a virtue, *Then Again, Maybe I Won't* is the story of one Tony Miglione, who's a Jersey City resident; lover of basketball; younger sibling of Ralph, a teacher crammed in upstairs with his wife, Angie, and Vincent, who died in Vietnam; son of Vic ("Pop") and Carmella ("Ma"); and grandson of Grandma ("Grandma"), who does all the cooking and cannot speak because she has no larynx, which doesn't creep Tony out, because he loves her.

The crisis in the novel occurs almost immediately, when Angie gets, insofar as one can, inadvertently pregnant. (I'm going to go out on a limb and assume, due to the presence of several Father Pisarros in the narrative, that she and Ralph are using the rhythm method.) Pop, heretofore a general contractor, also goes out on a limb and sells some electrical cartridge thingie to a businessman named J. W. Fullerbach, which immediately gives the family the means to move out of Jersey City to the leafy environs of Rosemont, Queens. (Literally a *deus ex machina*!)

Before he knows it, Tony has been transplanted from playing basketball at the Y with characters named Big Joe and Little Joe to hanging out with his polite shoplifting neighbor Joel, who has an inground pool, a hot older sister, and a mother who calls Tony's mother, Carmella, Carol because it's "easier."

As a novel of class, *Then Again, Maybe I Won't* is neither cutesy nor polemical: Rather, the pressures Tony experiences as he tries to adjust to the strangeness of newly being consumed with liking girls and having wet dreams is merely doubled, as now he must also contend with the strangeness his new home in Rosemont imposes on him. Blume depicts with mastery the peculiarity of that brief window of adolescence where one is held hostage not only by one's parents but by one's own body as well.

Meaning one might get yelled at for not putting the paper under the mat on one's daily route. Meaning one might lose said route and move to a new town, next door to a rich kid who makes prank calls from his parents' bedroom, which has a circular bed on a pedestal, and this STRESSES ONE OUT. Meaning one's mother might insist on one's calling adults "sir," pick up lint from the new carpets constantly, and acquire a maid that usurps one's grandmother's role such that she secretes herself in her bedroom except to visit one's brother's grave. Meaning one's dad might buy a new car because one's neighbors notice the truck and ask if one is having work done on the house.

One might have erections constantly and have to carry a raincoat or a stack of books at all times to conceal one's condition, and one might lie to one's parents to ask for binoculars for birdwatching, then use them to watch the older girl across the way undress. One might become an uncle, be forced to take piano lessons, decide everyone's a phony, go ahead and let one's friends get caught by a security guard for shoplifting and sent to military school. Pretty much everything might

STRESS ONE OUT so much that one might get terrible stomach pains out of anxiety and eventually wind up in the hospital, after which one's dad, cutting one a break, would prevent one's mother from imitating the neighbors and sending one to a military academy as well—after which finally, one might come into one's own enough, as it were, to put the binoculars away.

And You Give Me a Pain, Elaine
By Stella Pevsner
1978

Sister Act

In the pantheon of beings whose merest whim can wreak havoc in the life of the preteen girl, never forget the mighty older sister, whose halfway state between child and woman is dangerously unstable, two parts that can combine at any moment like warm and cold air to create a murderous thunderclap. One such thunderer is Elaine, who is too consumed with her own bad mood to even lord her willowy beauty over her stockier sister Andrea. ("Someday, if there was any justice on earth—which I was beginning to doubt—Elaine would be all flab with no muscle tone whatsoever. And I'd be slim.") As a bigger sister, whenever I'm feeling like I'm being a pain, I pick up my copy and look at the lithe body of Elaine, twirling her hair while she's talking on the phone in teeny-weeny cut-offs and dangerously narrowed eyes, and feel a rush of sympathy for illustrated Andrea, who, sitting dutifully at her desk without a glint of glamour anywhere, is obviously not even going to be allowed to finish her homework in peace.

In this tale of sisterly disaffection, two sisters differ in every other way they can. Elaine is a sullen, almost hostile scholar; Andrea gets straight A's (except from the teachers who, of course, still bear a grudge against Elaine). Elaine sneaks off to drink beer and carouse; Andrea becomes the dependable stage manager of the school play, *Dracula*. Andrea begins a low-key romance with the props guy; Elaine runs away with a bad boy who ditches her by the side of the road after she runs away. Elaine is her mother's favorite, and Andrea her father's, and Andrea is good-natured, understanding, and mellow—except when it comes to Elaine.

What's most interesting about *And You Give Me a Pain, Elaine* is how Pevsner resists making Elaine a character defined by *Lifetime*-worthy bad behavior. She's not an alcoholic; she's not dangerously obsessed with a boy; she doesn't have a boy who's dangerously obsessed with her; she doesn't have an addiction to painkillers or an addiction to pain. Her drama is simple—she's in a bad mood. But it's a bad mood that, like a gathering hurricane, pulls the hapless surrounding atmosphere straight into its moody, whirling vortex, and from the havoc she wreaks, each nasty word might as well come with a cudgel.

And more interesting still, the solution is *not* sisterly love. The girls' older brother, Joe, knows the only cure is to stay clear.

("I'm not her audience and I care nix about her performance.") Andrea doesn't realize she has a choice—until Joe dies, and she begins to see herself as a person apart, someone who exists as more than in opposition to Elaine—who has, miraculously, started to tire even of herself. Sisterly love doesn't help Elaine stop being such a fuckup—in fact, Andrea releases herself from all responsibility for Elaine's well-being: "It was something my sister would have to work out for herself." But in the quiet after the storm, sisterly love is something that can finally grow.

To Take a Dare
By Paul Zindel and Crescent Dragonwagon
1982

Homing Instinct

Despite having one of the most recognizable co-author names in all of history, Paul Zindel and Crescent Dragonwagon's joint foray may be the least remembered for either author. That's a shame, because this story of a bookworm masked in the body of a bad girl who runs away before she's even 14 is one of the most memorable, complex novels in the bunch. It was a book I found on my friend's shelf and borrowed over and over again, never able to find it in any used bookstore until I was finally saved by eBay, completely obsessed with the expression on the face of the girl on the cover and her terrific body, both lean and curvy in a way teen authors seemed insistent about, but few cover artists could accurately convey. Would I get that body, too? Would my teenage years be that striking and dramatic? (No and no; whatever.)

But Chrysta, who, like Elaine in *And You Give Me a Pain, Elaine*, is the girl at the party who takes a hit of the pot and definitely goes home with the bad guy, is the antithesis of the awkward, worried character who'd like to get puberty going so she can get a boyfriend already—meaning the antithesis of most of the girls, like me, reading her story over and over, wondering what it would be like to be let loose in the world and forced to find yourself before you could even drive. For Chrysta's part, she knows full well that if only her bra size had been a few cups smaller, she'd have been allowed to be left in peace to hang out at the library with the rest of us.

Chrysta Perretti, who hits the road after "my father called me a slut once too often, my dog was hit by a car, and I lost my virginity—what was left of it" is, unlike her milder Margaret counterpart, an abject victim of puberty, sporting a pair of breasts that cause her previously affectionate father to become suddenly hostile and the boys around her suddenly pursuant. (Her mother, not much help in either department, is a character straight from the pantheon of classic Zindel grotesqueries, obese and cloying, capable of polishing off a few packages of cinnamon roles smeared with diet margarine for breakfast.)

But where a classic Zindel novel might evolve into still more elaborate versions of the bizarro (which, don't get me wrong, I adore, in all their *The Undertaker's Gone Bananas* glory), *To Take a Dare* continues in a more measured, realistic direction. This paradoxically has the effect of making Chrysta's experiences seem more, not less, dramatic. Staring with incredulity at the white dress her parents have bought her for her birthday, one with teeny straps and a bodice that would never fit over her new body, Chrysta thinks, "This dress that my parents were giving me was made for someone else . . . They think they love me, but it's not *me*. It's some make-believe character called Daughter, not *me*."

> There was a half bottle of catsup in the fridge. I got it out. I took that frilly white dress with its pretty pink shoulder straps and I spread it out over the kitchen table with its skirt neatly flounced out. Then I took that bottle of red, red catsup and shook it out all over that frilly white dress.

But if the horrors of the first part of the book are made believable by their stark depiction, so too is Chrysta's improbable rise to independence, which takes place after a number of weeks on the road force her, for purely practical reasons, to shed the bad-girl persona she'd adopted in defiance of her family:

> But gradually, my life on the road began to change me. The Punk Queen started to get edged out. First, of course, my appearance changed—you can't wear Candie's if you're running down the shoulder of an interstate waving your hands excitedly because after two hours a car pulled over for you a few hundred yards down the road. You can't wear eye makeup if your only mirror is a jagged half mirror above a dirty sink in a Mobil station at three A.M. in North Dakota and the guy driving the Hev-in-Lee Yogurt delivery truck is waiting for you outside, his radio

tuned to an all-night country-and-western station for truck drivers.

And slowly I began to feel like there was more to me than just a good body, though I wasn't sure what. And sometimes I began to feel like somehow, I wasn't sure how, things might work out for me.

How they do work out—Chrysta settles in a small town in Arkansas, finds a job managing a kitchen in a hotel, and falls in love, though not without some pitfalls along the way—is, by all objective measurements, a fairy-tale ending. And it's certainly also a far cry from even the objectively *happy* endings of other runaway novels, which generally involve the character having been mistaken about the suitability of her family of origin or finding a family that's more suitable.

But Chrysta's story isn't about finding her true home—she's not a runaway, she's a pilgrim, and like all proper pilgrims, her story has to do more with self-discovery than discovering her true family. I've always thought it was bold of the authors to let Chrysta go ahead and just become an adult despite her age, which, by the time she finally settles down, is a mere sixteen. Our current obsession with creating the proper environment for children to learn and grow that makes us forget that, given the right circumstances and internal resources, they cease being children at all and—even more astonishing—might become adults who are healthy, productive citizens. Maybe it is a fairly tale, but I like the idea of a character who not only escapes a bad family—but also escapes the idea that she needs a family at all.

Caroline
By Willo Davis Roberts
1984

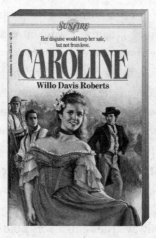

Either/Ore

As we touch on the topic of girls who are taking their first steps toward independence, I would be remiss if I did not include a "Sunfire"—the series that sent spirited girls traipsing across juicy historical periods long before *American Girl* had even had a chance to fasten its bonnet. Sunfire romances, distinguished by their eponymous titles, covered everything from the Civil War to the Salem Witch Trials, to the Suffrage era, but I am an unabashed fan of *Caroline*—oh, spunky, sun-kissed Caroline!—the girl who cuts off her hair and sports boys' clothing in order to follow her brothers to California, where they've joined that long wagon train to the Gold Rush. God knows what beach shack or dentist's office I swiped *Caroline* from, but by the end of several reads, I was as intimately familiar with the particulars of Gold Rush-era underthings and panning for gold as I was with the notoriously difficult nature of young love.

As the novel commences, it's not exactly clear whether Caroline's decision to not stay at home like a good girl instead of going off after them is motivated by curiosity, orneriness, or pure spite—"That's what everybody says anytime I want to do anything! If they wanted me to be one of those wishy-washy females, somebody should have thought of it before now." Still, her wise decision to do it in the guise of a boy means the reader can sidestep such tedious assertions of equality for a while and just concentrate on whether or not she's going to get caught.

Because, Reader, *can* Caroline's womanly curves be restrained by the merest straps and loose clothing? *Can* her smooth, dimpled face and hands belong to anyone secreting large amounts of testosterone? Can those charming curls cease beguilingly escaping and be brutally shorn to ordinary fuzz, and can she convince strangers that that soft, husky voice belongs to a young boy instead of one who is nearly a woman? Sure, whatever. But discovery isn't the thing Caroline has to worry about. Quoth the cover's tagline: "Her disguise would keep her safe, but not from love."

Ah yes! For, in *Twelfth Night*-style, Caroline is the confidante and right arm of another wagon-train inhabitant, Dan Riddle, virile and vital, who's also fond of the bright young boy—*he thinks*—he's taken under his brawny wing. This is inconvenient, as Caroline is full-on crazy in love with him. Night after night, she dreams of telling him, but she cannot—not only because it would expose her as a girl and get her kicked off the trail, but because it would reveal her to be a *liar. What man, Reader, could love a liar?* (Remember, she's safe from everything: but love.) One night, she finally puts on girls' clothes and steps out into a dance in her beloved's arms—thus imprinting herself on him enough that, 18 chapters later, he's still in love with the mysterious girl when he learns she's his young charge. Conveniently, the mysterious girl has also just happened on the biggest gold mine in creation, and everyone is too drunk with money to wonder about why Dan took the young boy under his wing in the first place.

Chapter 3

Danger Girls
I Know What You Did Last Summer (Reading)

Partners in Crime

Of all the mischief one worries your average young woman might get up to, being at the center of a conspiracy—vast! even multinational!—seems low on the list. (Stealing a sister's best dress, boosting a few lipsticks from Rite Aid, or making an old drunk buy her and some buddies a six-pack is probably closer to the conventional vision.) But, as fans of Lois Duncan, Ellen Raskin, or Robert Cormier know, the lives of young women and men can be as fraught with secrets both large and small, and as rocked by their revelations as any White House scandal.

The Westing Game may be the most beloved of mysteries for girls—and not only because it brought us the miraculous Turtle Wexler, braid flying behind as she bikes away from Samuel Westing's mansion, having spent her afternoon checking up on a dead man, but also because it was a sophisticated and hilarious send-up of a group of a adults as flummoxed by their own lives as by the clues they're given. We also have a character like Cormier's Adam Farmer, a pawn in a horrible game who can't avoid being taken. Then there's Duncan's *Daughters of Eve*, which dissects feminism even as, *Crucible*-like, it teaches us the dangers of the mob. And then there is L'Engle's *Dragons in the Waters* and *The Arm of the Starfish*, which somehow manage to combine cellular regeneration, ancient Indian tribes, helpful limo drivers, and the very nature of good versus evil with fisherman sweaters and very good coffee.

Which is not to say that there's anything wrong with Nancy Drew, Trixie Belden, or any other sleuth who can run rings around anything involving an old clock and a set of mysterious footprints. But these series' delicate, ticking works are to the mysteries and thrillers herein as a Swiss watch is to a nuclear power plant. Which is to say, not only are these serious business, but the complexity of the plots is matched only by the complexity of the challenges the characters face. In each case, there's a mystery to be solved, to be sure. But each protagonist is also a mystery to herself—and one we are just as eager to see her solve.

The Westing Game
By Ellen Raskin
1978

Identity Theft

The sun sets in the west (just about everybody knows that) but Sunset Towers faced east. Strange!

I'll admit up front it took me until my mid-thirties to notice the significance of that first line. But in a time wherein technology would obviate the plot points of most teenage reads, I can only be grateful for my continuing obtuseness. It's bad enough that the cell phone would have killed *Are You in the House Alone*, or e-mail allowed L'Engle's Zachary Gray to simply send Vicky

Austin opaque, enraging e-mails rather than showing up to coolly manipulate her in the flesh. I'd like to think Harriet M. Welsch, dedicated as she was to the power of the pen, could have resisted the glories of Facebook. But could the sleek inner assembly of *The Westing Game*, dependent on clues written, like highly absorbent cuneiform, on papyrus-like scraps of paper towel, ever have survived the gear-revealing powers of Google? Just try plugging in "FRUITED PURPLE WAVES FOR SEE" to any search engine, and see for yourself.

The story of—stay off Google! Then it won't ruin things to tell you what it's the story of—a ragtag group who is lured into renting apartments in a luxury apartment building under false pretenses, *The Westing Game* is a complex thriller to solve a murder—that of the multimillionaire Sam Westing, of Westing Paper Products, whose nearby mansion—and wide-flung life—casts a great shadow over all the tenants' lives.

Anyway, the new tenants of the building are as follows (at great—patience, please—length): The Wexler family, made up of mother and social climber Grace; father Jake, a bookie; daughter Angela, a beautiful fiancée of Denton Deere, med student; and her sister, Turtle, a clever shin kicker; the Hoo family, comprising Shin Hoo, proprietor of the building's unsuccessful Chinese restaurant; his son Doug, a long-distance runner; and his non–English-speaking second wife, Mrs. Hoo; Theo Theodorakis and Christos Theodorakis, aspiring writer and crippled birdwatcher, respectively, sons of the proprietor of the building's only successful restaurant, a Greek diner; Flora Baumbach, an unnervingly grinning dressmaker; Berthe Crow, a devoutly religious cleaning lady; Judge J. J. Ford, non-Magical Negro and judge; Otis Amber, idiot delivery boy; Barney Northrup, seething building manager; and Sandy McSouthers, the genial doorman. I am probably forgetting someone. Yes, secretary Sydelle Pulaski! Well, she was the mystery's "mistake" anyway.

Anyone with Asperger's has solved this whole thing by now, but let's continue for the rest of us.

The book commences as follows: the players learn of their mysterious fate—though not of the other players' connections to Westing—after the mysterious death of the man in question. Called to the mansion, they are declared heirs, then split into teams and given a series of five seemingly unrelated clues written, such as Flora and Turtle's SEA MOUNTAIN AM O (which, incidentally, would have had yielded nothing helpful on Google at all). The players' object, with this scarce matter, is to find Westing's murderer. The prize is his 200-million-dollar fortune.

What follows is less an *And Tween There Were None* than a Shakespearean farce, mainly because—aside from the fact that Turtle is the only tween—as the mystery unfolds, Raskin is less concerned with the exigencies of the plot as with the particulars of her characters. It's not a mistake that the first task of the heirs is to write down their professions. Angela Wexler, to the consternation of her fiancé, writes "none" ("Just what did Angela mean by *nun*?") while her mother chooses the more optimistic "heiress." As we will learn, Sam's murderer is not the only mystery. The players are, deliberately or subconsciously, hiding their true identities as well:

> Who were these people, these specially selected tenants? They were mothers and fathers and children. A dressmaker, a secretary, an inventor, a doctor, a judge. And, oh yes, one was a bookie, one was a burglar, one was a bomber, and one was a mistake.

Barney Northrup had rented one of the apartments
to the wrong person.

Alongside the sonorous tones of intrigue lies a subtler
theme: All of the players are gripped by identity crises. Grace
is terrified her clunky, explicitly ethnic maiden name, Wind-
kloppel, will be somehow revealed. Turtle knows her mother
likes her less than Angela, who is emotionally paralyzed by
how no one ever refers to anything but her looks or her impending marriage. Judge J. J. can't get over the fact that her
education—and career—was orchestrated by the tyrant Westing, while Flora is haunted by guilt over the death of her disabled daughter. Speaking of disabled, Chris is mortified by his
constantly flailing limbs, while Sydelle is triumphant over finally being noticed after a lifetime of secretarial invisibility.

But the tedious idea that we are a triumphant multi-culti
pot of unity is not Raskin's lesson. Instead, we see our culture's (generally humorous) warts: Mr. Hoo added the "Shin"
because he thought it would make him sound more Chinese,
Jake notes Grace conveniently forgets he's a Jew, people talk to
Chris like he's 5, and Grace compliments Mrs. Hoo for being
so "doll-like and inscrutable," then makes her hors d'oeuvres
in a cheongsam. (I can't blame Raskin for the straight-from-
P.C.-central-casting role of the female black judge—she's not
responsible for *Law & Order* running it into the ground.)

While *The Westing Game* is a wonderful, fun mystery, it's
also a profound meditation on how humans, given a set of clues,
miss what's actually missing right in front of them, and instead
project themselves onto the negative space. In future financier
Turtle's case, she's convinced her clues represent stock picks—
as Theo studies chemistry, he becomes convinced they're an
equation. Grace Wexler is so intent on proving she's Sam West-

ing's niece she doesn't even notice she actually *is* Sam Westing's niece, and in the unfolding of their race to the finish, J. J.
can only see the outlines of the chess moves with which Sam
repeatedly defeated her as a girl when she lived in his mansion
as the daughter of the maid.

But these self-generated projections don't trap the
participants—they're the keys to their freedom. At the last reading of the will, the sheaf of paper mysteriously defines them all
not as what they've been but as what they've become: Turtle,
financier; Flora, dressmaker; Theo, writer; Doug, champ; Mr.
Hoo, inventor; Grace, restaurateur; Jake, bookie; Mrs. Hoo,
cook; Angela Wexler, person. The real Sam Westing will die
many years from now on the Fourth of July, but the will wishes
the assembled a happy Fourth—to their great confusion—for
another reason: For all of the residents of Sunset Towers, the
end of the game is Independence Day.

Daughters of Eve
By Lois Duncan
1979

Lois Duncan

Author of *Summer of Fear* and *Killing Mr. Griffin*

Mad Libbers

The calendar placed the first day of fall on the twenty-third of September, and on the afternoon of Friday, the twenty-second, Ruth Grange walked slowly down Locust Street, her schoolbooks gripped by one hand, a brown paper sack by the other.

As I hit the midpoint of my third decade, I'm finally willing to admit that a large portion of my righteous indignation at the crimes of malekind stems not from things I've actually experienced, but from repeated, late-night readings of *Daughters of Eve*. Certainly the novel itself engenders enough rage at the patriarchy to fuel nationwide bra burnings. In a rare supernatural-free narrative (okay, there's one psychic character), *Daughters of Eve*, on the surface, is the story of Irene Stark, dark-browed, dark-hearted feminist faculty advisor, who leads her 10 unenlightened, high-school-aged charges into a twisted version of women's liberation. But despite Duncan's admirable efforts at parity, what emerges is only an unforgettable portrait of rank injustice.

We find the pre-lib girls ensconced in Modesta, California—a town whose name itself denotes placid submission—at the beginning of the school year, in the act of inducting three new sisters into the Daughters of Eve sorority. There are, as I've said, 10 of them, but let's keep our eyes on the big hitters: Bambi Ellis, an icy (is there any other kind?) homecoming queen; Ann Whitten, a dreamy artiste; Tammy Carncross, resident Cassandra; Fran Schneider, budding scientist; and the three novitiates: Ruth Grange, household drudge, Laura Snow, sweet, chubby outcast; and Jane Rheardon, holder of a terrible secret.

Yes, that's seven. Stick with me here! As the book commences, Duncan takes care to establish in *excruciating* detail the various levels of oppression under which the girls operate. And, although her problems are the most banal, I have always sympathized profoundly with Ruthie Grange, who is forced to babysit and pick up after her three cocky, filth-producing brothers in order that her mother may work a job to feed their college funds:

> The boys' cereal bowls from the morning sat out on
> the table with milk soured in their bottoms, and the
> egg plates were thick with yellow yolk dried onto

them like cement. There was a pool of some uniden-
tifiable liquid on the linoleum at the base of the refrigerator. . . .

The sticky intractability also stands as a symbol for Ruthie's
own position, where she is trapped like a fly in amber, not even
allowed to attend the weekly meetings of Daughters of Eve—
that is, until another member pipes up and reminds her that
she might as well go on strike and enrage her parents, since
she's already effectively grounded.

The other new girls, in ways large and small, are also locked
in their positions. Laura Snow, both "cringing" and overweight, is an easy target for a boy who lies to her to use her for
sex, while Jane Rheardon is the daughter of a brute who beats
his wife for anything—as when, in one of the most terrifying,
memorable scenes of wife-beating I've ever read, she refuses to
sing the secret song all Daughters of Eve are taught:

> "That sounds like a winner," Mr. Rheardon said.
> "Let's hear it."
> "Oh, I can't," Ellen Rheardon said. . . . "It's just
> that we took an oath. We would sing the song any-
> where except within the sisterhood. It was—sort
> of—sacred." Ellen gave a short, nervous laugh. . . .
> "But this is almost twenty years later! You're a
> grown woman, for God's sake, or at least you're sup-
> posed to be. You're a married woman whose hus-
> band is making a simple request of you, and you sit
> there and tell him—"
> *No*, Jane cried silently, *no, no, no!* . . .
> Jane pressed her hands against the sides of her

face to control the twitching. From the room below there came a thud and a high-pitched cry.

A moment later a thin, wavering voice began to sing.

That's a far cry from the sexism of the Grange household, which, besides enslaving Ruthie to devote all her labor, gratis, to her spoiled, obnoxious, messy, ungrateful brothers, is subtle, if no less dictatorial:

> "What Ruthie said was true, George; Peter and Niles don't lift a hand to help out. She was right when she said that it isn't fair. It's not fair."
>
> "What's unfair about it?" Mr. Grange asked impatiently. "Pete and Niles are boys. You can't expect them to put on aprons and flit around polishing the furniture. I didn't do that when I was a boy, and God help anyone who suggested it."
>
> . . . "How about some coffee?" her husband said now. His eyes were back upon the newspaper.
>
> "It's on the back of the burner, and the cups are on the drying rack."
>
> "I didn't ask you where it was. I said, how about some?"

KEEP CALM LADIES. It's the girls growing up in households like these that, in effect, lay the groundwork for Irene Stark—who, as we learn, has arrived in Modesta after being passed over for promotion in favor of a man who assures her it's better in the end, since she's going to need to devote her time to her babies any day now. (Also key to the physically plain Stark's twisted psyche: overhearing her father say, "We'd better get her all the education we can, because God knows, she's never going to find a husband to support her.") While Irene is fond of reciting appalling statistics on female hires, rapes, and domestic exploitation (facts I remember to this day!), her real arsenal is the built-in injustice the girls have already experienced, if they would only open their eyes to it: "You are not like your mothers! . . . You don't have to let yourselves be ground under foot as your mothers have been. You can rise—fight back—show the world that you know your own worth!"

When standing up involves refusing to hand over the money they've raised to get the boys' basketball team new warm-up suits when the girls don't even have a soccer team, this is terrific. (By the way, young ladies—have you thanked an older athlete for Title IX today?) Unfortunately, Irene is also fond of such methods as shaving the head of a male malefactor, trashing the science lab, and chopping up the wood-based objects in the principal's office. There is also the matter of Jane eventually bringing down a cast-iron skillet on her father's skull and killing him dead. (Oh, THAT'S why psychic Tammy, at the initiation, saw a candle dripping, as Duncan puts it, "BLOOD!")

However you shake it, Irene Stark is, like her name, a character far less scary than the world around her. (Okay, I admit the part where she threatens to bean poor old Tammy Carncross's dad with a glass bottle in the face for keeping Fran—justifiably, as it happens—out of the state science competition is a little rattling.) But with her bombastic pronouncements and gloomy indictments, she's almost a parody of a revolutionary—and of a monster.

What Duncan has to say about the ways in which the Daughters of Eve are oppressed is far more interesting. Mr. Rheardon beating his wife is clear-cut abuse. Also easy to object to is the sly way Peter deflects Laura's attempts to make their relationship public. ("Don't push me, Laura. I don't like being nagged at, okay . . . there are better ways to get a guy to do things than by nagging at him. A sweet, a loving girl can get just about anything she wants as long as she doesn't keep pushing and getting a guy irritated." Uh-huh.) But what about paternalism dressed up as love? Arguing with her husband again about letting Ruth join the group, Mrs. Grange thinks:

> Her husband's voice had settled into that solid, reasonable tone that she knew so well and liked so little. It made her feel diminished somehow, childish, as though nothing she said was of any real value, yet at the same time it contained affection. There had never been a moment in the duration of their marriage that she had doubted George's love for her, and that, in a way, made everything harder.

Being held down is hard—but being held down in the name of love is harder. In the case of Ann Whitten, the budding artist whose scholarship to art school, arranged by Irene, gets thrown off track by a (surprise!) pregnancy, Duncan takes the gray area even further. Her fiancé is disappointed by the idea of putting off the marriage, but he makes a solid effort at being happy about it. ("I'm trying. That's the best I can do. I'm trying.") Her father, noticing she's throwing up every morning, becomes a surprising advocate:

> "There's a friend who thinks I ought to have an abortion."
> She had expected a violent reaction, but she did not receive one.

"That's one answer, I suppose," her father said. "I hear they do them real easy and safe nowadays right in the hospital."

"Do you think it would be wrong?"

"What I think doesn't matter," Mr. Whitten said. "It doesn't matter what your mother thinks either, or what this friend of yours thinks. I don't know about Dave. I guess what he thinks ought to matter some, but then again, maybe it shouldn't. It all comes down to you. You've got to make a decision you can live with and once you've done this, you've got to accept it and go on from there."

"It's not fair," Ann said miserably . . .

"Of course, it's not fair," her father said. "Why should it be? Whoever said life is fair was a moron."

As far as I'm concerned, Mr. Whitten is the true feminist in the novel. And he's made a good point. As Duncan finally boils down the problem, it's not an issue of whether things are fair—it's whether they are *just.* Wife-beating, sport-fucking, attempted-raping, labor-stealing: unjust. Getting pregnant by accident: Them's just the breaks. It's not that men need to be punished. (I mean, they do, but whatever.) It's that no one should have to subsume one's life for another—unpaid, unthanked, and abused—merely because a set of cocky, entitled people (men! men! men!) prefer it that way.

Daughters of Eve may indict extreme feminism—but it's also as grim a tally as I've ever seen of a world without it. So what if Irene isn't actually a scary warning to would-be revolutionaries, but simply an avatar for the rage engendered when half the people get to leave cereal bowls on the table and the other half have to clean them up? "How could anyone know for sure what went on in all the neat white houses that lined the streets of a pleasant little town like Modesta?" Jane asks, hearing her mother being beaten downstairs. Before you lace up your steel-toed boots, ladies—if you could see what went on, you'd find quite a range of things happen. But Ms. Irene Stark's point still obtains—the people in houses leaving half-filled cereal bowls around for other people to clean up better watch out.

The Grounding of Group 6

By Julian F. Thompson

1983

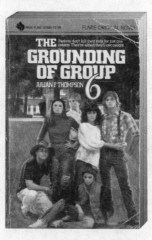

A Killer Course

> The people in their group, Group 6, were all sixteen,
> all five of them, and none of them was fat.

It's been a while since literature gave us a good teen slay-ing. I mean, parents in books kill their *young* charges all the time—or, rather, mothers do, generally by drowning them or letting them be drowned, if they can't manage to rustle up the funds to pay a fake abductor. (Men, in their *Gone Baby Gone* mode, tend to STEAL them away from such pitiable mothers . . . for their own good!) In any case, you are still hard-pressed to find a group of well-off parents offing their near-adult offspring—who have, by the way, *managed not to be fat*—for no good reason at all.

Not so in Julian F. Thompson's masterwork, the story of five high schoolers sent to a boarding school, Coldbrook Academy, for what they think is a brief coda to their so far vaguely unillustrious high-school careers. In fact it is meant to be the brief end . . . TO THEIR LIVES. Their parents have paid, from what my post-Algebra II brain can glean from the narrative, something like $1,500 to have their kids poisoned and thrown into deep crevasses, never to be heard from again. (With inflation, this is something like $57,235, which seems fair.) The service is offered by a select group of psychopathic faculty, including the dean of Coldbrook, who puts it to Nat Rittenhouse, the young man hired to ground said six, thusly:

> "We take them off their hands, those lemons. Once and for all. Quick and neat and clean and utterly untraceable. We have those limestone faults quite near the school—these fissures on the surface of the planet. Some of them seem almost bottomless. Drop a lemon into one . . . we never hear it hit. We call that 'grounding,' Mr. Rittenhouse. A natural and wholesome term, I hope you will agree. At Coldbrook, we are definitely . . . organic."

Something for Whole Foods to consider, perhaps. Anyway, the players are as follows: sassy Marigold, who has lightning bolts on her panties; dry, lanky Coke, who has vodka bottles stashed in his rucksack; sweet Sully, who is hot but unsullied; sporty Sarah, who is shy but secure; and Ludi, who is, as required by quota laws governing 99 percent of teen novels, psychic. On top of that is the still-young Nat—who has been thrust into this position by a small gambling habit and a run-in with an Italian character in the mafia who is not a stereotype *at all*. This is three boys and three girls. I wonder if any of them will get it on!

The characters are being shuffled off this mortal coil for the following:

Marigold: Sleeping with mother's boyfriend

Sully: Rejecting mother's gay boyfriend

Sarah: Plagiarism

Ludi: Psychic abilities

Coke: Unruly hair

I think! As near as I can tell, so knocked flat am I by a titanic flood of complex verbiage. (I have no idea how I followed any of this at age nine—*as I still cannot follow it now*.) In just the first chapter, we are graced with the following references: "*fleurs du mal de siecle*," Kir, a doorman named Porfirio, cannabis, "Moi?", and an Abenaki chauffeur. The weary worldliness of the characters—16, un-gay, un-fat—reaches its apex, I feel, as Coke raises a glass of smuggled rum to the crew and ironically declares, "Prosit." I'm not sure I knew what *rum* was.

But I am willing to overlook that the author has imbued his cast with age-inappropriate dinner-party game because they still totally have a bunch of YA sex to read aloud at the sleepover. Here's Sully, feeling up Sara:

Sully could hardly believe he was actually kissing her. Her lips felt wonderful under his, and—whoa—

he'd forgotten to move his hand off her breast. He
was actually *feeling* her breast with his hand and *it*
felt just fantastic, and then her lips were moving,
and, wow, that was her *tongue*. . . .

Italics TOTALLY not mine! Marigold and Coke, of course,
jump into bed right at the beginning, and somehow, Thompson
is even able to finesse Nat sleeping with Ludi—maybe if you are
psychic, you are not underage?—zipping their sleeping bags together so quickly time and the rule of law disappear entirely.

So, enter the emotionally sophisticated child, capable of
standing up to an adult world allied against her. But whither the
emotionally despicable parent, aside from the nasty stepmother?
What about tyrants like *The Cat Ate My Gymsuit*'s emotionally
abusive dad? The alkie mom of *The Long Secret*? The stage mom
of *I'll Love You When You're More Like Me*? Even Ramona's dad
brutally slicing his wife's as-yet-undone pancakes? Guardians
like Zindel's troupe of Bayonne parents—one of whom squeezes
margarine from the bottle, spreads it on an English muffin and
then tells her daughter, "I love you, kid. I just love myself a little
more"—have disappeared, and why?

Because now, parents are co-members of the narrative. We
have to deconstruct their little lives, we have to hang with
them at the breakfast bar, and love them like they're just like
us before heading off to a commercial break. So, as ascends
Gilmore Girls, so dies a golden YA trope—the parent who deserves to die.

Still totally no idea what an Abenaki chauffeur is, by the way.

Summer of Fear
By Lois Duncan
1976

Which Witch Is Which?

It's summer. Summer—again.

Over the course of the last decade I have been conducting a longitudinal survey on the works of Lois Duncan as experienced by other women my own age (old), often while trying on eyeliner at Ricky's or attempting to alienate someone's annoying new boyfriend. Amongst many unsurprising results ("I thought I was psychic until I was 32"; "Why are you talking about Lois Duncan to my new boyfriend?"), one surprising one is as follows:

Not one woman—one!—over the course of a decade was able to name the title of the book, *even though all had read it several times and confessed to attempting to remember the title in their own idle moments, frequently, and failing.*

Duncan fans will understand I owe those italics completely to her. Anyway, let's review the plot. After the tragic death of her parents, a long lost cousin comes to live with an innocent family, but then turns out to be an Ozark-bred, trash-talking, murdering witch who says things like "varmint" and totally STOLE THE IDENTITY of the cousin, whom she really killed, along with the girl's parents, in a fiery crash off a cliff.

That numerous women who can remember the names of people I don't even recall fooling around with or even knowing from, like, eighteen years ago could not scare up the title of a work they'd read at least 5 times WHILE ALSO HAVING read *Who Killed My Daughter* stems, I wager, from the fact that herein and herein alone, Duncan has taken the typical conceits of her other works of fiction and amped them up to an unsettling degree.

Just to refresh for you, some classic Duncan tropes:

1. The Malevolent Double
   Stranger with My Face, I Know What You Did Last Summer, Down a Dark Hall, Summer of Fear

2. Scary Ringleader
   Killing Mr. Griffin, Five Were Missing, Daughters of Eve

3. Perky heroine, just getting breasts, believes
   she has hotter boyfriend than she deserves
   *Stranger with My Face, Daughters of Eve,
   Summer of Fear, I Know What You Did Last
   Summer*

4. Psychokenisis/Telekenesis/*Deus-ex-machi-
   nesis*
   *A Gift of Magic, Down a Dark Hall, The Third
   Eye, Stranger with My Face, Five Were Missing*

5. Subtle Indictments of Reagan-era Feminism
   *Daughters of Eve, plus every mother character
   who's always like, "But I chose not to work"*

6. Helpful Old Person, Happens To Be Expert
   on Something Key to Plot
   Todo

7. Albuquerque
   Toujours

Summer of Fear does not deviate from the above. As I'm
sure you now recall, since I told you the title and the end and
everything already, 15-year-old Rachel is living the high life in
Albuquerque as a red-haired, freckly, prime-pubescent smarty-
pants with a hot boyfriend, Mike, a kindly sage of a neighbor,
Professor Jarvis, a spunky BFF, Caroline, two annoying brothers, and parents who inexplicably tolerate them all.

This all goes to hell, however, when Rachel's aunt and uncle
are killed in a car crash, and their daughter Julia (WATCH
OUT FOR THIS JULIA PERSON) comes to live with the
family permanently.

So far, we are on familiar, roseate-tinged territory. A gawky teen who has recently blossomed into love and B-cups (Mike to Rachel: "Let's face it, there've been some changes in the past year, and in all the right places"), Beave-like brothers ("Pretty soon, Bobby came in smelling like old tennis shoes and chewing gum"), a convenient plot device thinly disguised as an old-person sage ("Pine Crest?" The professor nodded appreciatively. "That's in the heart of the Ozarks, isn't it?"), a pet who knows the score before everybody else ("Julia's body stiffened. 'I'm not very good with dogs. They don't like me.'"), and subtle hints that something is terribly wrong ("When I think back I realize that this was the moment I received my first hint that something was terribly wrong").

As I reread the novel, all I could think was that my twelve-year-old takeaway from the entire novel basically was the whole scene in the shopping mall where Julia tries on a bikini and Rae cannot deal, the substance of which is apparently burned in my brain: " . . . she had the kind of figure I had always dreamed of having someday, maybe when I was about twenty."

I still dream of that! But what I had forgotten—let's say blocked—was everything else. First of all, one set of parents, plus one real-life girl your age and everything, is fully killed, thrown off a cliff. Killed! Second, a dog is killed. Killed! A dog! An innocent dog named Trickle! Third: A man is hospitalized and paralyzed and, like, has to send messages by blinking. Paralyzed! Fourth: Did I mention an evil Ozark woman kills and impersonates Rachel's cousin and moves in and steals her boyfriend and everything, KILLS? And fifth: Once Rachel calls her out as the witch she is, Julia is always wandering around with her eyes narrowing at Rachel and a smile dancing on her lips and saying evil shit like, "Maybe [your dog] choked on his own bad temper" and suggesting that at the end of the day she really wants Rachel's DAD, not her BOYFRIEND, and it is fucking *terrifying.*

We're not even getting into how scary the *witch* stuff is. Cuz not only does not-really-Julia kill Rachel's aunt, uncle, and the real Julia by just *marking a place on the map* where they should go off the cliff, she kills Rachel's dog, Trickle, by making a wax doll, and she gives Rachel hives (thereby decommissioning her for an evening so she can better steal her boyfriend) simply by splattering her picture with red paint. She makes everyone fall in love with her by sprinkling powder in their water. Oh yeah, also? She always avoids having her picture taken. Do you know why? Because witches *don't* show up in them.

But really, after Rae triumphs and saves her mom from driving off a cliff and gets her boyfriend back, the scariest thing I learned is that having not-really-Julia-actually-some-random-Ozark-person be a witch is the most manipulative plot device I had never seen coming at age 12. After all, there's not really any reason for not-really-Julia to be a witch. Murdering people, impersonating cousins and trying to sleep with their dads is already pretty scary. But, as a certain *Parents' Choice* winner must know, there is no way you are going to focus on any of that when you are twelve. Instead, you are going to make a wax figure of your biggest enemy and try to burn it with a candle. You are going to spatter a photograph of your brother with blue paint and be *freaked out by your powers* when he gets a bruise two weeks later and, like, NEVER do it again. And, after 22 years pass, you are going to see the cover, shiver, and be magically unable to remember the title at all.

I Am the Cheese
By Robert Cormier
1977

Don't Know Him from Adam

In general, the "it was all a dream" trope, that refuge for frantic writers in search of an ending everywhere, should be retired from fiction. That is, except for a few select cases like Robert Cormier's *I Am the Cheese*, which uses it not as a happy cop-out—hey, they didn't *really* die!—but as an avenue to discuss the unambiguous horror when one really doesn't know what's true about one's self.

When I started my grand reading tour of the teen shelf, there were only a few boys to be found there—hugely hungry 'Manzo, of course, brought to us care of our favorite pioneer, Laura—and Paul Zindel's misfit teenagers, manic and/or moody, whose inner thoughts were useful reading for anyone whose main back-and-forth with boys was filling out a biology lab.

Still, Cormier's Adam Farmer is the only one who still gives me a small pang of distress when I think of him. Maybe it's because he's so unconsciously kind and so unconsciously vulnerable, he rouses a sisterly sense of protection, one I never felt toward all the adventurers, wisecrackers, misfits, and other male-sexed characters I was perfectly happy to meet and find out about. They were there for the future, and frankly, a little too scary to think about beyond the biology-lab stage. But Adam's story has nothing to do with him rejecting the world—or any of the girls in it. Adam is kind and open and in a nasty situation—and he needs our help now.

When we meet him, the teenaged Adam Farmer is pedaling furiously toward Rutterberg, Vermont, having lit out hometown of Monument as well as his outspoken girlfriend, Amy Hertz ("*yes*, she sighs, *like the car*") under unknown circumstances. All the reader knows is that Adam is retracing the route he once took on vacation with his parents—also not on the scene for unknown reasons—and, between being menaced by toughs and the occasional pervert, he's trying to figure out why all of his calls to Amy—who is, ironically, fond of playing pranks where they pretend to be other people—are going unanswered.

These disturbing scenes, which occur not only in the present but in the first person, are interposed by chapters in the second person, which all begin with Adam being kindly grilled (ostensibly) by someone named Brinn:

T: And what did you find out, finally?

A: Too much. And not enough.

T: Do you really believe that or are you merely being clever?

(5-second interval.)

T: I am sorry to be so blunt. Please explain what you mean.

A: I wasn't trying to be a wise guy. I was telling the truth. I found out, for instance, about my mother's Thursday night telephone calls. And when I realized what the calls were all about, it was both too much and not enough. It was worse than just knowing the birth certificates.

T: Tell me about the telephone calls.

(10-second interval.)

A: I have a feeling you already know about them. I have a feeling you know everything, even my blank spots.

T: Then, why should I make you go through it all? Why should I carry on this charade?

A: I don't know.

T: You disappoint me. Can't you think of one person who will benefit?

(5-second interval.)

A: Me. Me. Me. That's what you said at the beginning. But I never asked for it. I never asked to benefit by it.

(4-second interval.)

A: I have a headache.

T: Don't retreat now. Don't retreat. Tell me about the phone calls your mother made.

(5-second interval.)

A: There really isn't very much to tell.

Like a doctor's chart made all the more horrible by its formal impenetrability, these transcripts of interviews create a horrid sense of foreboding. This is only increased by the periodic flashbacks of his loving family and childhood, which come in brief, lyric bursts:

> He curled up in the bed, listening. He always liked to listen at night. Often he heard his mother and father murmuring in their bedroom, the bed making a lot of noise, and there were the nice sounds of his father and mother together, making soft sounds as if they were furry animals like the stuffed animals he always slept with, Bittie the Bear and Pokey the Pig, his friends. His father would say: "Hey, boy, you're getting too old for all those toys, three and a half, going on four." The boy knew his father was joking, that he would never take his friends away. Anyway, his mother would say: "Now, now, he's a long time from four, a long long time." The tenderness in her voice and her perfume like lilac in the spring.

The revelation that Adam and his family are part of an early form of the Witness Protection Program, one he remembers himself during these interviews, is a welcome answer to

Adam's present quandary, but it's not really what this book—which anticipates *Memento* by more than twenty years—is about. It's a book about losses of all kinds—not only identity, but family, friends, one's love, one's home and connections in the world. The title comes from Adam's father's love for the song "The Farmer in the Dell," with its "The Cheese Stands Alone" refrain—and just like the song, *I Am the Cheese* shows how easily something innocent and guileless can be ripped away, without apology or warning. When the present is revealed to have been a dream, one usually wakes up to find the bogeyman gone. Adam only wakes up to the nightmare.

The Arm of the Starfish
By Madeleine L'Engle
1965

On the Straight and Sparrow

I am proud to say that everything I ever learned about cellular regeneration, I learned from Madeleine L'Engle. Oh, and the layout of Lisbon and any bits of Portuguese (*para* means "in order to"!), as well as the workings of the State Department and the proper treatment of shark bites. (I'd say I learned that from *Jaws*, too, but if you flip to the last chapter, you'll see that had more effect on my grasp of female arousal.) Speaking of female arousal, I also learned not to trust pretty girls abroad—and DEFINITELY to never let them get ahold of your passport.

Adam Eddington, making his first strong-silent-type appearance in a L'Engle novel, is a marine biology student headed to Gaea Island to study starfish regeneration with the now adult Calvin O'Keefe, a job he's gotten through the good graces of his mentor. (Starfish, for your information, contain a central nerve structure similar to that of humans, although they can immediately generate a new limb when one is lost. See what I mean by knowing everything?) Unfortunately, on a stopover in Lisbon, Adam is waylaid by the lissome and dangerous Kali Cutter, the blond daughter of the wealthy, craven tycoon Typhon Cutter, and Adam's summer morphs into a very different kind of dangerous experiment.

Cutter, bloated, with lean, trailing limbs like a spider's, is out to steal O'Keefe's research—and therefore control the phantom-limb-replacement industry until the end of time. (Cutter? Get it, Cutter?) But it's not so easy. As O'Keefe soberly tells Adam, the animals who've been injured naturally benefit by his research. But those injured deliberately by local villagers seeking the spare change O'Keefe pays become monstrosities. (O'Keefe takes the physique's wont to represent the psyche into the human realm in the case of Typhon: "The odd distribution of the weight is glandular," Dr. O'Keefe said, "but I don't think it's as simple as all that. It also reflects the choices he's made in his life.") It's a high-stakes game, one with horrifying implications if the research gets into the wrong hands. "So I guess this kind of thing makes enemies?" Adam asks. O'Keefe is perturbed. "They *are* enemies, Adam," he tells him. "You don't have to *make* enemies of them."

But this distinction is a lesson Adam, who is given to considering that even the enemy may have virtues, will have to learn. He's asked to look after O'Keefe's redheaded, spirited daughter Polyhymnia O'Keefe (who your dedicated L'Engle reader will know is not only truly good but also preternaturally wise), who is also an object of Cutter's for her familiarity with her father's research. But Adam, blinded by Kali's looks, can't choose between them.

Thus entereth Canon Tallis, L'Engle's jack-of-all-trades philosopher, clergyman, spymaster, and father figure to the rescue, hot on the trail of discovering whether or not Adam has gone over to the dark side—something, through the course of the novel, Adam himself must wrestle with, too.

Never one to be married to any particular genre, L'Engle creates in *The Arm of the Starfish* a happy melange of classic thriller, sci-fi, romance, and philosophical treatise on the nature of evil and forgiveness. Poly, on the cusp of love—clad in a red woolen swimsuit, despairing of her straight up-and-down figure—is the moral center of the novel, the adolescent who pushes Adam to be honest and good even as he's drawn in by Kali's genteel manipulations, as does the O'Keefe clan as a whole, who remain firm in my affections despite their propensity to burst into four-part harmony. It's a famous L'Engle combo of morality and philosophizing married to religion, topped with two shakes of science and served with some fantastic chase scenes. (And a dolphin!)

Also pulling Adam away from the arms of evil is Joshua Archer, who acts both as his protector against the Cutters and as the gentle interrogator, his questions designed to lead Adam to the truth—even though leaving himself so open that Adam finally comes back to haunt him. The book concludes in a series of chase scenes on the streets of Lisbon that don't really make much sense except that they allow shots to ring out and opaque quotations to be uttered, as well as lots of rattling of papers and mysterious numbers. But by the end, Adam has accepted not only that there is something called good and evil, but that he's responsible for both, especially when Archer is killed saving him—what Tallis Canon calls "the fall of the sparrow"—the necessary sacrifice in the face of evil. That doesn't mean good people have to knuckle under it in bitterness, though. As the wise village chief (there's always gotta be one) who's been helped by O'Keefe says, "It is not enough if you pray neither for nor against. You must pray. For."

Dragons in the Waters
By Madeleine L'Engle
1976

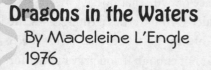

Phair Game

If there's a truth all mystery writers should take care to re-member, it's that the only better place to set a mystery than a dark, many-roomed villa in a remote location during an elec-trical storm is, of course, on a boat. Practically any boat but a kayak! Because not only does the boat achieve with dispatch all the mysterious and crucial advantages of the villa—isolation, crush of strangers, places to hide and suddenly appear, questionable power sources—there might also be some sailors! Try working a sailor—to say nothing of a crew—into a remote villa sometime.

Dragons in the Waters is one of L'Engle's more baroque formulations, and I love it even more because. The story of the young, Southern scion Simon Bolivar Quentin Phair Renier, it contains appearances of many of L'Engle's key players, including Poly O'Keefe, the flame-haired daughter of Meg (yes, *A Wrinkle in Time*'s Meg), Calvin O'Keefe, also of same, pianist Dr. Theo Theotocopulus of the Upper West Side and *The Young Unicorns*, respectively, and Canon Tallis, all-around problem solver in the lives of both the O'Keefes and the Austins.

Simon is being escorted to Caracas under the auspices of his newly declared cousin, the vaguely oily Forsyth Phair, who has nonetheless provided Simon's Aunt Leonis with a tidy little sum for the portrait of their mutual ancestor he is transporting. Unfortunately, someone keeps attempting to kill Simon, and Poly and Charles, named for his uncle Charles Wallace, keep irritatingly preventing it. Will Simon—and the portrait—make it to Caracas alive? And can solving the mystery of the initials in faint letters on the portrait keep Simon alive long enough to know what they mean?

Dragons is dreamy, vivacious, peculiar, and whimsical—as suits a novel with an Indian princess, a mysterious crew, more cellular regeneration, and a full crew. Alongside wonderful cozy visions of tea with the captain and thick fisherman's sweaters and saltwater onboard pools, there is a mysterious tribe called the Quiztano Indians, who have their own relation to Simon, and a large-scale kidnapping, as well as the revelation of certain heretofore unknown bloodlines. Yes, yes, as it happens, there is a return-of-the-great-white-prodigal relationship, but did you hear me when I said there was a tea service and a saltwater pool? Also a race of beautiful people who live with nature in houses on stilts. Perhaps someone should try to set a murder mystery in one of those!

Secret Lives
By Berthe Amoss
1979

The Portrait of an Artist

Every childhood reader has the book whose title she's forgotten, but whose particulars stay with her so strongly as to almost intersperse themselves with her own memories. That book for me is Berthe Amoss's *Secret Lives*, whose Tomato Surprise sandwiches cooked under a broiler have remained on my mind long past any reasonable browning. I've actually never met anyone who's read this book, which continues to astonish me. It's a marvelous mystery on its own. It's also, like, for instance, *Hangin' Out with Ceci* or *Starring Sally J. Freeman as*

Herself, a meticulous portrait of a period, down to the very last decoder ring. But most important, Adelaide Agnew is a heroine as smart, funny, and complex as any I've ever met in the *Booker*-nomination crew, one I demand be released into larger circulation immediately to take her place at the side of Vicky Austin, Blossom Culp, and Harriet M. Welsch.

Addie Agnew, growing up in 1937 New Orleans, is chafing under the care of her two ancient, rattling aunts, Eveline and Kate, who've taken over her care since the death of her mother, Aspasie. "It just seems to me that, this being 1937," Addie grouses, "there ought to be a hint of modern times around here, but Three Twenty Audubon Street and its occupants have been lifted straight out of the Dark Ages." She might as well have said "the graveyard," since that's where, after reciting their catechisms, Eveline and Kate often joyously look forward to relocating.

Drowning in slipcovers and shutters, Addie is also plagued by her next-door neighbor and first cousin, Sandra Lee, a perky blond with curls and turned-up nose who, to Addie's consternation, more closely resembles the ancient portrait of her mother, Pasie, hanging in the living room. There's also Tom, the freckled next-door neighbor who is sourly immune to her charms and schemes, as well as Holly, the theatrical, commanding daughter of Addie's housekeeper, Nini, who proves a welcome, if occasionally caustic, companion to Addie's flights of fancy. These mostly involve Addie reliving her circumstances of her mother's death through an imaginary character called Jane Whitmore, another glamorous blond who's died in dramatic circumstances.

In a story as old as Aunt Kate's cloves, Pasie's dramatic death has been recounted for Addie so many times she can almost remember it, though she was only a baby when it occurred: "I . . . wondered why I've never learned to say 'was' instead of 'is' for my mother. It has been such a long time since my mother, father, and I lived in Honduras. My father was manager of a banana plantation there and my mother painted landscapes, until one day, a hurricane came along, and a tidal wave swept most of Belize and our house into the Gulf. My father saved me, but, in Aunt Eveline's version of what happened, my mother was torn from his arms and hurled into the arms of the angels. I can't remember any of it—a strange, funny thing when I stop to think of how dramatic it must have been."

Yes—wondrous strange! Unfortunately, little is left of Pasie for Addie to remember her by, except a sheaf of old practice drawings and Eveline's rapturous recollections. (About her looks: "No, dear, I was never pretty. Your mother, now . . ." About her art: "Her professor considered her talented. Most talented!") Adelaide, despairing over her brown curls, snub nose, and poor painting skills, is desperate to find any hint of herself in her mother—or any hint that her mother loved her. Slowly, however, by overhearing stray bits of information, questioning everyone to distraction, breaking into a crypt, then decrypting her mother's recovered diary, Addie starts to find a Pasie very different from Eveline's recollections.

While the world Addie dreams up for her mother and stand-in Jane Whitmore is steeped in hyperbole, as purple as a silent film, the world Amoss conjures up for the reader is wry and funny, a vibrant portrait of a family and of New Orleans. For the reader, the slow uncovering of the mystery of Aspasie takes place at the same nail-biting pace as for Addie, as does our appreciation of her family, which Addie learns to love at about the same time we do.

Fearing her lowly place in the teen social ladder, miserably insecure, feeling she's fated to die unable to live up to her charming, popular mother, Addie as we first meet her is convinced both of the injustice of the world and the certainty that she will never take any kind of rightful place in it. But as the novel ends, Addie has come to terms with her mother, having learned that the woman she was looking for never existed. She's also come to terms with herself, but it's not because she's made peace with disappointment. Happily, like most adolescents on the cusp of growing up, she's only realized that the terms were entirely different than she'd thought. Jane Whitmore, indeed, exists. Addie was only looking at the wrong woman.

Chapter 4

Read 'Em And Weep
Tearing Up the Pages

No Answer, Try Again

Let's all just start crying now. Seriously, just get up, find a flat surface, put your head down and weep—because what follows, I must warn you, is very, very heavy. Children fall to their deaths. Honorable prisoners are shot like dogs in the street. Witty alcoholics in velvet smoking jackets expire, kindly old men's broken dreams are smashed by the callous young, young college students biking along lonely roads are no match for heedless vehicles. In fact, no one is a match, it seems, for a heedless world—and all in all, there is much to despair over, little justifiable cause at hand, and not a happy ending in the bunch to be found.

What we find in the drama, however, is a notable lack of the melodrama. Because, while those unfamiliar with the YA market might be surprised to find out it's chock-full, like the adult markets, of thrillers, comic novels, morality plays, highly naughty books, sci-fi, fantasy, and fluffy chick lit, what it lacks, unlike its counterpart, is a bunch of standard weepies. That's not to say slim tearjerkers like *The Bridges of Madison County* or agonized epics like *Cold Mountain* don't have their uses. But whatever those may be, they are as yet untested on the under–18 set.

What we have, instead, is a bunch of straightforward works that address, head-on, the *difficulty* of the world—revolutionary not because they show how it's different for the young, but because they show how often it's not. *Summer of My German Soldier*'s Patty Bergen finds out not only that her moral code can't save anybody—but in fact, that it endangers those she loves. *The Pigman*'s John and Lorraine learn how important a bit of vulnerability is when learning to be close to others—and then how easy it is to abuse, and *Bridge to Terabithia*'s Jess finds how difficult it is to shed guilt—even when one is not guilty.

But as much as I'm interested in pinpointing the "lessons" of these books, these authors, thank God, are doing nothing of the kind. Instead, they are fully caught up in the narrative, in drawing characters whose actions are as surprising or disappointing to us as they are to them, who do the best they have with what's left over, the kind of redemption no one welcomes but everyone has to accept.

And in that uncomfortable reality, the authors sidestep either easy answers or soppy melodrama. We know why it's brave of Ruth to stay in Patty's corner long after the country has abandoned her. But why does her visit to Patty's new jail break our hearts, exactly? We know it's sad that Leslie dies—but why is his father's awkward attempt to help Jess come to terms with that even more devastating? The books don't seek the answer—they ask the *question*. And thus we don't only know what the characters feel—we *feel* it ourselves. So, like the most profound works of literary fiction, these prompt—but ultimately elude—the best-laid lesson plans.

Jacob Have I Loved
By Katherine Paterson
1980

Coastal Erosion

As soon as the snow melts, I will go to Rass and fetch my mother. At Crisfield I'll board the ferry, climbing down into the cabin where the women always ride, but after forty minutes of sitting on the hard cabin bench, I'll stand up to peer out of the high forward windows, straining for the first site of my island.

This is your favorite book, right? Okay, just checking. (MINE TOO.) Why? Is it the island thing? The song thing? The twin thing? Falling in love with an old captain and your formerly nerdy friend and not getting either one? No. It's that there is no book more quietly, quietly sad, nor one that as brilliantly depicts the psychic disarrangement of childhood without falling prey to convenient justification—say, being funny or heartwarming, or instructive, as in by setting it in stultifying historical period—as this one, which takes sisterly jealousy as neither an object lesson nor a juicy starting point but as the painful, enduring state it is.

Jacob Have I Loved is the story of Sara Louise Bradshaw, christened ineluctably by her fraternal twin, Caroline, as "Wheeze," to her eternal consternation. Caroline is not only generally agreed to be lovely, but also possessed of the kind of shatteringly beautiful voice that makes others pay attention ("Caroline is the kind of person other people sacrifice for as a matter of course") and what Louise takes to be callous disregard for others. (I can now read this only as Caroline's rare—but fair—lack of adolescent self-hatred.) Louise is, of course, nearly paralyzed with envy of her sister—although it's less pure envy than rage and shame at how publicly pale in comparison Louise must seem to everybody else, including even her best friend Cal, a chubby, bespectacled nerd.

The girls have been raised on Rass, a teeny island on the Chesapeake off the Eastern Shore, where their father crabs and their mother, a former mainland schoolteacher, watches over them. Their grandmother, not the cookie-baking type, is suffering from the early stages of dementia and given to following Louise around the house and triumphantly offering damning passages from the Bible:

I struggled to pry the lid off a can of tea leaves, aware that my grandmother had come up behind me. I stiffened at the sound of her hoarse whisper.

"Romans nine 13," she said. "As it is written, 'Jacob have I loved, but Esau have I hated.'"

That's totally going to help you work through that insecurity thing about how no one even remembers your BIRTH because your sister almost died and they were all worried about her, especially when your grandmother whips that out right at the moment you're dying over your weird inappropriate crush on a 56-year-old sailor that's returned to the island and you know that no one, ever, not in a million years, would give up their life's savings to let you go study voice in Baltimore. And also: "Wheeze."

Paterson is unflinching about the pain Louise suffers by her second-best status without making Louise's frustration seem like anything but the unattractive, festering blister that it is. Yes, Louise's fundamental rage and pain is something that could probably be handled through a triple dose of CBT, Paxil, and a round of family therapy nowadays. But let's let the pain stand: the few minutes before Caroline exited the womb after her are, as Louise sees it, "the only time in my life I was ever the center of anyone's attention." Louise may be both the main proponent and victim of this belief, but it will take her until adulthood to realize that.

The first insight occurs at the nadir of Louise's adulthood. While Caroline has gone off to a brilliant career at Juilliard, Louise has left school to crab with her father, out on the water with the men in the hard weather, snapping at her mother when she suggests she might want to go to a boarding school on Crisfield—a cheap simulacrum of Caroline's life is far worse than a blatant rejection. Stuck in a deliberate limbo, hiding out from her friends, family, and any romantic prospects, she buries herself in crabbing:

> It was work that did this for me. I had never had work before that sucked from me every breath, every thought, every trace of energy.
>
> "I wish," said my father one night as we were eating our meager supper in the cabin, "I wish you could do a little studying at night. You know, keep up your schooling."
>
> We both glanced automatically at the kerosene lamp, which was more smell than light. "I'd be too tired," I said.
>
> "I reckon."
>
> It had been one of our longer conversations.

But, after Cal returns on leave, Louise finds herself pulling on a dress and smearing cheap lotion on her hands, desperately trying to wash off the smell of crab. For her pains, she receives the news that her newly handsome old friend stopped off in New York before coming to Rass to ask Caroline to marry him.

But it's not until a rare clear day in spring to wash the windows with her mother that the rage that's been building in Louise since childhood finally comes out. Unable to contain her bitterness at Caroline having escaped with the best of Rass while she is left only the dregs, she assails her mother and is unexpectedly rewarded:

> I moved my bucket and chair to the side of the house where she was standing on her chair, scrub-

bing and humming happily. "I don't understand it!" The words burst out unplanned.

"What, Louise?"

"You were smart. You went to college. You were goodlooking. Why did you ever come here?"

. . . "It seemed romantic—" She began scrubbing again as she talked. "An isolated island in need of a schoolteacher. I felt—" She was laughing at herself. "I felt like one of the pioneer women, coming here. Besides—" She turned and looked at me, smiling at my incomprehension. "I had some notion I would find myself here, as a poet, of course, but it wasn't just that."

The anger was returning. There was no good reason for me to be angry but my body was filled with it, the way it used to be when Caroline was home. "And did you find yourself here on this little island?" The question was coated with sarcasm.

She chose to ignore my tone. "I found very quickly," she scratched at something with her fingernail as she spoke, "I found there was nothing much to find."

Louise cannot contain herself:

"Let me go. Let me leave!"

"Of course you may leave. You never said before you wanted to leave."

And, oh, my blessed, she was right. All my dreams of leaving, but beneath them I was afraid to go. I had clung to them, to Rass, yes, even to my grandmother, afraid that if I loosened my fingers one iota, I would find myself once more cold and clean in a forgotten basket.

"I chose the island," she said. "I chose to leave my own people and build a life for myself somewhere else. I certainly wouldn't deny you that same choice. But," and her eyes helped me if her arms did not, "oh, Louise, we will miss you, your father and I."

I wanted so much to believe her. "Will you really?" I asked. "As much as you miss Caroline?"

"More," she said, reaching up and ever so lightly smoothing her hair with her fingertips.

And of course, now that Louise has to admit that she's held herself back more than anyone else has (again, some family therapy and a dose of Paxil), she finds that everyone around her, even the captain, whom she'd loved—to her shame—as a child, has only been waiting for her to notice:

I sat down on the couch near his chair. There was no need to pretend, I knew. "I had hoped when Cal came home—"

He shook his head. "Sara Louise. You were never meant to be a woman on this island. A man, perhaps. Never a woman."

"I don't even know if I wanted to marry him," I said. "But I wanted something." I looked down at my hands. "I know I have no place here. But there's no escape."

"Pish."

"What?" I couldn't believe I'd heard him correctly.

"Pish. Rubbish. You can do anything you want
to. I've known that from the first day I met you—at
the other end of my periscope."

It's admirable that Paterson refuses to deny Louise her pain,
though everyone around her knows it's unjust, unnecessary—
even self-generated. But that's the horribly ironic nature of
pain, of course—not that we can't help but be taken over by it,
but that, despite ourselves, we may be creating it.

Louise chooses to go to the mountains, to become a nurse
practitioner, and even though she marries and has her own
child, she still isn't able to let her sister go, until one night,
when she's called to help a young mother whose husband has
clearly been smacking her around give birth to twins. One
twin comes easily, and then the second, blue, is in danger, until
Louise finally manages to get him stable. But then she realizes
she's repeated her own past:

"Where is the other twin?" I asked, suddenly
stricken. I had completely forgotten him. In my
anxiety for his sister, I had completely forgotten
him. "Where have you put him?"

"In the basket." She looked at me, puzzled. "He's
sleeping."

"You should hold him," I said. "Hold him as
much as you can. Or let his mother hold him."

Louise realizes that Caroline's anointment at the moment
of their birth as the most valuable twin was not *personal*, not
some grim finger of fate consigning Louise to second-place
status. It was only practical—and she was as able to be guilty

of it as anyone. It was a harm leveled on her by distraction, not intention—and once she sees that and reverses it, she becomes her own redeemer.

But I was trying not to cry. Let's see: I just want to point out that this is one of my favorite covers of all time and I always thought Louise looked prettier than Caroline. So there.

Summer of My German Soldier
By Bette Greene
1973

Summer Camp

When I saw the crowd gathering at the train station, I worried what President Roosevelt would think. I just hope he doesn't get the idea that Jenkinsville, Arkansas, can't be trusted with a military secret because, truth of the matter is, we're as patriotic as anybody.

No one would argue that the Holocaust was not a world-class exhibition of hatred. But Bette Greene, in her novel about a young Jewish girl who harbors a Nazi escapee from a POW labor camp during the close of World War II, is also interested in the horrors of hatred on a person-to-person level— not only to drag out that old hoary butterfly whose unceasingly broken wing causes the destruction of the world, but to question why it's always the butterfly who gets it in the first place.

In *Summer of My German Soldier*, the horrors of World War II and concentration camps loom like black-bottomed storm clouds rapidly approaching, while on the ground a fine storm of hail is starting to sting—petty, small hatreds falling indiscriminately and without mercy on those without shelter. Patty Bergen, Jewish daughter of the South, is the actual daughter of Harry and Pearl Bergen, who own Bergen's Department Store in Jenkinsville, Arkansas, as well as the older sister of Sharon, who, though far younger, is generally considered the more beautiful and well-mannered.

It is not enough that, as a member of the only Jewish family in town in the 1940s, Patty is already barely tolerated among her Baptist peers. (Being the kind of precocious word lover who reads the dictionary for fun doesn't help, either.) But worst of all is Patty's father, who never hesitates to take his rage out on his eldest daughter, either with his tongue or his belt.

Mr. Bergen is a far cry from the typical Jewish dad found in old-school YA—who, when in evidence at all, is generally a turn-of-the-century hardworking *Tate* sort, stamping down rags and letting his children choose books from his store, or a kindly dentist receiving kisses on the news from his adoring daughter. Excepting stepfathers, in fact, genuinely *beastly* fathers are rare in YA: while they may switch their daughters to make a point (Oh, Pa!) or go so far as to call them fat and useless (*The Cat Ate My Gymsuit* comes to mind), I can't think of any other instance where one whips off his belt to beat his daughter by the side of the road . . . before he even knows she's sheltering a Nazi.

But then again, a Jewish girl who shelters a Nazi during WWII is not your standard fare, either. Even before Mr. SS enters the story, Patty's mother and father treat her with the sort of generic cruelty reserved for other people's (annoying) children—her father with tempestuous irritation: "Are you questioning me? Are you contradicting me?"—and her mother with an endless stream of politely pointed barbs meant to establish just how hideously unworthy to be her daughter Patty truly is:

> "When I was a girl," said my mother, turning towards Mrs. Fields, "I used to drive my mother crazy with my clothes. If my dress wasn't new or if it had the slightest little wrinkle in it I'd cry and throw myself across the bed."
>
> "You were just particular about how you looked," said Mrs. Fields.
>
> "I wish Patricia would be more particular," Mother said with sudden force. "Would you just look at that hair? . . . Here. Go look in the mirror and do a good job. You know, Gussie, you'd expect two sisters to be something alike, but Patricia doesn't care how she looks while Sharon is just like me."
>
> Didn't Mother know I was still standing here? . . . I took in my reflection: "Oh, mirror mirror on the wall, who's the homeliest one of all?"

But Patty, plagued with auburn curls and a persistent intellect, is ill-suited for the stiflingly Perma-Wave culture in which she finds herself:

Mrs. Fields smiled her adult-to-child smile. "How are you enjoying your vacation? As much as my niece, Donna Ann?"

I wondered how I could honestly answer the question. First I'd have to decide how much I was enjoying the summer—not all that much—then find out exactly how much Donna Ann Rhodes was enjoying it before trying to make an accurate comparison. Mrs. Fields' smile began to fade. Maybe she just wanted me to say something pleasant. "Yes, ma'am," I answered.

There are those who love Patty for exactly the singularity she would like to stamp out, chief among them the family's black housekeeper Ruth, who, knowing well that she is fighting a losing battle, tries to help Patty ward off her mother and father's abuse by training her to "act sweet":

"Hey, Ruth!" She looked up from her wash. "Ruth, know where I was? With the Germans going to the prison camp!"

She gave me her have-you-been-up-to-some-devilment look.

"I didn't do a single thing wrong!" I said. . . . "This is still my week to be good and sweet. I haven't forgotten."

Her face opened wide enough to catch the sunshine. "I'm mighty pleased to hear it. 'Cause before this week is through, your mamma and daddy gonna recognize your natural sweetness and give you some back, and then you gonna return even more and—"

"Maybe so," I interrupted her, and she went back to putting bed sheets through the wringer, understanding that I didn't want to talk about them anymore.

Patty's grandfather and grandmother also try to shelter Patty from their daughter and son-in-law, praising her on the family's brief visits and giving her money to buy books. (Patty's grandmother reacts with anger when Patty tries to refuse the gift, having been told by Pearl not to take anything. "But my mother said—" "Your mother!" A deep crease appeared on one side of her mouth. "This is not for your mother to know!")

But Patty's father's cruelty has a deeply disturbed side, one that frightens even her mother, Pearl, and the townspeople, whose acceptance of Jews has been hard-won, when her father releases it. When Patty hits a car with a rock by mistake and cracks the windshield, her father releases one of his all-too-common assaults:

> At his temple a vein was pulsating like a neon sign
> . . . He pointed a single quivering finger at me. "If you don't come here this instant I'll give you a beating you're never going to forget."
> . . . Fingers crossed, I stepped through the opening in the hedge to stand soldier-straight before my father.
> "Closer!"
> One foot advanced before a hand tore against my face, sending me into total blackness.

We never learn exactly why Harry is so angry, but we do know that his violent release is a horrifying effort to stamp out the individuality that Patty possesses without even thinking—her inability to participate in the town's casual racism, her rejection of the insipid nonthinking demanded of her, her curiosity, her giving spirit. Does Harry fear that Patty's outsiderness will upset the family's already tenuous position in the town's hierarchy? The only other minority, a Chinese greengrocer, has been chased out already: "Our boys at Pearl Harbor would have got a lot of laughs at the farewell party we gave the Chink," comments the sheriff, to which Patty's father laughs weakly. Meanwhile, the black residents of the town, like Ruth, who live in "Nigger bottoms," are subject to a constant level of seemingly banal persecution.

It is her parents' refusal to love Patty—to even recognize her—that puts her in the way of Anton Reiker, the POW who, like Ruth and Patty's grandmother, finds much in Patty to respect and like. When Jenkinsville becomes the site for a POW camp housing German prisoners, Patty, who is so open to the outside world that she instinctively waves at the prisoners, is disappointed by the ordinary nature of the crew: "In the movies war criminals being hustled off to prison would be dramatic. But in real life it didn't seem all that important. Not really a big deal. My stomach growled, reminding me it must be nearing lunchtime."

When she meets Anton at her father's store (the prisoners, put to work picking cotton, are brought in to buy straw hats), she is further confused by how different he is from what she has been led to expect:

> . . . He was looking at me like he saw me—like he liked what he saw.
>
> "I'll take the one you choose," said Reiker. He placed six yellow pencils and three stenographic

pads on the counter. "And you did not tell me," he said, "what you call these pocket pencil sharpeners."

"He was so nice. How could he have been one of those—those brutal, black-booted Nazis? "Well, I don't think they actually call them much of anything, but if they were to call them by their right name they'd probably call them pocket pencil sharpeners."

Reiker laughed and for a moment, this moment, we were friends. And now I knew something more. He wasn't a bad man.

Like Ruth, who likes to learn each new word from the dictionary along with Patty, or her grandfather, who praises her letters to the editor, her grandmother, who gives her money to buy books, and even Charlene Madlee, the reporter who helps Patty when it all comes crashing down, Anton is a seeker of knowledge, not a rejecter. (You can actually mark who will be Patty's friend simply by who is interested in words.) But Patty is right: Anton Reiker, the son of a historian who mocked Hitler and a devoted gardener from Manchester, is hardly the kind of conscript Himmler dreamed of.

So, when Patty finds him stumbling along the railroad tracks, having escaped from the camp, she takes him in, not caring what might happen to her family, who are, after all, a far greater danger to her than he could ever be. Even Anton, like some reverse Anne Frank, now housed, clothed, and fed by Patty, is perplexed—then amused—by the absurdity:

His mouth came open. "Jewish?" An index finger pointed towards me. "You're Jewish?"

I thought he knew. I guess I thought everybody

knew. . . . As I nodded Yes, my breathing came to a halt while my eyes clamped shut.

Suddenly, strong baritone laughter flooded the room . . . "It's truly extraordinary," he said. "Who would believe it? 'Jewish girl risks all for German soldier.' Tell me, Patty Bergen—"his voice became soft, but with a trace of hoarseness—"why are you doing this for me?"

It wasn't complicated. Why didn't he know? There was really only one word for it. A simple little word that in itself is reason enough.

"The reason I'm doing this for you," I started off, "is only that I wouldn't want anything bad to happen to you."

Unfortunately, it ends about as badly as you could expect (if you'd like not to know, stop reading now), with Anton dead, shot by the FBI, and Patty in juvenile detention—more estranged from her family than ever, having humiliated them in the eyes of Jenkinsville, the larger Jewish community, and America as a whole beyond reason.

But it's exactly this gross reaction to a small crime—trying to help another person in need—that shows Greene's point: it is dangerous to have a mob who can only react to a global bogeyman, not the person.

America sees a traitor—Patty only sees a man in need, a friend, someone who is no more an acolyte of Hitler than she is. And who is a worse traitor—she, or the man who beats his own daughter? Anton risks his life to come out of hiding to protect her from a beating—her father can't even protect her from himself.

But in the end, this does not matter, Bette Greene's work is stunning not only for its tragic proportions, but for the revelation of the great complexities of love and cruelty. When Ruth sees Anton run out, she finally accepts that Patty's refusal to hate will always put her in harm's way, just as her own protection of Patty will soon cause her to lose her job:

> "I want you to tell Ruth the truth about something. You hear me talking, girl?" I nodded Yes.
>
> "You tell me who is that man."
>
> . . . "The man is my friend," I said at last.
>
> Ruth sighed like she sometimes does before tackling a really big job. "He's not the one the law's after? Not the one from the prison camp?"
>
> "Yes."
>
> Her forehead crinkled up like a washboard. "You telling me, Yes, he's not the one?"
>
> "No, Ruth, I'm telling you yes. Yes, he's the one."
>
> Ruth's head moved back and forth in a No direction. "Oh, Lord, why you sending us more, Lord? Don't this child and me have burden enough?"

But Ruth also knows that Patty wouldn't be Patty if she could refuse Anton's friendship, and she also knows that Anton gives it back in kind: "That man come a-rushing out from the safety of his hiding 'cause he couldn't stand your pain and anguish no better'n me." Patty—and Ruth, and Anton—all have a funny kind of courage that is never recognized, the kind that never gets anyone the kind of medals brandished by the soldier herding the POW prisoners into the truck. Like the Jews in the concentration camps, they're not persecuted for what they do—they're persecuted for what they *are*. But somehow, however much they are hated, they are still not people who can hate.

The Pigman
By Paul Zindel
1968

Senior Moments

Now, I don't like school, which is what you might
say is one of the factors that got us involved with
this old guy we nicknamed the Pigman. Actually,
I hate school, but then most of the time I hate everything.

I'm glad nowadays that therapists and master's-in-teaching
programs are here to minister to the maladjusted amongst us,
but I'm not sure I love what they've done for literature. It's not

that the notion of the dysfunctional family has disappeared—obviously we are beset by a new indie film about the crushing complexity of family life set to a charming soundtrack every other week, with attendant guitar line gesturing toward some sort of plot. But Paul Zindel, former high-school teacher and avatar of a certain stretch of miserable adolescence, knew both plot and teen peril. In his garbage heap of a world, adults, pressed into a stratum of pure misery, wait calmly for the crush to descend on their children, who have little but their mordant wit and a fast-dwindling sense of good to hold it at bay.

John Conlan, high-school student, is a blue-eyed, good-looking career prevaricator who drinks too much and has a soft spot for any hint of enthusiasm, however hokey. (Planning a prank on yet another substitute teacher, he desists because the old guy is so excited about telling the students about commemorative stamps.) His friend Lorraine is obsessed equally with omens and psychoanalysis, worried about her weight, mildly in love with John, and equally given to ruminating about the destroyed adults around her:

> I mean, take the Cricket for instance. I mean Miss Reillen. She's across the library watching me as I'm typing this, and she's smiling. You'd think she knew I was defending her. She's really a very nice woman, although it's true her clothes are too tight, and her nylons do make this scraaaaaaatchy sound when she walks. But she isn't trying to be sexy or anything. If you could see her, you'd know that. She just outgrew her clothes. Maybe she doesn't have any money to buy new ones or get the old ones let out. Who knows what kind of problems she has? Maybe she's got a sick mother at home like Miss

Stewart, the typing teacher. I know Miss Stewart has a sick mother at home because she let me mark some typing papers illegally and drop them off at her house after school one day. And there was her sick mother—very thin and with this smile frozen on her face—right in the middle of the room! That was this strange part. Miss Stewart kept her mother in this bed right in the middle of the living room, and it almost made me cry. . . . When I look at Miss Reillen I feel sorry. When I hear her walking I feel even more sorry for her because maybe she keeps her mother in a bed in the middle of the living room just like Miss Stewart. Who would want to marry a woman who keeps her sick mother in a bed in the middle of the living room?

The question for John and Lorraine: how are they going to grow into any kind of a life without the miserable specter of their parents—basically, death writ large—smack in the middle of it? When we meet them, there is no aspect of John or Lorraine's life not entirely shadowed. Lorraine's mother is a home nurse ministering to people who are dying, from whom she steals the occasional can of soup. Obsessed with making sure Lorraine doesn't get loose with boys, she simultaneously reminds her she's not very good-looking. John's father, whom he calls "The Bore," and his mother, who is obsessed with deodorizing everything, are fonder of John's older stockbroker brother, Kenneth, than they are of their incendiary younger son. "Be your own man!" his father tells him, in a typical exchange. "But for God's sake get your hair cut—you look like an oddball."

All of which explains why John and Lorraine are quickly

drawn to Mr. Angelo Pignati, a man they befriend after prank-calling him as members of a fake neighborhood charity. As John says, the Pigman—so called because of his enormous collection of novelty pigs—is the absolute reverse of all the adults they know: not only filled with native good humor, but innocently trusting and loving of those around him in a world where the default mode toward them is antagonistic. The Pigman isn't trying to be on their level or drag them down, he just delights in their company: "In fact," says John, "the thing Lorraine and I liked best about the Pigman was that he didn't go around saying we were cards or jazzy or cool or hip. He said we were delightful, and if there's one way to show how much you're not trying to make believe you're not behind the times, it's to go around saying people are delightful."

This delightfully oddball friendship includes all kinds of activities John and Lorraine have never experienced: visiting baboons at the zoo, shopping for exotic foods at Beekman's, roller-skating through department stores, playing pen-and-pencil shorthand psychology games meant to reveal one's true nature. It's a childhood compressed into a few months, one that John and Lorraine treasure: "One part of me was saying 'Don't let this nice old man waste his money,' and the other half was saying, 'Enjoy it, enjoy doing something absolutely absurd'— something that could let me be a child in a way I never could be with my mother, something just silly and absurd and . . . beautiful," thinks Lorraine. John has an even more violent feeling of protection:

"John, turn your radio down."
    "John, you're disturbing your father."
    "John, you're disturbing your mother."
    "John, you're disturbing the cat."

"John, please do whatever you'd like. Make yourself comfortable. If you want something out of the refrigerator, help yourself. I want you to feel at home."

And always with a big smile so you knew he meant it.

That was the Pigman, and I knew I'd kill Norton if he tried to hurt the old man.

Yes, there is a bad thing, and it happens with Norton. You know how I am about the bad endings. But Lorraine and John aren't bitter at their parents—"My mom is a very pretty woman when she has her long brown hair down," Lorraine says, "and when she smiles, which is hardly ever. She just doesn't look the way she sounds, and I often wonder how she got this way"—but they do, as Lorraine says, wonder how they got this way. If they could find out, maybe they could keep it from happening to them. There's an important scene in the middle of the novel where Lorraine observes an attendant at the zoo:

The thing that made me stop going to the zoo a few years ago was the way one attendant fed the sea lions. He climbed up on the big diving board in the middle of the pool and unimaginatively just dropped the fish in the water. I mean, if you're going to feed sea lions, you're not supposed to plop the food in the tank. You can tell by the expressions on their faces that the sea lions are saying things like "Don't dump the fish in!"

"Pick the fish up one by one and throw them into the tank so we can chase after them."

"Throw the fish in different parts of the tank!"

"Let's have fun!"

That's Lorraine and John, looking for any sign of life from the adults around them on whom they depend not only for nourishment, but for love, interest, smarts, play—any sense of joy in the world. It's not until they meet Mr. Pignati that they find it—and it's only after losing him that they realize it's up to them to create it again: "There was no one else to blame anymore—no Bores or Old Ladies or Nortons, or Assassins waiting at the bridge. . . . Our life would be what we made of it—nothing more, nothing less." John and Lorraine want to avoid being crushed. But their roller skates are gone, and it's just not certain that they can.

Bridge to Terabithia
By Katherine Paterson
1977

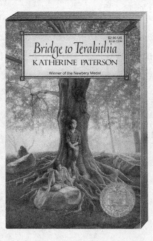

Crossing Over

Ba-room, ba-room, ba-room, baripity, baripity, baripity, baripity—Good. His dad had the pickup going. He could get up now.

The life-changing friend is a standard trope of teen fiction, but rereading *Bridge to Terabithia*, it occurs to me that one does tire of the all-too-common morally bracing appearance of a Pollyanna (as in my beloved *An Old-Fashioned Girl*, or, you

know, *Pollyanna*.) An outsider who is revolutionary purely
because of her strangeness (*The Secret Garden*, *Iggie's House*)
is a great variation, but I'm not sure I've ever seen, outside
Bridge to Terabithia's Leslie Burke, a character who manages
to be both moral and strange—both wholly herself and wholly
strange, and wholly a revelation to protagonist Jess Aaron.

Jess Aaron is a fifth-grader whose elbows are bumping up
against both his own limitations and those of his outside life
(insofar as a fifth-grader has an an external and internal life—
but, you know, if anyone can make you understand how they
do, it's Katherine Paterson). The oldest boy in a working-class
family with four girls, he's a budding artist, which goes over
poorly with his trucker dad ("'What are they teaching in that
damn school? Bunch of old ladies turning him into a—'"), as
well as with the old ladies, in fact ("The devil of it was that none
of his regular teachers ever liked his drawings. When they'd
catch him scribbling, they'd screech about waste—wasted
time, wasted paper, wasted ability.") His mother, overwhelmed
with his sisters, is too busy to pay much attention to him, but
Jess, who's asked to stand in as the man of the household when
his father is gone to work in D.C., feels the loss of his father the
most keenly:

> Jess watched his dad stop the truck, lean over to
> unlatch the door, so May Belle could climb in. He
> turned away. Durn lucky kid. She could run after
> him and grab him and kiss him. It made Jess ache
> inside to watch his dad grab the little ones to his
> shoulder, or lean down and hug them. It seemed to
> him that he had been thought too big for that since
> the day he was born.

His new neighbor, the life-changing Leslie Burke, could not be more different. A transplant from D.C., child of noblesse oblige who've taken a house in rural Virginia because they're "reassessing their value structure," Leslie meets Jess in the meadow where he is practicing his running in anticipation of winning one of the lunchtime heats to make him the fastest runner in the school. Leslie's comment, very far from typical girlish admiration, is, like herself, both artless and unwittingly incisive:

"If you're so afraid of the cow, why don't you just climb the fence?"

As it happens, Jess is afraid—although he doesn't realize it until he sees his new schoolmate Leslie flout all of the conventions that have held him back heretofore. On her first day of school Leslie shows up in old tennis shoes and shorts, in stark contrast to all the country children in their faded best. A child of a world where pride would keep anyone from showing up that way in public unless they had to, Jess is embarrassed for her—but then finds himself defending her when she breaks yet another barrier:

> Gary stopped walking and wheeled to face him. Fulcher glared first at Jess and then at Leslie Burke. "Next thing," he said, his voice dripping with sarcasm, "next thing you're gonna want to let some girl run."
>
> Jess's face went hot. "Sure," he said recklessly. "Why not?" He turned deliberately toward Leslie.
>
> "Wanna run?" he asked. . . .
>
> . . . For a minute he thought Gary was going to sock him, and he stiffened. He mustn't let Fulcher suspect he was scared of a little belt in the mouth.

But instead Gary broke into a trot and started boss-
ing the threes into line for their heat. . . . See, he told
himself, you can stand up to a creep like Fulcher.
No sweat.

Of course, Leslie then goes on to beat the pants off all of
the boys in the school. It's not a particularly feminist moment,
though: she is honestly confused when they refuse to accept
her win, as they will refuse to accept every other aspect of her
that doesn't fit in with their world. Beating them in running,
they must understand, is only one of the examples in which
Leslie is literally ahead—not due to her economic and cultural
advantages, but in how those freedoms have enabled her to be
utterly herself.

Jess, attempting to break boundaries himself, is bitterly
disappointed to lose, but still differs from his peers in that he
can see that Leslie's open embrace of life isn't something to be
feared, but admired: "She ran as though it was her nature. It reminded him of the flight of wild ducks in autumn. So smooth.
The word 'beautiful' came to his mind, but he shook it away
and hurried up toward the house."

And here Jess makes a decision to no longer be bound by his
distracted parents or by the teachers in the school, to embrace
the people in his life who seem to be interested in other aspects
of him than in how well he's milking the cow: not only his
"hippie, peacenik" music teacher, Mrs. Edmunds, with whom
he's been in love for ages despite the scorn of the school for her
hippie pants and makeup, but Leslie herself. This happens, appropriately enough, as they're singing "Free to Be You and Me"
in class (and did you KNOW that those lyrics were by Bruce
Hart of YA titan Bruce and Carol Hart fame, by the way?):

Caught in the pure delight of it, Jess turned and his eyes met Leslie's. He smiled at her. What the heck. There wasn't any reason he couldn't. What was he scared of anyhow? Lord. Sometimes he acted like the original yellow-bellied sapsucker. . . . He felt there in the teachers' room that it was the beginning of a new season in his life, and he chose deliberately to make it so.

And thus begins a friendship in which Jess finds a freedom to be himself he hasn't considered before, and Leslie finds a friend in the sea of a school population with a knee-jerk scorn for girls who don't wear dresses, own TVs, or stand on the sidelines cheering during races. This friendship finds its apex in the imaginary world of Terabithia, a kingdom in the woods conceived by the visionary Leslie, reached only by a rope swinging across a river, located physically and philosophically just on the cusp of where Jess's fears begin:

> There were parts of the woods that Jess did not like. Dark places where it was almost like being under water, but he didn't say so. . . . Jess agreed quickly, relieved there was no need to plunge deeper into the woods. He would take her there, of course, for he wasn't such a coward that he would mind a little exploring now and then further in amongst the ever-darkening columns of the tall pines. But as a regular thing, as a permanent place, this is where he would choose to be. . . .
>
> . . . There in the shadowy light of the stronghold everything seemed possible. Between the two of

them they owned the world and no enemy, Gary Fulcher, Wanda Kay Moore, Janice Avery, Jess's own fears and insuffiencies, nor any of the foes whom Leslie imagined attacking Terabithia, could ever really defeat them.

As has often happened when I'm rereading the novels in the 1970s period, I'm struck by how the class distinctions are far more explicit than I noticed as a child. Take, for instance, the Burkes, whose world cannot be further than Jess's and those in the town, a world of milking, hard-earned dollars, canning, trucking, beating your children, and then dressing up for church on Sunday:

> Leslie's parents were young, with straight white teeth and lots of hair—both of them. Leslie called them Judy and Bill, which bothered Jess more than he wanted it to. It was none of his business what Leslie called her parents. But he just couldn't get used to it.
>
> Both of the Burkes were writers. Mrs. Burke wrote novels and, according to Leslie, was more famous than Mr. Burke, who wrote about politics. It was really something to see the shelf that had their books on it. Mrs. Burke was "Judith Hancock" on the cover, which threw you at first, but then if you looked on the back, there was her picture looking very young and serious. Mr. Burke was going back and forth to Washington to finish a book he was working on with someone else, but he had promised Leslie that after Christmas he would stay home and

fix up the house and plant his garden and listen to music and read books out loud and write only in his spare time.

They didn't look like Jess's idea of rich, but even he could tell that the jeans they wore had not come off the counter at Newberry's. There was no TV at the Burkes', but there were mountains of records and a stereo set that looked like something off *Star Trek*. And although their car was small and dusty, it was Italian and looked expensive too.

They were always nice to Jess when he went over, but then they would suddenly begin talking about French politics or string quartets (which at first he thought was a square box made of string), or how to save timber wolves or redwoods or singing whales, and he was scared to open his mouth and show once and for all how dumb he was.

But what's interesting to me now is how, especially after the tragedy of Leslie's death, Paterson refuses to judge either family. (I think there must be a hint of the Patersons themselves in there.) Yes, the Burkes with their Italian car, their love of books and art and all that is beautiful and deeply thought, the Burkes who are not ashamed to paint their living room gold, are a revelation to Jess, but then, so is the kindness of his own parents in the face of Leslie's death—his mother making him pancakes and refusing to allow his sisters to torment him, and his father reassuring him, albeit roughly, that whatever his mean older sister says, Leslie didn't need to be baptized to be all right in the afterlife. ("Lord, boy, don't be a fool. God ain't gonna send any little girls to hell.")

One of the book's beautiful, delicate illustrations of Jess's father carrying him home (does ANY book besides this and "A Taste of Blackberries" have more weep-inducing artwork?) showcases the stability and love Jess doesn't realize he has at his own disposal at home, as well.

Leslie, who is unafraid of scuba-diving, who is not afraid of the dark woods, of the world of imagination, of striding out on the edge, distant and alone, does die because she's unafraid. But she's also given Jess life:

> He thought about it all day, how before Leslie came, he had been a nothing—a stupid, weird kid who drew funny pictures and chased around a cow field trying to act big—trying to hide a whole mob of foolish little fears running wild in his gut.
>
> Leslie was more than his friend. She was his other, more exciting self—his way to Terabithia and all the worlds beyond.

But Jess has also learned something very important—that Leslie was scared, too. Rescuing his sister May Belle from the same river in which Leslie drowned, he forgives himself for not saving Leslie and for being too cowardly to be there for her the day she died. "Everybody gets scared sometimes, May Belle. You don't have to be ashamed." He saw a flash of Leslie's eyes as she was going into the girls' room to see Janice Avery. "Everybody gets scared." After Leslie's death, the bridge Jess builds to cross the river into Terabithia isn't only to protect anyone else from falling into the river and drowning. It's to make the leap he's made—into a world of art, imagination, life beyond his small town—safe for anyone else who's afraid.

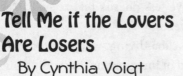

EXTRA CREDIT

Tell Me if the Lovers Are Losers

By Cynthia Voigt
1982

Blind Faith

I have an ignominious history with this odd Cynthia Voigt classic, one based entirely on an offhand remark I made before having read it at all. During sixth-grade recess, as my friend, turning back the page, flipped the cover my way—three girls intently conversing on a college green, while behind them the leaves turned gently yellow and shadows lengthened on the grass—I said, almost without volition, "She dies at the end."

My friend gasped angrily and (because it was, of course, true) didn't speak to me for nearly two weeks.

By my second year of high-school English, I probably could have told you my prediction was based on several transparent aesthetic signifiers—the sun almost setting, the world turning to winter, hint, hint—and could have probably pinpointed the girl in question: a blond whose hair was already charged with light as if haloed, and who leaned forward on her bike as if impatient to get going on this journey to the hereafter, already.

But just the evocation of a genteel New England college campus might have been enough, since, if you judge by similar work, it hardly seems worth placing young women in such close quarters—the female equivalent of army barracks—unless, as with soldiers, you could guarantee that one would lose either her virginity, her timidity, or her life.

Voigt, in fact, achieves all three, although not in the traditional fashion. If we look at the history of similar works, like Mary McCarthy's *The Group*, Marilyn French's *The Women's Room*, or Rona Jaffe's *Class Reunion* (even nonfiction college memoirs, like *Loose Change*) we see several inviolate categories: the frigid preppy; the mousy, sexually neuter intellectual; the sultry, often Southern, siren; and the wholesome creature who'll have her rose-colored glasses knocked off by the world, just you wait. These avatars have crept into prime time in shows like *The Golden Girls* and *Sex and the City* for good reason—we women are sure to relate to one another (or all) of them, at some point in our lives.

But in her triumvirate of Ann, Niki, and Hildy, first-year students at the Seven-Sisters-esque Stanton College, Voigt creates three characters who are distinctly themselves. When the reader meets them, instead of feeling the automatic shock of recognition, we, like trembling freshmen ourselves, have to swallow our trepidation and get to know the other girls.

Ann, a trim preppy bookworm with good shoes and an impressive knowledge of Shakespeare, is the biggest "type" of the work—something her new roommate Niki makes sure to point out: "Don't kid yourself. You are a type." (Told you!)

> "And you aren't?" Annie was growing tired of denigration.
> "No, ma'am. Not me. There are lots of you around, with tans and square jaws and that wavy hair. You all move the same way, muscular but not strong, somebody's idea of femininity. It's a prep-school type."

Um . . . nice to meet you, too! But although Ann—unlike Niki and her other new roommate, Hildy—has a built-in peer group already from her private-school past, she is the most insecure of the three. Niki, whose parents are divorced, is both bold and scornful, competitive and judgmental (see above). She falls just shy of being a bully—but only because, at the end of the day, all Niki demands is that people be better than themselves, not worse than her. An almost obsessive athlete, on the first day she challenges Ann to a tennis match, then proceeds to beat the more skilled Ann simply by fighting with sheer grit for every point—a pattern she continues anywhere she can, incredulous at Ann's seemingly endless capacity to say uncle.

Hildy is another story. Tall, blond, and beautiful, Hildy was raised on a farm in a small rural community, and she speaks not only with an oddly formal syntax (there is not a contraction that can be found), but also with the kind of patient, humorless commonsense that can nonetheless easily poke a hole in a more ironic, antic intellect, like Niki's:

"Didn't anybody ever tell you you talk funny?" Niki demanded.

"Oh, yes," Hildy said.

"What did you say?"

"I asked if they could understand me," Hildy answered patiently, "and like you, they said yes."

Voigt also departs from the standard formula for what causes a conflict among the girls—namely, boys, of whom there is not one to be found. (Niki loses her virginity somewhere off-scene, and Hildy, as it turns out, already has, to the local farmer she plans to marry.) Instead, the girls work out their relationship on highly unnatural turf: a volleyball court, which is an arena they all scorn, until Hildy, who knows its mysterious and dig-deep laws, introduces the other girls to it.

Volleyball is a stand-in for what Hildy herself represents—the underappreciated skills of teamwork, as well as balance, between one's own side and the enemy's. For Niki, accustomed to beating people down in one-on-one sports or simply making team sports one-on-one by grabbing every shot and taking it, having to acknowledge that she can be part of something larger than herself is humbling—and a bit terrifying. For Ann, it's quite the opposite. She's used to being part of something—a "type"—but only when it helps her to disappear. She may not be center stage in volleyball, but she'll be called up for service on a regular rotation, like everyone else, and what happens to the team will depend on her. Ann learns, with surprise, that at first this is almost unbearably frightening—but then that she can't imagine living without it.

More interesting—as the girls learn, Hildy, in fact, plays blind, which she's legally been for years. Ann, after much urging and manipulation, finally forces her to buy a pair of glasses, but as the freshman team rises in the college matches, Hildy, unaccustomed to twenty-twenty vision, finally throws them away. Ann compares her mind to that of a forest, "wild and profuse in its growth . . . accidental, at least in human terms, in its self-management." Ann knows she's a type, but Niki, as much as she fights against it, is as well—as prosaic a radical, and as prosaically ambitious, as Ann is, in her own way. Only Hildy, whose entirely unique mind comes from an equally unknown world to which she'll soon return, is outside the mainstream.

Which is why, of course, she has to die. (Dang, I did it again!) It's rare for radical thinkers to be able to survive until the end of novels—like wild spores, they impart their crucial DNA to more well-rooted characters, then drift onward toward oblivion. But Hildy's skilled deflection both of Ann's inhibitions and Niki's irritating exhibitions—very similar to the deadly way she rises up to block all the spikes headed her way—is almost a refutation of the limitations of the entire genre. When Niki, fresh from losing her virginity and thereby dismissive of the whole operation, declares she'll master sex like the volleyball court, Hildy firmly stops her—"It is not like practicing volleyball. It is a human experience,"—then responds to Ann's gleeful assertion that she's taken the wind out of Niki's sails by saying, "I hope not. I wanted to put the wind back in them." Voigt, in presenting us with the entirely unquantifiable Hildy, has done something very similar.

A Day No Pigs Would Die
By Robert Newton Peck
1972

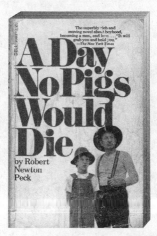

Trough Times

I can say this with complete confidence: There are probably as many novels about Shakers as there are Shakers still rattling around. But Robert Newton Peck's autobiography—written much like a novel—of his boyhood on a Vermont farm with a father who teaches him, alongside pig farming, how to not confuse "need" with "want" is a quiet, gentle story about how sometimes, when it involves your own family, you can't choose between the two. It's one of those strange books where the totality of the circumstances are so likely beyond anything

188 Lizzie Skurnick

you're familiar with—pig slaughtering, deep religiosity, a rural, barren surround—that the minds of the characters are almost more vivid, as if to make up for the difference. It's also a stark story of a son and a father—one that takes on the difficulties of parenthood without lionizing anyone or making anyone the enemy.

Beat the Turtle Drum
By Constance C. Greene
1976

Horse Sense

When I picked it up again, I was surprised to see how slight this novel about a younger sister, Kate, whose eldest sister Joss dies after falling off a horse, is—it's almost skeletal in plot. When I read it as a girl, it seemed to me a full, many-chaptered epic, but in fact it's but a series of small, brilliant characterizations and elegantly wrought scenes, ones that are as touching as the grayed-out, elegant illustrations that open each section. Characters I thought loomed large in fact only appeared in the narrative once or twice, but—as in the case of the woman Joss rents the horse from—visually unforgettable, spilling out of her silky top and offering the girls their first cup of creamy, sweet coffee. I also hadn't remembered how sharp a tone Kate has for a child—"They said everybody's born and everybody dies." "That seems obvious."—but her observations are born from a deep watchfulness that is the reverse of Joss's ephemeral enthusiasms. It may well be that that stark difference is what really stays with you—not only how different we can be from those we love and are close to, but how the small choices we make can actually have enormously dangerous consequences. You're much less likely to die talking about a tree than climbing it (or, for that matter, reading about it).

The Gift of the Pirate Queen
By Patricia Reilly Giff
1982

Blood Kin

I always loved this story about Grace, whose younger sister has diabetes and who, after the death of her mother, has to get used to her new cousin Fiona, who her father has brought over from Ireland to watch her. Throughout the story, Grace is absolutely tormented by breaking a beautiful china angel her teacher kept on her desk—one given to her by her first class, one she's evidently loved much more than the one she has now. It's a stand-in for everything Grace has lost—the family that was better than the family she has now, one she's as unwilling to adjust to as her teacher is to let go of the dream of her original class. But it's also such a moving portrait of the small griefs and worries of childhood—how doing something as small as breaking a piece of china can take over your entire psyche, or how having someone else cooking dinner in the house looms larger than a presidential election. (I could break all the china in my friends' houses and they could cook forever in mine, and vice versa, and I dare say none of us would much notice the difference.) There's no romance in adjusting to strange, old Fiona; and there's no real natural affection in her frightened teacher—but that makes this year of change, in which Amy learns to take her diabetes seriously and Grace to stop taking everything so seriously—far more affecting.

Chapter 5

You Heard It Here First
Very Afterschool Specials

It Could Happen To You

It is part of the perverse logic of childhood that, as far as the fictional world goes, the greater the horror of the story, the greater the greedy reading glee. Parents dead, left in poverty in a garret? Terrif. Intense privation, wandering around with wolves? Done. Persecuted unjustly for witchcraft? Lay it on us.

But it goes without saying that a story that can tell us an entirely new horrible thing we've never heard has unparalleled possibilities for enjoyment. Who knew your spine could grow in an *S* shape, nearly crippling you forever? That some people are beaten in private by their parents—and no one cares? That you can be raped—*by someone you know*—or just want to stop eating? (Wait—do *I* want to stop eating?)

There is an unavoidable sensationalistic bent to fictionalizing any pathology—the anorexia, the scoliosis, the date rape becomes its own separate character, a relentless bogeyman that we had no idea was even lurking on the horizon. (How many girls bent over to ask a friend to measure if their hips were even after reading *Deenie*?). There's also the Very Important Problem aspect, the novel serving the same purpose as an AA pamphlet with a built-in scare story. (Now you know if you ARE an alcoholic . . . and you know what happens to *alcoholics*, don't you?)

This is probably why reading plans tend to tout these books' value as useful vessels for history, society, tolerance, and other bracing assaults to human depravity. But I have to imagine their appeal is far more basic—simply, to imagine one's own capacity to respond to the same situation, given the shot.

That's because they were more than spokesmodels for hotlines. These girls were living, breathing characters who emerged from their situations intact. Some had stories that were primers for the disorder, the DSM-IV meets Dostoevsky. Some took that same primer and turned it around to show us that the problem was nothing like what we'd thought. Either way, however sensationalist the story, there was a clear result—it got us information we might need. In a country where Betty Ford's acknowledgment that she was an alcoholic was still a shocking revelation, these were almost revolutionary in their candid disclosures—and their refusal to condemn their characters or let them be condemned. *Yes, this can happen*, they all said. *It happens.*

Deenie
By Judy Blume
1973

Brace Yourself

My mother named me Deenie because right before
I was born she saw a movie about a beautiful girl
named Wilmadeene, who everybody called Deenie
for short. Ma says the first time she held me she
knew right away I would turn out the same way—
beautiful, that is.

Oh, how I wanted to look like the girl on this cover. She might
be the only cover girl I ever wanted to look like, actually. (Those

legs! That skirt! That thin salmon SWEATER!) But kudos to the cover artist for catching an essential part of the story. Deenie Fenner, as envisaged, is that rare kind of beauty who can be appreciated equally by her high-school-aged peers and by New York modeling agencies. In short, she's a girl readers can relate to exactly as the other characters do: with admiration, jealousy, and an involuntary sense of possession.

When we first meet Deenie, she's an ordinary high-school girl, complete with a less pretty older sister, Helen; two best friends, Janet and Midge; a dishy crush, Buddy Brader; and an actual stalker, Susan Minton, who wears whatever Deenie wore last week. Her place in the social circle is secure if not exactly, like your typical beauty, all powerful. She by no means torments her social inferiors, like Gena Courtney, her wheelchair-bound neighbor, or Barbara Curtis, a new girl whose eczema Deenie privately calls "Creeping Crud." But she's not exactly rushing to sit with them at lunch, either.

Her mother is a different story. While her father—albeit affectionately—reacts to the events in Deenie's life with baffled, genial detachment ("I didn't make the cheerleading squad." "So you'll find another activity."), her mother takes on Deenie's beauty as a spiritual mandate. "Deenie, God gave you a beautiful face," she says, poo-pooing any reluctance Deenie has to become a model. "Now, he wouldn't have done that if he hadn't intended for you to put it to good use."

Deenie treats her own beauty with admirable equanimity, even a few qualms. When she's trying out for the cheerleading squad, she tells us, "Most times I don't even think about the way I look but on special occasions, like today, being good-looking really comes in handy. Not that a person has any choice about it. I'm just lucky." But when she thinks about her mother's confidence in her future profession ("Deenie's the beauty, and Helen's the brain!") a fault line emerges: "One thing I'm sure of is I don't want to spend my life cleaning house like Ma. Sometimes I think Helen's lucky. She'll be a doctor or a lawyer or engineer and she'll never have to do those things. But if I don't make it as a model, then what?"

Still, it's important to remember that Deenie's no queen bee, though she's well-received in all the modeling agencies despite complaints about her posture. (Foreshadowing, foreshadowing!) In another narrative, Deenie might lord a trip to New York to see a modeling scout over her friends. But this heroine is stubbornly a product of her age-appropriate present, irritated that she's missing, of all things, a trip to Woolworth's:

> When we go to Woolworth's Janet's the best at trying on junk without buying. You're not supposed to do that but Janet always gets away with it. The one time I tried on some nail polish the saleslady caught me and I had to buy the whole bottle.
>
> "And we saw Harvey Grabowsky," Midge said.
>
> "You did?"
>
> "Yes, we followed him all around the store."
>
> "Did he say anything?"
>
> "He never even noticed."
>
> "Oh."
>
> Harvey is the best looking guy in the ninth grade. He's also on the football team and President of his class. Harvey has never said one word to me. I guess he doesn't talk to seventh-grade girls at all.
>
> As soon as I hung up the phone it rang again. It was Janet.
>
> "We followed Harvey Grabowsky in Woolworth's," she said.

"I know. I just talked to Midge."

"Did she tell you what he bought?"

"No . . . what?"

"Three ballpoint pens and a roll of Scotch tape. And once I stood right next to him and touched his shirt sleeve!"

I just knew I'd miss out on something great by going to New York.

It would have killed me to miss this, too, naturally. But the social drink of adolescence is like a delicate, primordial soup into which the introduction of a foreign agent can alter the composition forever, causing unexpected, irreversible roils in the resident organisms. Which is exactly what happens when Deenie—heretofore heading in a predictable evolutionary direction—finds out she has adolescent idiopathic scoliosis; or, in Deenie's words, "adolescent and something that sounded like idiotic."

Suddenly, Deenie goes from having her photo snapped and practicing her walk in front of agents to having her X-rays taken and walking around in order for the doctor to better pinpoint her infirmity. It's portfolio to pathology, something Deenie comes to realize almost immediately when she starts chattering with her new doctor about the pictures on his examination-room wall:

"Were you a good football player?"

"I was fair," he said. "Are you interested in football?"

"I'm not sure. I don't know much about it yet. I wanted to be a cheerleader, but I didn't make the squad."

He didn't say anything about that. I thought he
would. I thought he'd say "Well, you can try again
next year" or something like that. Instead he said,
"Bend over and touch your toes with your hands,
Deenie."

No more cheerleading, no more modeling—and no more
"you'll find another activity." Instead, it's a race to figure out
what activities the new, highly unimproved Deenie actually
can do, and who's to blame for the situation:

In the car, on the way home, Ma told Daddy, "Your
cousin Belle had something wrong with her back
. . . remember?"
"That was different," Daddy said. "She had a
slipped disc."
"But I'll bet that's where this came from."
"I don't think so," Daddy said.
"Because you don't want to think so!" Ma told
him.
I wanted them to stop acting like babies and start
helping me. I expected Daddy to explain everything
on the way home—all that stuff Dr. Griffith had
been talking about—that I didn't understand. Instead, he and Ma argued about whose fault it was
that I have something wrong with my spine until we
pulled into the driveway. It was almost as if they'd
forgotten I was there.

In a way, Deenie is *not* there anymore. As the doctor marks
her plaster cast with a felt pen to show the braceman where he
should put the straps, he might as well be marking the spot

in the narrative where Deenie must also fit herself into a new role: whoever was beneath the pretty face that was going to be such a successful model. When Deenie is cut out of the cast, she even finds that her body stocking has disappeared, leaving her nearly naked. She's a babe born into a new life, running, mortified, for the closet.

It's also no coincidence that the first thing Deenie does when she gets home is masturbate. This passage, I am not ashamed to admit, went right over my head at age 8, but I still got the gist: whatever she was doing meant Deenie *did* have a private life, and private desires—and also, presumably, some socially acceptable public ones that would soon be made manifest: "I have this special place and when I rub it I get a very nice feeling," Deenie tells us. "I don't know what it's called or if anyone else has it but when I have trouble falling asleep, touching my special place helps a lot."

Deenie's first step is breaking free of her mother, who's devastated to see the future she'd wanted for Deenie decimated by the wrong kind of fitting:

> The brace looks like the one Dr. Kliner showed us three weeks later. It's the ugliest thing I ever saw.
>
> I'm going to take it off as soon as I get home. I swear, I won't wear it. And nobody can make me. Not ever! . . . I had to fight to keep from crying.
>
> Just when I thought I was going to be okay Ma started. "Oh, my God!" she cried. "What did we ever do to deserve this?" She buried her face in a tissue and made sobbing noises that really got me sore. The louder she cried the madder I got until I shouted, "Just stop it, Ma! Will you just stop it please!"

Dr. Kliner said, "You know, Mrs. Fenner, you're making this very hard on your daughter."

Ma opened the door and ran out of Dr. Kliner's office.

Daddy hugged me and said, "I'm proud of you, Deenie. You're stronger than your mother."

And it's not only that Deenie is stronger that her mother—it's that suddenly, this outward manifestation of difference makes Deenie realize she really *is* different: not only from what everyone thought of her, but what she thought of herself.

Part of this involves accepting the idea that she, the former beauty, is "disabled." As the nurse shows her illustrations of her own scoliosis, she sees a drawing of kyphosis, or hunchbackism—what the woman who mans the newspaper stand near her bus stop has. "It was hard to believe I really had something in common with Old Lady Murray," Deenie thinks. After she's handed a form for the handicapped bus, she throws it away—then wonders if her wheelchair-bound neighbor, a former friend to whom she never speaks, thinks of herself as a "handicapped person or just a regular girl, like me." She stops worrying about catching Barbara's creeping crud in gym, after she can't lean over to tie her shoelaces and Barbara wordlessly does it for her: "When she told us to choose partners Barbara and me looked at each other and grabbed hands."

But she has her best insight about the brace after wearing it for a few days and responding to endless questions, not knowing whether she should feel sorry for herself or worried about being considered "different":

When Harvey saw me he asked, "What happened to *you*?"

He would be the only one in school who didn't already know. "I have scol . . ." I stopped in the middle. I didn't feel like explaining anything to anybody. Instead I looked straight at him and said, "I jumped off the Empire State Building!" After I said it I felt better. I usually think up clever things to say when it's too late. From now on, when people ask me what's wrong, I'm going to give them answers like that. It's a lot smarter than telling the truth. No one wants to hear the truth. "I jumped right off the top!" I forced myself to laugh.

"Oh, Deenie!" Janet said. "Tell him the truth."

"I just did."

"Hey, that's a good story," Harvey told me.

It is, and it's a much better story than the story her mother had planned for her. It's also better than the one she had planned for Helen, whose love life she meddles in after deciding it also doesn't fit into her plans for her other daughter. But with Deenie chucking her part, the center cannot hold, and the entire beauty-and-brains scheme comes crashing down:

"Oh Ma . . . you're impossible! God didn't give me a special brain. You made that up. And you almost convinced me, Ma . . . you almost did. . . . I used to tell myself it didn't matter if I wasn't pretty like Deenie because I have a special brain and Deenie's is just ordinary . . . but that didn't help Ma . . . it didn't help at all . . . because it's not true!"

Helen turned around and looked at me. Then she did the craziest thing. She ran to me and hugged me and cried into my shoulder. "It's not your fault,

Deenie . . . don't let them make you believe that . . . it's really not your fault."

I started crying too. Helen doesn't hate me, I thought. She should, but she doesn't. We both cried so hard our noses ran but neither one of us let go of the other to get a tissue. And right through it all, Ma kept talking. "I wanted better for you," she said. "Better than what I had myself. That's what I've always planned for my girls . . . is that so wrong?"

Oh, jeez, now I'M CRYING. Focus. But this isn't a comeuppance story about a conceited beauty who gets brought low by her own flaws, it's a more subtle point about the perils of any gift, including good looks. They can give one opportunities, but they can also be their own kind of cage. While Deenie's not conceited, she's passive—a very minor flaw in the scheme of things that unchecked, as Blume knows, can have far more dire consequences. Deenie's brace, ironically, frees her from the invisible brace her mother was setting up for her, which was a life she hadn't chosen for herself, however well meant. A plastic cage, with its collar and straps, chafes. But Deenie's brace is far better than the one her mother had in mind—and one Deenie can emerge from with her standing intact.

Don't Hurt Laurie!

By Willo Davis Roberts

1977

Hit and Miss

> Laurie sat on the edge of the table, not looking
> around her because it always frightened her to see
> all of the emergency room equipment.

Don't Hurt Laurie!, the story of a young girl whose mother has
been assaulting her for years with the same energy with which
she evades detection will seem to modern readers so completely
of the *Lifetime* pathology-meets-story tradition—dire warnings
mounting as if for an approaching hurricane system—that it's

important to remember that in its day, both the revelation of the problem at all—to say nothing of its features—were largely unknown by the public, including young readers.

When we meet Laurie, she's sitting on the table at the emergency room, having her hand sewn up by a kindly physician. The knife wound has been delivered by her manifestly unkind mother, Annabelle, and, we soon learn from the girl at the desk's gentle inquiry, Laurie has also recently been in for burns and either a broken collarbone or arm, wounds carefully put down as "accidents." "If she'd be more careful, she wouldn't have so many," Annabelle snaps back at the girl's hesitant observation, then drags Laurie away.

Laurie's father has abandoned the family, and her new stepfather, while jocular, has two other children and little attention to pay to Laurie. Still, after pointing out that Laurie is the "readingest kid I ever saw," he buys her a dictionary for her birthday at the urging of her new, younger stepbrother, who's the only one in the family who has any idea what Annabelle does when her husband is away on business trips. One of the few luxuries, in fact, that Annabelle allows her daughter is trips to the library, where Laurie picks out books "where everybody had adventures with nice mothers and fathers, and there were horses and dogs for pets. She's always wanted a pet, but Annabelle didn't like animals."

Annabelle, in fact, won't even let Laurie have friends, since anyone who became close to her daughter might threaten to expose her. (An unlikely invitation to a birthday party from a girl Laurie's just met prompts this sour grape: "More likely she's just looking for as many presents as she can get. Honestly, when she hardly knows you!") After Laurie receives the invitation, she knows exactly what's coming—Annabelle is going to insist the family move to a new school district, where the children don't know Laurie enough to like her and the people at the hospital have no records of recent burns and broken collarbones.

Laurie, highly attuned to her mother in an effort to not be beaten within an inch of her life at every turn, knows to watch Annabelle for the telltale twitch at her mouth that means she's about to get walloped, and she knows that Annabelle, despite seemingly losing control with each violent eruption, is able to control herself enough that she never beats Laurie when any adult is around. What Laurie doesn't know is why she's being beaten in the first place: "Not for the first she wondered what had made Annabelle the way she was. And as always before, she couldn't come up with an answer to that."

Roberts is careful at the beginning to lay out exactly the way Annabelle, by all appearances a pretty, happy stepmother and housewife, is able to avoid detection even though she wounds Laurie violently enough that the librarian, upon seeing Laurie, exclaims, "What happened to you?" But she also has to establish why Laurie doesn't tell the other adult who lives right in the house with her, yet has no idea what's going on—her stepfather:

> How would he react if he knew about the things Annabelle did to her? It wasn't the first time she'd speculated on that, of course. He'd never been there when anything happened; but what if she went up to him when he came home and said, "My mother deliberately cut me with a knife today because she was angry with me"? . . . Naturally, it wouldn't be the same as if it happened to his own kids. He thought she was a funny girl, an odd one he didn't understand. But he was kind, if you didn't let yourself be scared by his loud voice . . .

But of course, Annabelle wouldn't just stand there and let Laurie tell her story without offering her own version, the way she did with doctors and the nurses and the teachers. She'd remind him of how careless Laurie was and how clumsy, and probably she'd even say Laurie was lying.

If she did that, who would he believe?

I'm also interested in how little Roberts stints on presenting the actual beating, even though this is a book for young children. The scene below, where Laurie is beaten with a hairbrush simply for making too much noise playing with Annabelle's curlers one night, has stayed with me my entire life, since it so clearly depicts the nature of absolute, inexplicable rage:

Annabelle never did her hair when she had a headache, but Laurie reached up a trembling hand to remove the first one, anyway. Her mother reached out as if to help her, but instead of removing the little pins that held the curls in place, she jerked curler, hair and all, so that Laurie let out a yelp of pain. And then Annabelle's hand came around in a hard blow against Laurie's cheek as she exploded in low-voiced fury.

. . . Eyes blurred, head stinging where the hair had nearly been pulled out, Laurie bent over to pick up the nearest of the curlers on the floor. And Annabelle kicked her . . . hard enough to send her sprawling, hitting her mouth against the edge of the bathtub. Laurie felt a tooth go through her lip, tasted the blood in her mouth, knew the old, familiar terror and helplessness.

She was almost unaware of the blows that rained on her back as she crouched on the floor, her hand to her mouth, watching the blood run down her arm and into the tub. She just closed her eyes and waited until it was over.

When after Annabelle finally delivers a beating that no one can explain away—it involves an iron poker—Laurie is able to get help, and is lucky enough that her stepfather and step-grandmother want to keep her a member of the family. Her stepfather, handily enough, also is the one to finally let Laurie know why Annabelle treats her as she does: "The doctor said maybe what she does doesn't have anything to do with you at all . . . You see, many parents who mistreat their kids do it because they, themselves, were mistreated by their parents, years before. And it makes a sort of sickness in them that they can't control. It doesn't mean that she hates you. It just means she's unhappy and she can't help it, the things she does."

Well, okay not *exactly*. As Laurie points out, she's never beaten, or wanted to beat, anybody. Through Laurie, we get answers to these small questions, valuable for their (God forbid) application in the real world, or just for the creation of empathy and awareness. But I keep coming back to that brutal scene. Nowadays, such explicitness can easily veer into the sensationalistic, the salacious, a kind of over-the-top entertainment. (What child today, after all, isn't being abused by an authority figure in some novel and horrible way?) But Roberts's scenes of beating fully display their horror, and *Don't Hurt Laurie!* walks a tightrope nothing on *Lifetime* ever does. Yes, we understand Annabelle—and are even more determined to take that brush from her hands.

Are You in the House Alone?
By Richard Peck
1976

Can You Hear Me Now?

Without exaggeration, I can say with confidence that any child
of the 1970s and 80s can confirm, in a sizable swath of mainstream TV, they raped everyone. First it was *Differ'nt Strokes'*
Kimberly, locked up by that old man and nearly molested while
Arnold banged on the door. Ditto Punky Brewster. *The Facts of
Life's* Natalie had some bus-station incident with Tootie banging helplessly on the door (doors blocking what happened apparently were the way to go on prime time), and *Fame's* Irene

Cara had to show her breasts to the pervy guy—and a girl in the *Fame* spin-off TV series got raped.

I'm not done! *Family Ties'* Justine Bateman got perved on by her dad's best friend. The pretty daughter on *Gimme a Break* had her sweater half ripped off and, if I do not mistake myself, then they raped *Hunter's* Dee Dee. They raped Cagney. They may have raped Cagney *twice*. (I'm surprised they didn't rape Kit.) And there was of course, the infamous *Lipstick*, with Mariel Hemingway screaming, "He *raped* my *sister*!" which we weren't supposed to watch, but of course did.

I cannot emphasize how disconcerting it was, in the era of *Love Boat* followed by *Fantasy Island*, to see the sit-com characters one was accustomed to living vicariously through in very unfunny peril. As I sit here rocking in my cane chair, I am dimly aware that, nowadays, there are shows *devoted* to rape and the procedural accoutrements thereof. The impulse to raise awareness on a Very Important Issue remains high, as does the salacious lure of insta-drama. (Witness the entirely gratuitous rape of *The Sopranos'* Dr. Melfi.) But I'm not here to retroactively wrist-slap the media. I lay out the Rape-In-Our-Times roundup only to emphasize how Richard Peck's *Are You in the House Alone?* was such a departure from the one-episode treatment of its era, and to wonder, given the temporary cultural fascination of that time, why there weren't more books like it.

The story of Gail Osbourne, whose parents have moved from New York to the Greenwich-esque Oldfield Village in Connecticut just as she enters high school, *Are You in the House Alone?* is a commentary not only on the laws that govern the nation but society. Gail is dating Steve Pastorini, a hot working-class brainiac given to sending her notes with quotes from *Othello*. Her best friend, the doggedly social-climbing Allison, is dating

Phil Lawver (ironic name alert!), the scion of the richest family in town. Anyone who can add two and two can probably predict how the foursome will add up.

Other social conventions will probably be more jarring for the modern reader. First of all, Gail, horror of horrors, is having sex with Steve—but it's not a big *deal* that she is. It takes place alongside doing homework, going to each other's house for dinner, or any other normal activities of a near-adult relationship—in short, it's central and important but not controversial. But alongside this laissez-faire (and short-lived) sexonomics lies a less palatable artifact: Allison's grim determination to marry Phil straight out of high school, something that's become far more the exception than the rule—and certainly nothing that most girls would choose to do anymore to make their way *up* in society.

And Peck upends a bunch of stereotypes on his own, as each character reacts to the rape in unprecedented ways. After Phil Lawver rapes Gail—having stalked her through a series of increasingly sick notes, frightening calls and, finally, a horrible unsolicited visit—Allison all but rejects her, accusing her of lying. (Then, she inadvertently reveals she knew it was him from the beginning. What kind of a teen-novel best friend *is* that?) Gail and Steve predictably break up—but for the unpredictable reason that they were simply falling out of love already. Mrs. Montgomery, the hip and likable divorcee Gail babysits for whose house she's raped in, tells her she can't let her babysit for her anymore because it's too much of a reminder. (A set of conservative parents, sure, but the hip *divorcee*?) Gail's parents neither go vigilante nor blame Gail but are simply powerless, locked in an odd kind of stasis. Even Phil's behavior is surprising: cocky and at ease, he continues to ask Gail out as if she's merely playfully holding him off.

Even more surprising for readers of the time must have been Peck's brutal depiction of the ways Gail was trapped even from the time Phil started harassing her. As she explains to the lawyer, even letting people know about the early harassment didn't work: "It was like running a film in reverse. The events skipped back in a blur, jumbling up. Allison saying, 'It never happened, Gail.' My mother saying, 'What has that Steve Pastorini done to you?' Connie saying, 'Men can't afford to fail. It's like bred into them.' It seemed that everybody had turned blind ears and deaf eyes to me." After the actual rape, Gail learns, it becomes impossible to prove that she, already sexually active, hadn't just decided to cheat on her boyfriend—despite looking like she's gone 10 rounds. "Why does the law protect the rapist instead of the victim?" she asks the lawyer. He gives my favorite answer ever, unglossed, which is also the last line of the chapter:

"Because the law is wrong."

Is how Gail reacts realistic? When all is said and done, she's able to go back to school in fairly short order, weathering the loss of her boyfriend and best friend, and holding on to the horrible secret that nobody knows. She's bloody but unbowed: When Phil approaches her on a deserted road, she picks up a rock and smashes his windshield: "Just knowing I could give Phil Lawver a little hell, even if that only meant scratching his surfaces . . . What can I say? That thinking made me feel better? No, but it got me through the moment." She's angered but not consumed with rage; bloody but not shattered; frightened but not crippled. In the midst of a welter of Very Special Episodes, Peck created a character who was neither overwrought nor unnecessarily bleak, and the horror of what happens to Gail is all the worse for the prosaic details:

> Later, in that winter, Mother said, "It could have all been worse." . . .
>
> "It could have been worse, Mother, but not much." She was sitting at her desk in a little pool of light, composing a real-estate ad for the newspaper. "Not much worse. We were all trying to protect ourselves as individuals and families instead of organizing to make everybody safe. There are more Phils out there, you know."
>
> "Don't talk that way," she said.
>
> "Well, there are. We should have done something else. We still should."
>
> "But what?" Mother said. "What could we do?" And then she turned back to her work.

Go Ask Alice

By Anonymous

1971

Smoke and Mirrors

You are just going to feel dumb if you reread this debunked diary, which purported to detail the downfall of an "Alice," a nameless girl growing up sometime during the 1970s who is yanked out of a comfortable middle-class existence where "ten globby pounds of lumpy lard" are the worst problem she faces into a life of drugs, prostitution, chaos, and disrepute. BECAUSE IT IS TRULY THE WORST-WRITTEN BOOK IN THE WORLD. According to the author, fatness, family, social alienation, and hair issues are credible reasons to start taking drugs in earnest, and Alice's life, filled with parties, new friends, boyfriends, clothes, and a benign, caring family, is a plasticine ideal of the idea of a teenage girl's existence, a teen mass-produced for a public who needed to know, with all these people spelling establishment Establishment, how they ticked and how to stop them ticking. I know, I know, I know, in our grammar-school years, it seemed incredibly dangerous and real. This is why they call it propaganda. It's not a mistake that the part where she rolled up her hair in orange-juice cans was just as hard to picture as the part where it seemed confusing that a man and a woman would take turns raping someone all night. On reread, though, was my particular fave, the middle-school student she sells some acid to, then comments he's probably pushing it on grammar-school-aged kids. No, sadly—we were all too busy reading this book.

It's Not the End of the World
By Judy Blume
1972

SURE, PEOPLE GET DIVORCED
BUT IT'S DIFFERENT WHEN
THEY'RE YOUR OWN PARENTS

IT'S NOT THE END OF THE WORLD

A NOVEL ABOUT LOVE AND REAL LIFE

BY JUDY BLUME

Splits and Starts

In these days where the statistic that fully 50 percent of marriages end in divorce doesn't yield so much as a blink, it seems hard to remember that a simple divorce was once as enormous an event as any other brutal and unplanned death. But the depiction of Karen's parents is all the more striking because of how ordinary it is, exactly the kind of simple loss of affection that drives children, who would like a more earth-shattering explanation for the dissolution of their family, completely insane. *It's Not the End of the World* immediately assumes the kind of familial intimacy you get when sleeping over at a friend's house—and there we are, watching the family fight, fall apart, stomp off angrily, and finally make peace, wondering if we should call a parent to take us home.

Chapter 6

Girls Gone Wild

Runaways, Left Behinds, and Ladies Living off the Fat of the Land

Eating Our Words

Do you know exactly how much money is in your wallet? How much food is in your fridge? How long you'll be able to stretch the cache of dried abalone near the cliff that's only reachable during the summer season? When to pick those little purple flowers that look so nice in a summer salad? No? And you call yourself independent? Tell me at least you can *knit*.

I am convinced more than ever that once the great global climactic catastrophe has destroyed the earth, when the stragglers dig themselves out from their damp bomb-shelter hovels and go hard-core low-tech, readers of young adult fiction will make up the core of the new society . . . because we are the only ones who will find living off the land fun.

Imagine, if you will, a Hamlet who spent hours on how one prepared the funeral meats and elided the whole dead-father-mother-betrayer theme in a few paragraphs, and you will have a sense of the nature of the true girls' survivor narrative, wherein the point isn't *if* you get there, but how. ("Fortinbras! What is your method for removing mud from your boots after days of marching in the rain? I use a decoction of sunflowers and saltwater . . .")

The *ne plus ultra* of all skimming-the-cream narratives is, of course, *Little House in the Big Woods*, where Ma goes so far as to color the butter with squeezed carrots before she shakes it out into neat pats. But Karana of *Island of the Blue Dolphins* is no slouch—able, as she is, to not only create beautiful skirts for beach-purpose strolling but also to tame wild dogs, birds, and other animals, and then to make spears and hunt the animals she does not care to tame. *The Witch of Blackbird Pond*'s orphaned Kit makes a brave show of stirring the corn for mush with her new Puritan cousins, then seriously considers marrying a lump of a man just to have to *never* do that again. *The Endless Steppe*'s Esther Hautzig tears apart a skirt to remake it into a sweater, laboriously plucking out each stitch to then card and spin her own wool. (She may take the cake here.)

From whence comes our obsession with churning, straining, boring, sewing, scraping, stirring, carding, pulling, picking, boiling, and scrubbing? Certainly not from any domestic instinct. These children do not simply flit around cooking, cleaning, and readying the slippers for the approaching salary earner. But they are also not simply vagabonds who hunt, moving across the land, sleeping on pine needles and drinking from streams as they go, leaving the litter of kills in their wake.

They are some lovely amalgam of the two, picking, like conjurers, perfectly civilized meals, clothing, and shelter as if from thin air (or dirt, for that matter). It's one thing to simply drink from streams and sleep under the stars. It's quite another to take a cow and a plot of dirt and transmogrify it into yellow, flowery pats of sweet creamery butter. These girls kill the bacon, bring it home, then fry it up in a pan they hacked out of a gourd on a hearth they built out of rocks they gathered painstakingly, striking the fire by rubbing sticks of wood together to create a spark.

I know, that is kind of long for a slogan! But I think it has a nice ring to it.

Island of the Blue Dolphins
By Scott O'Dell
1961

Feather Wait

I remember the day the Aleut ship came to our island.

All I want for Christmas is a skirt of black cormorant feathers that shimmer green in the sun! There. I've said it. While we're on the subject, I also want a yucca skirt of tightly woven fibers, a sealskin belt, some sealskin sandals, a necklace of glittering black stones, a bull-elephant-tooth wristlet spear to kill devil-fish with and—oh, what the hell:

- Three fine needles of whalebone

- an awl for making holes

- a good stone knife for scraping hides

- two cooking pots

- a small box made from a shell with many earrings in it

Did you hear that, Mom? A *good stone knife*. Basically, I just want the possessions of one Won-a-pa-lei, secret name Karana, last inhabitant of the village of Ghalas-at, located on the outcropping of earth known to you as *Island of the Blue Dolphins*.

For those of you too fond of the weekly teen-pregnancy revelations in *US* to remember the days when girls only bore awls, *Island of the Blue Dolphins* is the true-ish! story of a young girl left behind on an island off the coast of California in the mid–1800s when her entire village clears out for the mainland, surviving alone in a far less annoying way than Tom Hanks, even if you remove the whole volleyball thing from the equation.

Which brings me to the following question . . . which is stranger? The propensity of actors, when cast in a film depicting an ancient culture, for speaking in English accents, irrespective of the country being portrayed (see *Troy, Rome, Hunt for Red October*), or for all Native-American characters in novels to maintain an internal narrative of affectless formality, occasionally peppered with quietly authoritative reverse syntax? (To wit: "He was small for one who had lived so many moons, but quick as a cricket. . . . Below me lay the cove.")

But I forgive Karana for that, because her father and brother are totally about to die. In fact, it's striking how quickly *all* the men in this book are killed off. (Probably because if they were left in the narrative they would have just crowded it out by telling Karana it's bad luck for women to use weapons and whatever, but more on that later.) Here's how it goes down: Karana's father, Chief Chowig, totally pulls a boner by giving his secret name to the Aleuts, who have come to the island to hunt seal. Chief Chowig also refuses to share his fresh fish with the visitors, and when it's time to go, Captain Orlov, the Aleuts' Russian compatriot, starts a huge fight and most of the men of the village are killed.

Events thereafter lead up to one of my favorite encapsulations of the female condition, ever:

> Life in the village should have been peaceful, but it was not. The men said that the women had taken the tasks that rightfully were theirs and now that they had become hunters the men looked down upon them. There was much trouble over this until Kimki decreed that the work would again be divided— henceforth the men would hunt and the women harvest. Since there was already ample food to last through winter, it no longer mattered who hunted.

Note to self: *always be so competent that by the time men figure out we've completely obviated them, it won't matter.*

Next comes the horrible death of her brother Ramo, which occurs after both of them are left alone on the island because—OF COURSE—as the entire tribe is about to ditch the island for the mainland, Ramo goes back to get his special spear, and Karana has to jump into the ocean and swim back to take care of him. (When I was younger, every time I read this scene, I suffered a nearly unbearable anxiety attack at the thought that Karana would drown even though I knew *there would be no book then*.) Unfortunately for Ramo, in an equally anxiety-provoking way, he is killed off immediately by a pack of wild dogs.

And now you are just *dying* for Karana. But don't worry— this ties into my next vaguely holiday-related point. Girls don't really want to play with dolls; they want to perform *tasks*. (They do still care about clothes, however—after she plunges into the sea to swim back to Ramo, she says: "The only thing that made me angry was that my beautiful skirt of yucca fibers, which I had worked on so hard, was ruined.") Because after she is left to fend for herself, Karana displays a dizzying competence that might even trump Ma's comprehensive mastery over the pig.

She gathers abalones and dries them like a champ. She kills a bunch of wild dogs and tames another one. She builds a huge fence out of whalebones and catches a billion *sai sai* fish to burn for light. She builds canoes, she outwits Aleut visitors, she almost manages to kill a bull elephant (hippo?) and a devilfish (octopus!). She is alone, so alone that she winds up catching wild animals and snaring them for company, thinking how funny her boy-crazy sister would find the "children" she's managed to gather.

One night she paddles into a cave filled with creepy figures with abalone-shell eyes made by her ancestors, *and a skeleton*, and is forced to spend the night when the tide comes in. She does not a) freak out or b) make a daring escape. She just makes peace as the tide comes in. Her Aleut dog, Rontu, who is with her for years and years, dies. (" 'Rontu!' I cried. 'Oh, Rontu!' I buried him on the headland." It's horrible.) A ship comes back for her, and she misses the ship and they leave without her AGAIN. Are you kidding me?

One of the saddest parts of the narrative occurs toward the end, as Karana tells us how she fills her days alone:

> During the time I was taming the birds, I made another skirt. The one I had made of yucca fibers softened in water and braided into twine. I made it just like the others, with folds running lengthwise. It was open on both sides and hung to my knees. The belt I made of sealskin which could be tied in a knot. I also made a pair of sandals from sealskin for walking over the dunes when the sun was hot, or just to be dressed up when I wore my new skirt of yucca twine.
>
> Often I would put on the skirt and the sandals and walk along the cliff with Rontu. Sometimes I made a wreath of flowers and fastened it to my hair. . . . I also made a wreath for Rontu's neck, which he did not like. Together we would walk along the cliff looking at the sea, and though the white men's ship did not return that spring, it was a happy time. The air smelled of flowers and birds sang everywhere.

Of course, we know this cannot stand. Soon, missionaries are going to come to bring her over to the mainland, where, like some prisoner falsely convicted and freed too late, she finds herself out of step with the world she doesn't even remember why she tried to get to. (Sorry, you have to read *Zia* for this whole part.) Everything she's missed is lost to her. Just as girls like her are lost to us.

Little House in the Big Woods
By Laura Ingalls Wilder
1932

Fresh Kills

Once upon a time, sixty years ago, a little girl lived in the Big Woods of Wisconsin, in a little gray house made of logs.

Did you know that a black physician, Dr. George A. Tann, saves the lives of the entire Ingalls family from a bad attack of Fever 'n' Ague, a.k.a. malaria, in *Little House on the Prairie*?

I state this not because this is the most salient point at

hand—or even a point, really—but I think letting just one out of the thousand, strange moments that have stuck with me my entire life from the entire Little House series is as good a way as any to enter into a discussion of The Most Important Work of Our Time.

But before I get into it, let me lay some still more super-charged imagery on you. Blacking on wallpaper. Black-eyed papoose. Sugar snow. Vanity cakes. Water splashed on freezing plants. Bad wells. Real white sugar, wrapped in brown paper. A tin cup and two pennies. Sprigging. Jigging. Jack, the brindle dog. Baths in used bathwater. School for the Blind. Common Taters on the Axe.

I'm just going to end there, because if you remember that last one, you deserve some sort of valedictory bonnet. But my point is, more so than the Madeleine, the Little House series (which, at age 8, I used to take to bed on the weekends and read, propped on a pillow, in its entirety, like some bonbon-popping lady of leisure), is a wholly sensual experience for the reader, frontier porn for the underaged. Those schooled in its world (said school being, of course, a clean, cozy room with fresh-cut planks, sun shining through its real-glass windows, a metal object bolted to the teacher's desk, a *mechanical pencil sharpener*) are forever molded by its voluptuous embrace.

The Big Woods lays the groundwork for all the sublimated sensuality that comes thereafter, including Mary and Laura's epic, savage rivalry. Speaking of which, I have to lead with the fact that I had forgotten quite how much of *The Big Woods* is devoted to animals and the disambiguation thereof. That is, my friend, the pig's bladder. That Mary and Laura are bat about. Because, when you were 8, could you think of anything more fun than playing with the bladder of a freshly slaughtered pig? Why, that might be even more fun than getting to watch Ma skim off cracklings from the drained fat, then boil a whole hog's head and chop the meat to make headcheese! But you know what it could never be more fun than? ROASTING A PIG'S TAIL. That would be, and mark the quotes, "such fun that that it was hard to play fair, taking turns." Even before it was cool enough to devour entirely down to the bones, you and your sister would have to take turns tasting it—licking it!!!—as it cracked and boiled on a spit, and *burn your tongues.*

But I could go on forever about the deer, bear, muskrat, mink, foxes, wolves, and other cadavers bloodily splayed, like so many credulous Trojans, across the narrative. So I will just note that, to be fair, Pa is a trapper, another fact I had forgotten while I was wondering whether he just kept wandering off all day so he wouldn't have to hang in the house with Ma, molding butter. That's why it makes complete sense that the chapter "The Long Rifle" begins with the wholesome image of him teaching the girls to make bullets.

But in Wisconsin's big woods, there is more to life than slaughtering, chopping, trapping, molding, and making beds. There is also thrusting hollow sticks into the mighty trees, letting the succulent sap drip out, then boiling it until it can be consumed in all its rich, slow-cooked delight. Because it is time for the maple-sugaring dance at Grandma's! It's going to take all of my strength not to type the passage below in its entirety—it's taking all my strength to not type the *book* for you in its entirety—so bear with me as I recount Laura watching her Aunts Docia and Ruby get dressed:

> Laura sat on their bed and watched them comb out
> their long hair and part it carefully . . . they had

washed their hands and faces and scrubbed them well with soap, at the wash-basin on the bench in the kitchen. They had used store soap, not the slimy, soft, dark brown soap that Grandma made and kept in a big jar. . . . They fussed a long time with their front hair . . . They brushed it so smooth on each side of the straight white part that it shone like silk in the lamplight. The little puff on each side shone too, and the ends were coiled and twisted neatly under the big knot in the back.

Then they pulled on their beautiful white stockings, that they had knit of fine cotton thread in lacy, openwork patterns, and they buttoned up their best shoes. . . .

"Caroline says Charles could span her waist with his two hands, when they were married."

Then Aunt Ruby and Aunt Docia put on their flannel petticoats and their plain petticoats and their stiff, starched white petticoats with knitted lace all around the flounces. And then they put on their beautiful dresses.

Aunt Docia's dress was a sprigged print, dark blue, with sprigs of red flowers and green leaves thick upon it. The basque was buttoned down the front with black buttons which looked so exactly like juicy big blackberries that Laura wanted to taste them. Aunt Ruby's dress was wine-colored calico, covered all over with a feathery pattern in a lighter wine color. It buttoned with gold-colored buttons, and every button had a little castle and a tree carved in it.

Aunt Docia's pretty white collar was fastened in front with a large round cameo pin, which had a lady's head on it. [Talk about disambiguation.] But Aunt Ruby pinned her collar with a red rose made of sealing wax. She had made it herself, on the head of a darning needle which had a broken eye, so it couldn't be used as a needle anymore.

I am so sorry. But obviously, I had to get the buttons with the whole castle carved on them in there.

But, as in the case of all charged imagery, the sprigged dresses and molded bullets would be all for naught did they not hide the great conflict in the narrative—viz, Laura's despair that everyone thinks Mary is prettier than she is. While Mary's curls are "golden and beautiful," Laura's hair is "dirty and brown." The storekeeper tells Ma and Pa that Mary is pretty—he says nothing about Laura. Laura gathers too many rocks by the shores of a lake and tears out her pocket—Mary is clean and neat and keeps her hands nicely folded in her lap. (Of course she does, the fucking bitch!)

Across the entire series, one of the major themes is Laura coming into her own alongside that shadow—somewhat mitigated, of course, by the fact that Mary goes blind in book three or four—and growing into her own marriage, which closes with its own books, *The First Four Years* and *These Happy Golden Years*. (One of them you have to buy outside the boxed set, cheapo.) But the intimations of the conflict are laid out over and over again—most poignantly, I think, when Laura has slapped Mary for telling her "Golden hair is lots prettier than brown," and been whipped. Tearily crawling onto Pa's lap afterward, she asks, "You don't like golden hair better than brown, do you?"

And do you know what Pa says?
"Well, Laura, my hair is brown."

Going off to weep now. Tell me when the bladder balloon is prepared for play.

The Witch of Blackbird Pond
By Elizabeth George Speare
1958

Stock Characters

On a morning in mid-April, the brigantine *Dolphin* left the open sea, sailed briskly across the Sound to the wide mouth of the Connecticut River and into Saybrook Harbor. Kit Tyler had been on the forecastle deck since daybreak, standing close to the rail, staring hungrily at the first sight of land in five weeks.

"There's Connecticut colony," a voice spoke in her ear. "You've come a long way to see it."

I've only read *The Witch of Blackbird Pond* something like 34 times, and the yellow spine of the cover I had—a dark, moony head rising up mistily from a swamp—is ineluctably seared in its place in my memory of my 8-year-old bookshelf. Still, whenever I fail to reread it every few months, it hodgepodges itself in with the tar-and-feathering scene in Scott O'Dell's *Sarah Bishop*, *The Crucible*, and a TV movie where a young girl accused of witchcraft gets felt up by her examining judge.

It may be that my poor brain has only so much room for Revolutionary-grade persecution and does-the-witch-float tests, but it never matters. Because upon reread, like some annoying little brother who keeps repeating everything you say exactly as you say it, my memory keeps catching up with the text in front of me until the entire text becomes but one self-pleasuring session of *déjà vu*.

Viz: The *Dolphin*! (Always ital'd.) "Turn back, Captain! T'will be an easy enough thing to catch." Tarring and feathering. (Shit. Wrong book.) A blueberry corncake and a kitten: Hannah's cure for all ills. Diamond-paned windows. A hornbook. A green silk dress. A soft blue shawl. A red ear of corn. Staggering in from the cold to put your head in Mercy's lap. Sprinkling the floor with sand. Her thin face transformed by the bonnet. Prudence Cruff. Nat. Goody Cruff! Stocks. A dirty blanket thrust through an opening. Kit! Frippery! Quakers! Livestock frozen in place! The *Dolphin*! Nat! Kit! Kit! Nat!

But back to the story. Kit Tyler, orphan, is the kind of character flap-copy writers live to call "headstrong." Raised in Barbados by her grandfather after the death of her parents, she has come to colonial Wethersfield, Connecticut, after his death to live with her aunt Rachel, her mother's sister, whom she's never met. Raised reading Shakespeare with her grandfather and frolicking in the blue waters under swaying palm trees, she's been forced to sell off all the property and its attendant hundred slaves—even, as she laments, her own "Negro girl"—to pay off her grandfather's debts and gain passage on the ship.

This display of wealth, as you can imagine, goes over tremendously with the Puritan settlers, whom she manages to horrify before even setting foot on land when she dives overboard to rescue a young girl's doll:

> "Such water!" she gasped. "I never dreamed water could be so cold!"
>
> She shook back her wet hair, her cheeks glowing. But her laughter died away at the sight of all of their faces. Shock and horror and unmistakable anger stared back at her. Even Nathaniel's young face was dark with rage.
>
> "You must be daft," the woman hissed. "To jump into the river and ruin those clothes!"
>
> Kit tossed her head. "Bother the clothes! They'll dry. Besides, I have plenty of others."
>
> "Then you might have had a thought for somebody else!" snapped Nat, slapping the water out of his dripping breeches. "These are the only clothes I have."

Kit! Shhhhhh! That's your love interest! But don't worry—as a narrative convention to prevent us from realizing he's your love interest too soon, the author is going to make him torment you up to the penultimate page. Here he is, like, two pages later:

> "I'll wager you're wishing you'd never left Barbados," he said. "'Twas unfair of me to tease you."

"How I envied you!" she exclaimed. "To get into that water and away from this filthy ship for even a moment!"

In a split second a squall darkened Nat's blue eyes. "Filthy—the *Dolphin*?"

"Oh," she laughed impatiently, "I know you're forever scrubbing. But that stable smell! I'll never get it out of my hair for as long as I live!"

Nat's indignation found vent in scorn. "Maybe you think it would smell prettier with a hold full of human bodies, half of them rotting in their chains before anyone knew they were dead!"

Don't fret, Kit, once you hit land to join the somber household of your aunt Rachel, her husband, Matthew, and their daughters, Judith and Mercy, this whole scrubbing thing is about to loom large enough in your life that you'll forget about Nat for a while. Here's Kit on her first day in her new household:

By the end of the first day the word *useful* had taken on alarming meaning. Work in that household never ceased, and it called for skill and patience, qualities Kit did not seem to possess. There was meat to be chopped, and vegetables to prepare for midday meal. The pewter mugs had to be scoured with reeds and fine sand. There was a great kettle of soap boiling over a fire just behind the house, and all day long Judith and her mother took turns stirring it with a long stick. . . . Kit tried to keep a gingerly distance from the kettle. . . . Her stirring became more and more half-hearted till Judith

snatched the stick in exasperation. "It will lump on
you," she scolded, "and you can just blame yourself
if we have to use lumpy soap all summer."

But I don't want to go too much more into colonial porn (oh,
all right—here's when Kit unpacks her seven trunks and Judith
is consumed with envy at what passes for daily wear in Barbados: "Imagine!" cried Judith, pulling out a handsome gown of
filmy silk. "Five slits in the sleeves!") because the actual plot
is such a vibrant machine that you don't want to waste all the
time on the trappings—just as Kit's colorful personality is, at
times, outshined by the splendor of her clothes.

Kit arrives in Wethersfield during the beginning of the Puritan colonists' breakaway from England. (For those of you,
like myself, with deeply uneven public-school educations who
studied this roughly a quarter century ago, Puritans can be
differentiated from Pilgrims in that they sought to "Purify" the
church from within, not feast on turkey ceaselessly.)

As we soon learn, Kit has been forced to leave Barbados not
only because she is penniless, but because a friend of her late
grandfather's with "pudgy red fingers with too many rings on
them" wanted to forgive the debt and marry her instead. Not
so much. But not so fast with escaping from the wealthy, stocky
suitors, either! Kit soon catches the eye of William Ashby, one
of the wealthiest young men in town, unwittingly tearing him
from the hands of Judith.

Judith doesn't care, however, because, on the boat, Kit met
the handsome scholar John Holbrook, and, after Kit introduces
him to the family, Judith "sets her cap" for him, inconveniently
failing to realize that he is desperately in love with her gentle
sister Mercy, whom no one really notices because she's so pure
hearted and crippled and everything.

Taking place outside the environs of *Wethersfield Place* is, of course, the formation of America as we know it—complete with Indians, Quaker separatists, Royalists, Puritans, slaves, and the explosion of persecution and resistance betwixt and between. (The majority of which makes it unsurprising that settlers might go a little nuts and seek to mitigate their anxiety by seeing if a woman floats before killing her.) What's wonderful about *Witch* is that the narrative isn't a flimsy cover for a history lesson, and neither is Kit a stand-in for heroic, spunky girls resisting the powers-that-be everywhere.

True, Kit tutors poor Prudence Cruff and makes friends with Hannah Tupper, the older Quaker woman. But she's also a former slaveowner who seriously considers marrying William Ashby simply to escape the cycle of hard labor of her uncle's house. She acts impulsively, which means she saves people with her kindness, but she also endangers them at the same time. Yes, she takes Prudence Cruff away from the poverty of her upbringing and teaches her to read, but her insubordinate inclinations also nearly close Mercy's school. Yes, she saves Hannah from the angry mob who comes to torch her house, but her visits are partly what has drawn attention to the woman in the first place. Yes, she's brave to go see Hannah, but she also exposes her entire aunt's family to the condemnation of the community. But worst of all, even though Elizabeth George Speare mentions that Nat's eyes are twinkling and blue and smiling and that William Ashby is stocky a million times, Kit takes like *900 years* to figure out she's in love with him.

By the time Nat has saved her from hanging in a courthouse scene reminiscent of those boardroom wrap-ups in 1980s movies like *The Secret of My Success*, we've truly grown to love Kit and her surrounding cast, not in spite of their flaws or for their lack of flaws but for how truly they all embody the contradictions of their time. In other words, it is all right, my dears, if you jump overboard in all of your fine clothes to save a young girl's wooden dolly like a nitwit, too. FYI, I am available to make soap, tutor worthy children, and be confounded by any suitors at first light.

Homecoming
By Cynthia Voigt
1981

Traveling in Steerage

The woman put her sad moon-face in at the window of the car. "You be good," she said. "You hear me? You little ones, mind what Dicey tells you. You hear?"

Is there anything better than having to count out your every meal? I don't mean in real life (that's horrible, of course) but stretching foodstuffs to match your difficult situation is—you will forgive me—a staple of a certain brand of teen fiction. Take Julie (*of the Wolves*) and her dried seal meat rations. Take Claudia (of *Mixed-Up Files*) stretching the coins hard earned by scraping the bottom of the Met's fountain to get her and Jamie a hearty breakfast at the Automat. Take *A Little Princess*'s Sarah Crewe managing to pull together enough pence for four large, fragrant buns—then realizing she is not going to be able to enjoy them if that really poor street urchin keeps looking at her wolfishly.

Thirteen-year-old Dicey Tillerman's mastery over milk, bananas, donuts, clams, and throwaway fish makes her no less an illustrious follower of this tradition. When we meet up with Dicey, she, along with smart, bookish brother James, gentle sister Maybeth, and rebellious youngest brother Sammy, have been left in the parking lot of a mall in Peewauket, Massachusetts, by their mother, with only the address of a distant relative in Bridgeport, Connecticut, that the woman has pressed into Dicey's hand to go by.

Before I get into their adventure, I'm going to swing into the first meal at the mall, which sets the gustatory heights from which the four are about to plummet:

> . . . They were drawn to restaurants that exuded the smell of spaghetti and pizza or fried chicken, bakeries with trays of golden doughnuts lined up behind glass windows, candy stores, where the countertop was crowded with large jars of jelly beans and sourballs and little foil-covered chocolates and peppermints dipped in crunchy white frosting; cheese shops (they each had two free samples), where the rich smell of aged cheeses mingled with fresh-ground coffee, and hot dog stands,

where they stood back in a silent row. After this, they sat on a backless bench before the waterfall, tired and hungry. Altogether, they had eleven dollars and fifty cents, more than any one of them had at one time before, even Dicey, who contributed all of her baby-sitting money, seven dollars.

They spent almost four dollars on supper at the mall, and none of them had dessert. They had hamburgers and french fries and, after Dicey thought it over, milkshakes.

Ah, poor fools! It's a last meal in a very real sense, since this plasticine, industrial Agora and everything it represents is about to be left behind by the Tillermans, perforce—and Dicey will be thinking it over at every meal, from now on. After making a call to find out how expensive buses to Bridgeport are and almost being nabbed by a guard at the mall, Dicey decides they'll set off to walk to Bridgeport, to their Aunt Cilla, whom they've never met, because Dicey thinks there's a chance their mother will be there.

But it's not completely clear why Dicey runs from the guard, instead of marching right up to him and telling him exactly what's happened. Partly it's dim understanding that doing so would mean they'd be split up, and certainly taken away from their mother and put into foster care. There's also the fact that, since the children were raised in a rambling shack in Provincetown, out of the mainstream, their father absent, their mother (almost certainly) bipolar, they're used to acting on their wits and whims, not on the say-so of adults. But mostly it's Dicey's pure instinct—something in her resists handing over their destiny to someone in authority who doesn't know them. It's her family. She's the authority, even if she doesn't quite know what she's going to do with it. "Sometimes I think we can do anything," Dicey tells James, once they're on their way. "Because we're the Tillermans."

So they set off, on foot, on Route 1, "mostly garages and small shopping centers and discount stores and quick food places. There were no green patches and few sidewalks." James comments that it was probably a "nice road once, a country road," and soon, Dicey realizes they'll be better off sticking to actual country roads, where they can camp out and forage for their own food. So they begin a pattern—she'll buy them donuts, bread, apples, and other cheap, filling things during the day, and then they'll stay in parks at night. Sometimes, they stay in abandoned houses in developments. She buys them hooks to fish, and Sammy (who is SIX—they built six-year-olds better then, obviously) actually proves to be a good fisherman. Maybeth is skilled at gathering wood and suchlike. Dicey, having grown up on the beach, knows how to build a driftwood fire and roast whatever they catch. And when they need more money, she asks for work at gas stations and supermarkets, washing windows (she's big on washing windows!) or carrying other people's groceries.

Still, the adult world continues to conspire to confound them. After a big catch of fish, she's told by a sports salesman that it's illegal to fish in the park where they're hiding out:

> How were they supposed to eat then, Dicey asked herself. By buying food, she answered. The whole world was arranged for people who had money— for *adults* who had money. The whole world was arranged against kids. Well, she could handle it. Somehow.

Julie (of the Wolves) was unencumbered on the tundra, able to hunt whatever she needed. Subsisting on the land is all Dicey wants to do, but one may not, unfortunately, hunt in a Grand Union:

> So, she had to earn some money. But how? There was that shopping center. It had a big parking lot, and a supermarket. She pictured it carefully, and then pictured herself coming out of the market with two big bags filled with fruit and meat and breads and cans of vegetables and a pan to cook things in. And a can opener; it would be just her luck to forget the can opener.
>
> In her daydream, the Dicey she saw walking out of the store with enough food for her family to eat for days, with her eyes smiling and a big grin stretching her mouth, that Dicey tripped and fell. The food scattered over the ground. The wheels of cars squashed the scattered oranges and bananas. A dog took the package of hamburger meat and ran away with it. The people around went off on their own ways, carrying their own heavy bags of groceries.
>
> Was this how Momma felt? Was this why Momma ran away?

Usually, in the books where the need to be fed overrides—usually mercifully—the opportunity to mope over one's circumstances, the child in question also finds, surprisingly, that she *can* survive by her own wits, something she didn't know before. Dicey is a bit different. In a way, she's always been a survival machine, with instincts that automatically allow her to make the best of any situation, almost unconsciously. As she tells James when he's telling her how much he loves school, "It takes different things to make me glad. . . . Like knowing we've got food . . . the ocean . . . and lots of room outdoors. But mostly the ocean. And the food too. . . ."

Throughout, there are also those who help—and, not infrequently—feed them as well. There is, of course, Windy, the Yale student who is amused by the ragtag group and, after taking them to several meals at a diner, arranges a ride to Bridgeport for them. There's Cousin Eunice, the only living relative of the deceased Aunt Cilla, whose cloying pressing of religion on the children becomes overwhelming, as does her old-lady food, which Dicey must prepare. ("Cousin Eunice's house wasn't free, it was expensive—and the price was always remembering to be grateful.") There's the totally creepy child molester who almost traps them on his tomato farm once they've made it to the Eastern Shore to try to find a grandmother they've only just learned about. And there's Will, the itinerant circus director who saves the children from creepy tomato man, and who, along with his partner, Celia, takes a shine to the children, and makes sure they have a good meal in their stomachs.

And though she's grateful to all the adults they meet along the way, Dicey finally realizes, like all those nearing the end of a quest, that in fact there's no need to stop:

> "You know," Dicey said, "we don't have to go any-where. We could always travel like this, following the warm weather, like Will said he did. We can take care of ourselves."
>
> "Yeah, but what's the point?" James asked.

"There doesn't have to be a point," Dicey said. "Just doing it. Like sailing."

Could a kid with three siblings in tow manage nowadays to walk from Provincetown to Bridgeport, then get from Annapolis to the Eastern Shore? Could a *person* do it? (I can't even walk through my whole CITY.) Would our 21st-century prices make room for kids to eat, to make even enough money for a day, even eating off the dollar menu?

I don't think the point of *Homecoming* is how realistic it is, although, for its own purposes, it's realistic enough. Still, what's wonderful about *Homecoming* isn't only that Dicey and her siblings finally succeed. It's also the understanding that the world has forces, and resources, that we can marshal to our side if we're courageous and competent enough. When Dicey and James manage to convince two boys to take them across the bay to Easton, Maryland, Dicey realizes what she's been doing the entire journey:

> Boats, waves, water, wind: through the wood she felt them working for her. She was not directing, but accompanying them, turning them to her use. She didn't work against them, but with them; and she made the boat do that too. It wasn't power she felt, guiding the tiller, but purpose.

You'd be wrong to sum Dicey up as a "spunky" adventurer. She's not. She simply is—as her name suggests—a natural sailor.

The Endless Steppe: A Girl in Exile
By Esther Hautzig
1968

Miss Steppes

I must have read this autobiography of a girl being sent to the gulag by Stalin 100 times, feeling, upon each reading, more and more put upon that no one, whatever my parents did, was EVER going to come and take us from our house so we could live on a strange, windswept region in Siberia, piecing together a life bit by bit as we struggled against both the political winds and the elements. OUTRAGED, really. (We'll see if this country ever gets around to giving my children a shot.) Esther, a young Jewish girl from Vilna, Poland, and her mother and grandmother are lucky enough to only be sent to Siberia (for the dubious crime of being "capitalists"), forced to leave a comfortable middle-class existence to become terrified homesteaders in the windswept nothingness. For all that it involves the divestiture of all one's goods and identity, *The Endless Steppe* is a strangely uplifting narrative, told in amusing episodes, like the one in which Esther promises to make a sweater to trade for a cow, rips apart a skirt and labors over the sweater for months, then finds it no longer fits the buyer, who has, of course, become fat off the milk of the cow in the meantime. (You would think, being so taken with the ripping apart of this skirt, the painstaking carding of the wool, the knitting, and the washing, I would just go to H&M and replicate it, but alas, when it's not being bought by a beautiful, wealthy Siberian to get the family a cow, it loses that special something.) As the book closes and they find they will be returning to Poland, Esther breaks away from their years of near-starving scrimping and insists on buying *sapogy* and a *fufalka*, high leather boots and a green quilted jacket that is the height of fashion in Poland. Her father's first words upon greeting them back in Lodz? That the first thing they will do is buy her some new clothes. Me? I am in possession of the closest the mall could offer to a *sapogy* and a *fufaika* to this day—all I need is a Stalin to give them meaning.

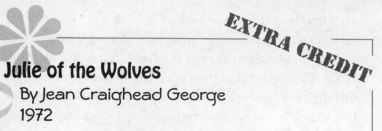
Julie of the Wolves
By Jean Craighead George
1972

Packed and Sealed

It's tough to say if you gave a group of school-aged girls an animal to shoot, butcher, dry, store, and carry, if it would turn them off the stuff forever or have a kind of friendship-bracelet effect, spreading through the community like Miley Cyrus's next album. Truly, nothing SOUNDS more fun, which is probably why the story of Miyax—"American" name Julie—a young Eskimo girl who, after the death of her mother, is raised by her father, Kapugen, out in the wild, is so absorbing. Truly, little else happens. As the author tells us, even Miyax's body is part of the landscape, as she's a "classic Eskimo beauty, small of bone and delicately wired with strong muscles. . . . Unlike the long-limbed, long-bodied animals of the south that are cooled by dispensing heat on extended surfaces, all things in the Arctic tend toward compactness, to conserve heat." Sadly for Miyax, her dream to "live with the rhythm of the beasts and the land" is no longer supportable, since the Indians are being brought into the towns for special Indian schools and western hunters are taking over the landscape. Not only are the "seals scarce and the whales almost gone," Kapugen himself has gone from an Alaskan hunter to a western one, using a plane to shoot animals that he doesn't even bother to collect. Perhaps he has killed Amaroq, the last wolf hunter of the tundra, the one who has sustained his daughter in her time of need, and the only company Julie has as she putters around sustaining herself off the fat of the land. Is it partly that we know it's not longer possible to live off the land, to never have school, to be on one's own, that makes it so appealing? By the end of the book, the only thing left for Julie, and for Alaskan culture, is a bastardized version of their old way of life. Exit dried flesh, enter the airplane.

Understood Betsy
By Dorothy Canfield Fisher
1917

Town and Country

Weight gain, confidence-building, and a breakdown in all fear-based mechanisms is the order of the day in this adorable tale, in which spindly, sickly orphan Elizabeth Ann has to be sent away from her two spindly aunts to the house of some more robust cousins, and suddenly realizes she is not as shy, delicate, and useless as she had been made to fear. When she arrives, she's barely able to untie her own shoes, but, at the kind behest of cousin Abigail, the less kind behest of cousin Ann, and the dutiful silence of Uncle Henry, she goes from mastering the simple art of washing dishes to becoming a girl who can fetch another out of a ravine and save the day. Throughout, the act of labor is paramount—at the beginning, she cannot even remember how the asphalt in her own city was laid, which Henry wants to hear all about. By the end, she is milking, cooking, cleaning, gathering, sugaring—the best antidote to being "thin and nervous" ever invented. Who could get through this book and NOT wish to have been skinny and useless, then be made into a hearty and useful creature who has the admiration of her tough, rural cousins, and now is in possession of a bunch of useful skills involving milk and freshly shaved wooden pencils? It's Eliza Doolittle, to be sure, but a much more wonderful Eliza Doolittle, since she's ditched the bone-china culture for one where they talk about apples being hard enough to shoot through an oak plank.

Chapter 7

She Comes by It Supernaturally
Girls Who Are Gifted and Talented

Second Sight-geist

Let's first get the reason there is a preponderance of the supernatural in girls' literature out of the way: It's fun. It's fun to know what the future holds, it's fun to be able to float forks around the room, fun to go back in time, fun to inhabit someone else's body, fun to know what people are thinking, fun to talk to animals, fun to see ghosts—fun, fun, fun, fun. Even the official terms used to discuss the powers— Second Sight! Precognition! Telekinesis! Astral Projection!—are, in their grandeur and glory, fun.

But why, thus bewitched, one must ask, with exactly *this* type of fun? Providing the definitive verdict on why your average girl spends hours in front of the bathroom mirror chanting "Bloody Mary" and intently thinking of trees, squares, and ovals while a friend across the room attempts to channel them in the correct order on a scrap of paper and a third girl serves as a control in the hall may be beyond my puny powers. But I think looking at a few other times fork-floating exists in literature is helpful.

One of the classic conceits of the poltergeist, a house spirit that bangs ominously in rooms and, depending on your vengeful spirit—think *The Exorcist*—makes blood slide down the wall and sets heads to spinning, is that the upheavals are caused not by a ghost but by a resident girl going through puberty. (Her hormonal upheavals, apparently, yank their diminutive host roughly along like a dog on a choke chain trying to escape a puny captor.) Authors like Stephen King take the problem directly to the source with characters like Carrie, whose special powers arrive alongside a gushing menses—a rush of blood that morphs into a crimson deluge by the end. (*Throw a tampon at me now, motherfucker!*)

As amusing as these scenarios are, they are not, to say the least, ones to which your first-time feminine-product buyer can, or wishes to, relate. But traditional boys' fantasies—say, *The Hobbit*, or *The Chronicles of Narnia*, both of which, by the way, I am extremely fond—are almost aggressively bloodless, each fantastic species stuck in ageless eternity, the only sex sublimated in lightning-swift elfin arrows and the like. They also take as their setting the entire world—underworld included!—in stark contrast to the books in this chapter, in which the supernatural occurs when one is doing something as ordinary as setting the table or brushing one's hair.

And therein, I think, lies much of their appeal. As opposed to Bilbo Baggins's charge to save the world, the utility of these powers is, like the best politics, local. *Stranger with My Face*'s Lia Stratton, whose body fills out just as she learns to hop out of it, learns to accept a different kind of family and a different kind of boyfriend. *The Girl with the Silver Eyes*' lonely Katie Welker finds a new group of friends who also can talk to cats and like to take books out of the library (both are actionable, apparently), while Blossom Culp finds yet another use for her incisive insights, becoming closer to people, including Alexander Armsworth. But it's *Hangin' Out with Cici*'s Victoria whose time-travel jaunt produces, in my opinion, the most desirable power of all: She becomes able to get along with her mother.

If we take the girls' new powers as a metaphor for puberty, we find that these changes, with their physical aftereffects, can be occasionally disconcerting. Still, they rarely threaten to swamp a town in their all-encompassing evil. In fact, they herald new insights about one's self, as well as a host of inviting developments on the horizon for friends, family, and future prospects, both romantic- and work-related. They are, in short, *good* news for the girls. And that's good news for Tampax users everywhere.

Ghosts I Have Been
By Richard Peck
1977

Ferry Me Across the Water

I tell you, the world is so full of ghosts, a person
wonders if there's a soul to be found on the Other
Side. Or anybody snug in a quiet grave.

It can be generally agreed that any story is improved by the
addition of a) a wry Southern narrator, b) an aggrieved ghost,
and c) anything, *anything*, involving the *Titanic*. Hitting
on all cylinders is Richard Peck's *Ghosts I Have Been*, the turn-
of-the-century story of would-be spiritualist Blossom Culp

and her sudden rise from an adolescent Madame Blavatsky to a genuine, undead-espying psychic.

In the first book of Peck's quartet, *The Ghost Was Mine*, Blossom Culp, of the genteel, fictional Bluff City, is a brash secondary character and sidekick to narrator Alexander Armsworth, the far more well heeled neighbor who fights both his second sight and Blossom's undeniable affections. In *Ghosts I Have Been*, Blossom takes center stage as a troublemaker, schemer, and seeker of attention, but even she is mildly taken aback when she learns that she is actually in possession of the same powers of second sight as her mama, a gruff, toothless gypsy given to speaking to Blossom mostly in grunts. The world fame that accompanies her newly found powers, however, she handles with relative aplomb.

But I am, as Blossom often informs us she is, getting ahead of myself. We must first touch on the delights of the narrator herself, who has a knack for being around when curious events occur—or, as she puts it, "nearby, as I often am." Bluff City, the small town where she's lived her whole life, is "mainly divided into two camps: those who have already arrived and those who never will," and even after she becomes a celebrity, she remains "something of a misfit."

When we meet her, however, she's still grasping the short end of the stick, heading off to school unfed and leaving her home, a hovel by the streetcar—"Ours is a two-room dwelling which we have rent free, it being abandoned," she informs us— then passing the Armsworths' house nearby, from which drift pleasant, bacon-oriented smells. "Some people live high on the hog and no mistake," she says:

> I consider that I was always well off without such
> advantages, as they tend to kill your initiative. As

the poet says, necessity makes the mule plow. And I
for one would not care to pass my life up on a porch,
gazing into an embroidery hoop.

Naming no names, there are some people who
still say I do not know my place. How wrong they
are. I know it well and always did. But I have always
meant to better myself, and when you are on your
own in this life, it is uphill work.

Now, I am not vain when it comes to looks. If I
was, a trip to the mirror would cure me. But I am
vain about my resourcefulness. There is more to be
learned about a town from the wrong side of the
tracks than from the right. I made a study of this
town long before I had the power to see beyond it.

The revelation of Blossom's powers—and the appearance of
the ghost whereof the title speaks—are set off, as it were, by
a scene involving an outhouse, a gang of boys, Blossom in a
sheet, and an old man with a shotgun filled with rock salt. The
events of the night are too various to relate in full, but I hope
you will forgive my placing the scene below, where Blossom
bursts in on the old man in question, as it is one of the funniest
in modern literature:

My intention was to step just inside the privy and pull
the door shut. Then when the gang approached to tip
it over, I planned to step out, with the lighted candle,
and moan eerily. If this wouldn't strike them half-
dead with horror, what would? I grinned under my
mosquito bar at my plans. Alas, I grinned too soon.

As there was no breeze that night, I fished the

matches out of my shoe top and lit my candle as I stepped up to Old Man Leverette's privy door.

At this point, things went seriously wrong. I had one foot inside when I come face to face with Old Man Leverette himself. He was in his privy, using it. His nightshirt was hitched up above his hips. My candle threw dreadful shadows in the tiny room, and light fell on Old Man Leverette's startled face and on the torn pages of the Montgomery Ward catalogue in his aged hands.

Near enough to the grave himself, he let out a kind of Indian war whoop. He rose up, thought better of it, and flopped back down on the seat. I was as startled as he was, and the wind from his gasping breath set the candle flame bobbing.

"Whoooo, whoooo, whooo in the Sam Hill are *you*?" Old Man Leverette howled.

"I beg your pardon, I'm sure," I said, not wanting to identify myself. " . . . I just happened to be passing."

"So was I!" Old Man Leverette roared.

As Blossom would say, "Remember this. It bears on the story later on." (Blossom's syntax may be even more catching than HARRIET M. WELSCH'S CAPS.) In a roundabout way, the twists and turns of which are too various to relate at present, Blossom's prank results in an extremely begrudging invitation to the house of the school's queen bee, Letty Shambaugh (and a free wardrobe from her parents' Select Dry Goods Company, in another twist too complicated to relate). Blossom accepts, thinking it will simply be a champion opportunity to torment the prissy, obnoxious Letty, something she does as often as possible. ("'You mean you won't come?' [Letty] said, brightening. 'I mean I will,' I said. And I did.")

At Letty's house, Blossom turns events around so that she can give one of her famous faux seances, planning to use the opportunity to reveal that two girls in the assembled group cheated on a recent test, a piece of information she picked up on one of her many visits to the office of the long-suffering Miss Spaulding, the school's principal. However, it's she who's shocked by what happens:

> "Don't be too long," Letty warned, "or we'll give you a broom, and you can fly home on it, ha ha."
>
> I began to sway in my chair then, starting up slow. I have always been able to roll my eyes up into my head so only the whites show. As a kid I practiced that by the hour. "Oh, look what's happening to her eyes, isn't that sickening!" somebody said.
>
> I moaned low in my throat, wishing I'd thought to ask for a candle. Candlelight always adds a touch. But I proceeded without it. . . . But then something happened that even I could not explain. My eyes did not roll back, yet I seemed to go blind for a second. There was a peal of thunder that nobody else seemed to hear. Then a strange flash, like lightning at night—jagged and blue. The room and the girls flickered and faded from me, and I spoke without conscious thought:
>
> "Oh, dear," I said. "Newton just fell off the back of the trolley and was run over by Miss Dabney's electric auto."

It's true. Letty's plump, braying brother has just fallen off the trolley (he emerges unscathed) and Blossom has been revealed to have the Second Sight, much to the consternation of her mama, who had long groaned with unconvincing regret that the gift had died with her. Beyond gaining her some small recognition among her peers—including Alexander, who is displeased to have the supernatural rear its ugly head again—it also gains Blossom somewhat of a protectoress in the form of the elderly but sharp Miss Dabney, who has a supernatural problem of her own she asks Blossom to clear up—namely, a maid who hung herself in the pantry nearly 100 years ago, who's still hanging around in the back kitchen, banging pots ominously:

> "Minerva, I've come to tell you something to your advantage." She waited. I was reminded of how a cat will freeze on a fence with one paw drawn up, to see if you are friend or foe. I was exploring new territory . . . "Mr. Dabney, he won't send you packing. He died . . . here a while back."
>
> "In 1892," Miss Dabney whispered behind me.
>
> . . . "And so you're to settle down and quit your fretting. Mr. Dabney's little girl—"
>
> "Gertrude," Miss Dabney muttered.
>
> "—Gertrude is all grown up now, and she would consider it a privilege to share her home with you."
>
> "But tell her to be quieter, for Heaven's sake," Miss Dabney murmured.

After successfully changing Minerva from an angry spook into one who likes to bake spectral cakes and set them out at teatime (" 'I really ought to pay her a wage, if I knew how,' Miss

Dabney would often say in a vague way"), Blossom is on a roll, ridding the town of a traveling spiritualist huckster in a spectacle that is universally successful, except in that it lands her yet again in Miss Spaulding's office. This time, the weary principal is at her wit's end, and decides that the best way to tamp Blossom down is to engage journalist Lowell Seaforth, the husband of Alexander's older sister ("What he ever saw in Alexander's big sister, Lucille, is the deepest mystery of this account") to write a story on Blossom's spiritual powers for the daily *Pantagraph*. Miss Spaulding, not the spiritual type, is quite certain that this will solve the problem of Blossom's being "nearby" at any given conflagration. First, it will give her the attention she is obviously desperately seeking. Next, it will reveal that she has no special powers, as such a thing would "fly in the face of Science."

Miss Spaulding accomplishes the first of the goals with great dispatch. Unfortunately, the second eludes her when Blossom slips "through a crack in time, like a termite through splintered floorboard." She lands in a cabin on the swiftly sinking *Titanic*, where a British couple is fighting violently over how best to escape the icy looming mountain while their son, Julian—the ghost Blossom has been seeing around town—lies sleeping, totally unaware of the events unfolding around him:

> With no thought of anything but themselves, his own flesh and blood had left poor Julian for fish bait. . . . If this was an instance of English child care, I for one would settle for Bluff City and my mama.
>
> There's no fighting fate, or changing what's over and done with. Still, I struggled to wake Julian and send him flying for the lifeboats. I yanked on his blanket, but my poor transparent fingers poked

right through it. I darted over to where his life jacket hung on a peg, but my hands scooped through it like a fork into whipped cream. I couldn't have lifted a matchstick, let alone a life jacket, for I was a ghost, haunting the past. History can be very cruel. . . .

Then the first bodies hurtled past the porthole as people dropped into the sea. I tumbled back across the cabin and threw my weightless body across Julian. . . . He woke and struggled against the band that held him fast. His mouth was a startled circle. And in that moment I knew he saw me. Working one hand free, he reached for where my face was, and his fist closed in the air.

The electric lamp failed and water roared through both portholes under heavy pressure. In the last second I found I could clasp Julian's small hand. He clung tight. This was a miracle, but we were soon parted.

The rest of *Ghosts I Have Been* involves much in the way of fun, including a transatlantic journey, a meeting with the queen of England, and an unauthorized dramatic exhibition at Madame Tussaud's. But whatever happens, I still keep coming back to that touching last scene where Blossom attempts to grasp the boy's hand, and is able to hold it only briefly before he's swept away to his end, and she back to her own world.

While Blossom is surely delightful as a comic character, and impressive as a spirited pioneer (as her mama puts it, "She's a willful little . . . thing"), Blossom's true power lies in her ability to bridge worlds of all kind. Between this world and the next, yes, but also between her side of the tracks and Alexander's side of the tracks; between Miss Dabney's barren spinster life and the queen of England's; between formal Miss Spaulding and the world of the yellow press; and between loneliness and intimacy.

Because, while Miss Spaulding fears Blossom leaves a trail of chaos in her wake, but actually, Blossom's exploits set to rest wounds that have been raw for far too long. (What is a ghost, after all, other than the embodiment of unfinished business?) There are actual ghosts, like Minerva and Julian, whom she puts to rest as best she can, but the world is full of people stuck in a life that needs a drastic nudge to get set to rights. She may, as she proclaims, be a misfit. But her most miraculous power is the ability to put people, living or dead, in a better place.

A Gift of Magic
By Lois Duncan
1971

Options and Futures

Nancy pulled herself awake and sat up in bed. "Mother's crying," she said.

If every author has their redheaded stepchild of a book (John Updike's *The Witches of Eastwick*—WTF?) every author also has the book that, whether it's a reader favorite or not, seems the purest expression of their very authorial being. For Lois Duncan, *A Gift of Magic* is that work—and all the more strikingly for eschewing the trademark of her many other beloved novels (namely, being *fucking terrifying*). Instead, it takes an ordinary character dealing, as most of us were, with the changes of puberty right alongside changes in her family. In *A Gift of Magic*, there's no evil twin, no menacing stranger—only a girl who can see the past, future, and present far, far away, fighting with a power she does not yet understand or control.

When we first meet our pre-, present-, and post-cogriffic heroine Nancy Barrett, she, older sister, Kirby, and younger brother Brendon have just been taken by their mother, Elizabeth, back to Elizabeth's childhood home in Florida. Elizabeth has amicably separated from their father, a war photographer who dragged his entire family all over the world on an endless international heat-seeking jaunt that left them global travelers but curiously sheltered. So sheltered, actually, that the entire family takes Nancy's gift for knowing who's on the phone or that someone is coming to the door completely for granted. Even the reader, in the first line above, learns about Nancy in a blink-and-you'd-miss-it way.

Like all (sigh) middle children, Nancy is the emotional lightning rod for the family, and while Brendon and Kirby handle the separation with relative equanimity, Nancy's violent reaction to their new circumstances is rife with Duncian foreboding:

> It was a stupid question. Of course, there was something wrong. There had been something wrong for days, for weeks, for months even. Now that the words had actually been spoken, Nancy could feel, with a sick kind of acceptance, the great wave of wrongness rising higher and higher above

them, ready to come toppling over to swamp them all. With a violent effort she braced herself against it and made her mind go closed.

Okay, so Nancy's kind of intense. But by the time we've gathered the basic situation through Duncan's convenient use of dialogue-as-backstory ("But Dad?" Brendon said. "What about him? How can he work here? His job is to travel all over the place writing articles and taking pictures . . ."), we've moved on to Nancy handily locating her father in Paris to check in on his emotional situation:

> She closed her eyes tightly and reached out—out— across the miles, the hundreds and thousands of miles—to the place where their father was. . . . It was a business lunch and he was getting briefed on the next assignment. There was a notebook by his plate and a pencil, but the page of the book was empty, for he had not been taking notes. His mind was away from the conversation. . . .

No Twitter required! But Mr. Barrett's staying away from the family, ironically, gives the kids more of a chance to settle in and spread out. Now Kirby, a passionate dancer, is finally in a place where she can study it seriously. Brendon, who's been rambling solo with two sisters, can finally make a friend and get into normal-boy activities, like building a boat out of an old door and orange crates and chewing gum (more on that later). And Elizabeth—astonishingly, to her children—reveals all sorts of new items for the children to digest, like that she can actually drive, and hold a job—even date someone, like

Tom Duncan, a guidance counselor at their new school, who's her old boyfriend and still totally in love with her.

In fact, the change is only severe on Nancy, who must deal with the new problem that her ESP—which she does not even know is called ESP, EVEN THOUGH SHE HAS ESP—does not fly as easily in the world of the public high school. As this is a pre-*Blubber* era narrative, when teacher abuse still trumped peer abuse, Nancy's harsh debut into the world of the unbelieving takes place when she mistakenly starts putting the answers to a geography quiz down before the teacher has even asked the questions:

> "No, Nancy, you did not imagine these questions," Miss Green said. "They are exactly the questions that I asked the previous classes. I would be very interested in learning how you knew what they would be."
>
> There was a long silence. All around them, heads were raised and turned in their direction. Thirty pens were held, suspended, over thirty sheets of paper as thirty students waited to hear Nancy's explanation.
>
> "I—I don't know," Nancy said slowly. "I just sort of—knew. I do that sometimes."

How very convenient. (That's what the teacher says, too.) However, this is the part where it becomes even more extraordinarily convenient to have a guidance counselor who has been in love with your mother for 20 years:

> "Wait," he said. "Now, let's wait a minute, Miss Green. I would like to hear a bit more about this ability of Nancy's. There is such a thing as extrasen-

sory perception, you know, although we don't run into it too often."

"Extrasensory perception?" Miss Green's mouth fell open. She stared at the counselor as though she thought he had gone crazy. "Oh, come now, Mr. Duncan, surely you can't be serious!"

"Indeed I am," Mr. Duncan said firmly. "ESP does exist. I am quite positive of it. I have known these girls' family for years, and I have often wondered if their grandmother didn't possess the gift. . . ."

I cannot tell you how much I love the part in any Duncan novel where the wise old sage, upon hearing some supernatural activity has been occurring, instead of being, like, "That sounds batshit," nods oldly/wisely/sagely and says, "Yes, there are many studies from first-rate universities showing that there are [witches/ghosts/people who can astrally project themselves into other bodies]," etc.

With Tom Duncan's revelation, Nancy has a name for what has always been—and starts to realize that she, like Kirby, may also have something that distinguishes her as an individual:

"Well, what is it exactly?" Kirby asked. "Is there more than one kind?"

"There sure is." Nancy referred to the book. "There's one kind called telepathy. That means being aware of what the other person is thinking. Then there's clairvoyance; that means knowing when something's happened. There are two other kinds two—precognition means knowing about the future, and being able to tell when something is

going to happen. Retrocognition is knowing about
the past. . . ."

" . . . It's your gift, isn't it? This ESP thing? Like
my gift is dancing?"

Have I mentioned my second-favorite part of the Duncan
oeuvre is when the heroine goes to the library and retrieves
a book about whatever supernatural event is occurring, then
handily recites its particulars for another character?

It's no mistake that, one page later, Nancy goes to the mirror
and notices she's not quite as flat anymore: "She might never
look like Kirby, but she was finally, at long last, beginning to
look like something other than a boy." Taking responsibility
for her ESP is also about her growing up, and being able to
listen in on what one's father is doing thousands of miles away
in Paris should also leave room for noticing what's going on,
literally, under her nose.

Because *A Gift of Magic* isn't only about a girl with ESP. It's
also a novel about members of a family who, plopped like spores
in a new environment, have to learn how to grow without destroying the entire culture. Kirby, given the freedom to study
all the dance she desires, has to learn to not become completely
anorexic and starve herself in order to look like a dancer, then
fall down and break her leg and almost lose the gift because of
nerve damage, but then triumphantly be okay. Elizabeth has
to learn that it's all right to let go of the past and marry Tom
Duncan and be her own person, even if her daughter Nancy
isn't thrilled about it. Brendon, whose gift is music, has to learn
that even if he's going to squander that gift, it's still not a good
idea to make a boat out of a door and old crates and set sail
into the Gulf, and that if he does, he'd better shout loudly at

his psychic sister's mind so she and Tom Duncan can save him before he drowns. And it's Nancy, most of all, who has to learn that her powers aren't evil, and they're not all encompassing—they're a part of her, like Kirby's gift for dance, or Brendon's for music. (And, for that matter, Lois Duncan's gift for story-telling, which comes up at the end of the novel in a way that's too fun to be spoiled.)

But if the novel is truly about learning to grow within and without one's family, why the ESP at all? I've always wondered if perhaps these novels bloomed in the 1970s and 80s because it was a time before a fractured family became a given, and that, if it's the case, for the daughters growing up in that new hierarchy, they struck a particularly hopeful note. Because Nancy's family has undergone a turbulent dissolution, true, but it doesn't crush her. In fact, it gives her the ability to learn more about herself and what she can achieve than she would have had her mother stuck out an unhappy marriage. Duncan may have fun with ESP, sure. (She also has a bit of fun at the end, when we learn who Nancy's storyteller daughter turns out to be.) But at the end of the day, *A Gift of Magic* isn't only a novel about special powers. It's also just about power.

The Girl with the Silver Eyes
By Willo Davis Roberts
1980

Life on the Pharm

> Katie sat on the small balcony of apartment 2-A, looking out over the sidewalk.

As a champion squirreler of old books, I am rarely in the position of having my memory happily jogged by the cover photo. But not so with *The Girl with the Silver Eyes*, which fell out of my possession in the early 1980s, after which all I could call up was a dim memory of an apartment complex with brown balconies overlooking a pool. (There 'tis!) But what reams of crucial essentials had been forgotten! Those calico Clark Kent glasses! That white-ringed tee! That man's groceries tending skyward on their own! How *it is fun to make things move, just by thinking about them*!

Willo Davis Roberts also wrote, among the other 987 books she published, *Don't Hurt Laurie!*—which has a scene of young Laurie, wearing rollers, being beaten with a hairbrush and knocked out against a bathroom sink by her mother. *The Girl with the Silver Eyes* is not nearly that dark, although it does have Grimmsian intimations about the sorry fate of children at the hands of adults. Luckily, in this case, Roberts has given our heroine, the polyester-orange snappily knife-creased Katie Welker, a weapon against them—not only the aforementioned silver eyes, but their handy corollary: telekinesis, and the ability to know what animals are thinking.

When we first meet Katie, her grandmother Welker has just died, and she's been returned to the custody of her mother, Monica—living in splendor in the apartments you see pictured. Her time with her grandmother as a young girl, however, was by no means sanguine, as Katie's ability to float Social Security checks in from the mailbox to the dining-room table without moving rattled the old lady beyond reason:

> It had taken her awhile to learn how to be careful about what she moved. She knew the name for the moving, now; she'd read it in a book [more on that later!]. *Telekenesis.*
>
> As time went on, this peculiar ability of Katie's made more and more problems between them. When Katie learned how to turn off the light from the wall switch after she'd gotten into bed and turn the pages of her book [moooooore on that later!]

without touching them . . . and smooth her hair
without using the hairbrush, she made Grandma
Welker nervous. . . .

. . . The same was true of the kids at school. She
was good at games, but there was always someone
who didn't like the way she played them. She didn't
like balls coming at her. . . . That was before she
learned how to make the ball veer off to the side.
She knew that could spoil a game, but somehow,
like other things she did, she couldn't help doing it.

Katie's odd eyes, her controversial page-turning methods, and her champion poker face ("She knew it bothered
the adults around her, the way she could keep her small face
perfectly expressionless, yet it seemed the safest thing to do,
most of the time") go over equally unevenly at the new apartment complex, where she alienates Mr. P, the snarly resident
bachelor whom she torments with errant rocks, drives away
two loathsome babysitters, and weirds out Monica's boyfriend:

"What kind of kid is this one of yours, Monica? I
never saw one like her before."

He didn't lower his voice. He was one of those
people who talk about kids as if they weren't there
or couldn't hear. Of course, it was probably true
that he'd never seen anyone like Katie. She hadn't
met anyone like herself either. She wished, quite
sincerely, that she would.

Katie's alienation is somewhat mitigated by two new
friends: Jackson Jones, the paper-delivery boy whom Mr. P

routinely stiffs, and Mrs. M, the batty old neighbor who loans Katie *The Scarlet Pimpernel* while Katie mind-melds with her cat, Lobo. (Brief aside: Do they still only refer to adults by the first letter of their last name nowadays? All through the 1980s, I never knew any adult's actual last name!) Still, Katie knows she is different and it pains her—and when she overhears Monica's boyfriend Nathan put forth, in a tell-don't-show exchange too tedious to relate, the theory that Monica's exposure to a drug called Ty-Pan-Oromine while working in a pharmaceutical factory might have spawned Katie's unusual condition and that there may be *others like her*, she goes hunting for answers:

> And if Nathan was right—Katie forgot to eat, engrossed in the idea—that she was the way she was because of the stuff Monica had worked with, what about the babies those other women had had? All about the same time as Katie herself had been born? Was Ty-Pan-Oromine responsible for her silver eyes and this ability to move things by thinking about moving them? And if it was, were those other kids like herself? Somewhere out there in the world, were there more "different" kids, who would be her own kind?

It's unsurprising that *TGWTSE* is a stealth favorite of readers everywhere, since it is the implicit *cri de coeur* of those yelled at in English classes for reading *one* book under the desk because they finished the *assigned* reading two months ago. Forget talking to cats or moving rocks across the sidewalk to smack irritating neighbors—in *TGWTSE*, Katie's reading, full stop, is a deeply suspicious activity:

"It's like you were drugged or something, you don't even know what's going around you," Grandma Welker used to say in annoyance about Katie's reading.

Drugged. As in, ON DRUGS, people! And that's not the worst of it:

> Grandma didn't value books that much; she'd even burned one, once, when she'd caught Katie reading it after she was supposed to have been asleep. Katie had had difficulty forgiving her for that. She'd had to fish the remains out of her fireplace late at night and carefully lay out the brown pages with the charred edges to find out how it ended.

Does that make your stomach hurt? That actually makes my stomach hurt. But, as in *Summer of My German Soldier,* you can tell Katie's friends from her enemies by who likes words— Jackson Jones, Mrs. M—and who doesn't. That's why the letter Katie decides to send out to the probable offspring of one of her mother's old coworkers to feel out if they're co-kenetics is so stupendous:

> Katie chewed on the end of her pen for a minute, wondering if she should specify anything, and decided not to.
> "I like to read, and I like animals," she wrote then. "And I'd sure like to hear from you."

Likes to read, likes animals—*are you a mutant, too?* But Katie's quest to find out if she's the only one of her kind—a quest in which she is ultimately successful—will be familiar to those who might also primarily use telekinesis to turn pages and push up their glasses without lifting a finger, too. Normal children might use telekinesis to float a ball, you know, INTO the soccer goal. But Katie is un-bubbly, unprepossessing, happy to hang with a septuagenarian and paper boy, and completely unfamiliar with the rites of the slumber party. Left to her own devices, she'll read *The Scarlet Pimpernel* with one eye and diligently dissect the adults around her with the other. She is, to put it briefly, a big nerd. Yes, just like you! Floating forks is fine, but this is sweet justice for those of us who suffered having a book yanked out of our hands at the dinner table every night. In my next telekinetic life, I will float those back, too.

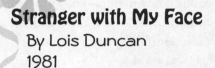

Stranger with My Face
By Lois Duncan
1981

Stop Projecting

My name is Laurie Stratton. I am seventeen years old, and I live at the Cliff House on the northern tip of Brighton Island.

Would it have been so hard to let me astrally project, God? I know the telepathy was not a possibility, as by second grade, my peers and I were already running numerous controlled studies using the means of scrap paper and different corners of the room, and to succeed would have granted me far too much power amongst them. I know you gave me precognition that one time about winning that contest in 8th grade and it was so spooky I could never have handled any more spook. I am way too OCD to move things with my mind, and I know, as I am not the seventh daughter of a seventh daughter, I cannot be a witch. *However.*

I don't see what the PROBLEM would have been with allowing me to freaking LEAVE MY BODY FROM TIME TO TIME AND TRAVEL THE WORLD, BOUND ONLY BY AN INVISIBLE CORD LINKED TO MY TRUE SPIRIT WHILE MY BODY WAS TEMPORARILY A HUSK, A SHELL, TO ALL APPEARANCES DEAD!

In any case, Laurie Stratton, unbeknownst-to-self-child-of-the-Navajo-with-twin-sister, is far more blessed than I. In *Stranger with My Face*, Duncan has ditched her typical Southwest setting for the rocky shoals of coastal New England, where our heroine lives with her mother and father, a painter and writer, respectively, and two sweet younger siblings, Neal and Megan. Also in the mix is Laurie's so-psyched-to-no-longer-be-gawky prize of a ripped boyfriend, Gordon; a brooding, darkly handsome acquaintance, Jeff, whose face was half-burned off by an exploded can of lighter fluid; and, of course, an expert outsider WITH insider extrasensory knowledge, Laurie's schoolmate Helen Tuttle, who has recently moved from the Southwest and becomes Laurie's new friend.

Interestingly, the first few scenes of the novel, as befits the events to come, are rife with splits in which one element is not only the opposite of the other, but also the veritable photo negative. First is Laurie's passage from gawky to glamorous—a constant Duncan trope at the beginnings of her novels. Laurie's improved looks not only alter her appearance but her entire social currency:

In every girl's life, I guess, there must be one special summer that is a turning point, a time of stretching and reaching and blossoming out and leaving childhood behind. This was the summer that had happened to me. The year before, I had been awkward and gawky, all pointed knees and sharp elbows and bony rib cage, hiding my shyness behind a book while girls like Natalie Coleson and Darlene Briggs wriggled around in their bikinis and got boys to buy them Cokes and rub them with baby oil.

This summer it had all been different. The first day I walked out onto the beach, clutching my book and my beach towel, I heard a wolf whistle.

Another split is found in Jeff Rankin, a former crush of Laurie's who has been moody and withheld since the summer when a can of lighter fluid exploded in his face:

The left side of his face was fine. If you saw him at a certain angle, you'd have thought he was the best-looking guy you'd ever seen. If you saw him from the right, you had to stop and swallow hard.

It occurs to me that even the fact that Laurie is recounting, not experiencing, the events in question, leads to a sort of narrative split, the dreadful present aftermath merging with a golden past. (Does not "There was a time when I, too, loved Cliff House" have more than a whiff of "Last night I dreamed I went to Manderley again"?)

However, the biggest initial split is with Laurie and her own family—from whom she is inherently estranged, just as Jeff is to his old face, by looks:

I didn't have the sort of looks you found just everywhere. Gordon kidded sometimes that I could be
part Indian with my dark coloring, high cheekbones
and almond eyes. "Bedroom eyes," he called them,
meaning they were sexy. My father referred to them
as "alien" because they were the same shape as the
eyes he gave to the maidens from other worlds in his
novels. When I looked at my parents—both of them
so fair—and at Neal and Meg with their light blue
eyes and freckled noses, I wondered sometimes how
I had managed to be born into such a family.

Well, duh. You weren't! However, we don't learn this from
Dad and Mom. (Who, P.S., are a "night person" and a "day
person" whose schedules only briefly coincide.) Instead, we
learn this from a sepulchral presence around town whom
people keep mistaking for Laurie. As the days pass, "Laurie"
appears at a party the actual Laurie has begged off of, enraging Gordon; in the house, confusing Laurie's parents; at the
Post Office, where she accepts a birthday invite that she fails to
pass on, enraging the birthday girl; and in various lonely poses
around the dunes surrounding Cliff House.

Laurie is beside herself at how this could be happening, but,
luckily, Helen Tuttle, child of the Southwest, holder of knowledge
of the Navajo, and former girlfriend of Luis, a Navajo, is there to
point out an explanation other than Laurie's going crazy:

"You weren't using astral projection, were you?"
Helen asked.

"Using what?" I said in bewilderment.

"You know—sending your mind out from your
body? Luis's father used to be able to do it."

This seems like a good time for somebody to take a book out of the library related to the issue at hand! Okay, but getting ahead of myself. Laurie finally gets the answer to her question, when she is visited, in a profound dream, by Lia, who claims to be her twin sister and leans across and gives her a spooky astral-projection kiss. At this point, in possession of a towering mountain of supernatural proof, Laurie confronts her parents, whose reaction is, to put it mildly, not open. "The trend today is toward total openness about adoption," her father says. "Still, that idea has been upsetting to your mother. . . . Laurie, it's not that big a deal. You're the same person you always were. You're our beloved daughter. . . . Now that you know your background, there's nothing left for you to wonder about. Can't we just file this away and get on with our normal lives?"

Sadly, this kind of secrecy was once the norm, young *Juno* fans! Also key for the plot is her mother's explanation of why, confronted with a set of beautiful, mixed-blood Navajo twins to adopt, they did not just snag both:

> "Then, why—" The question rose to my lips without my even realizing that I was going to ask it. "Why did you take me instead of her?"
>
> "We couldn't raise both of you," Dad said. "We were going out on a limb to take even one dependent at that point in our lives."
>
> "That's not what I asked," I said. "What I want to know is, why did you choose me over my sister?"
>
> There was a moment's silence as my parents exchanged glances.
>
> Then Dad said slowly, "Your mother—your mother, well, she thought—"

"I didn't want her," Mother said. Her normally gentle voice was strangely sharp. "I just didn't want her. I wanted you."

"But if we were just alike—"

"You weren't alike," Mother said. "You looked just alike—both of you so beautiful with big, solemn eyes and all that thick, dark hair. The people at the agency wanted us to take you both, and despite what Dad says, I really think we might have done it. It seemed wrong to separate twin sisters. I picked you up and cuddled you, and I knew I never wanted to let you go. It was as though you were meant to be ours. Then I handed you to Dad to hold and picked up the other baby, and—and—"

"And what?" I prodded.

"I wanted to put her down."

BECAUSE LIA IS EVIL! Arg! And, of course, the machinations of Lia's evil, as they unfold in the novel, are great fun. Not only does she put Helen Tuttle in the hospital (the ability of specters to put people in hospitals in the novels of Lois Duncan must only be exceeded by the ability of the shark in the *Jaws* franchise to increasingly have the ability to handily kill people on dry land), she lures Jeff and Laurie to a near-death experience, and, having alienated Laurie completely from her peers and those who love her, manages to invade her body and steal her entire life.

BUT NOT SO FAST, LIA!

Because Lia doesn't weaken the bonds Laurie holds to the world—her takeover of Laurie Stratton from all the elements strengthens them. When Lia easily ruins the friendships she gained through Gordon, it only makes her realize how glad she can be for Helen's loyalty. Her interruption of the placid family structure of the Strattons forces Laurie's parents to realize how damaging their inability to face Laurie's adoption was, which in turn allows Laurie to realize she is, in the end, a Stratton who loves and is loved by her family. And, most important, when Lia splits Laurie and Gordon apart, she actually brings Jeff and Laurie together—not coincidentally because Jeff, unlike Gordon, is willing to face the question of Lia and Laurie's adoption. He's also willing to talk about the weirder question of what Megan calls Laurie's "ghosty":

> "Look, Jeff, there's no sense in our discussing this. You don't believe in astral projection, and I don't blame you. I couldn't accept it myself until just recently." A question occurred to me. "What were you doing here the night you thought you saw me? There's no reason for anyone to come out this way unless he's coming to Cliff House."
>
> "I walk here sometimes because you live here," Jeff said.

Shades of *Pretty in Pink*! But, even though the ostensible point of the novel is that looks don't matter because those who love us, like Laurie's savior and little sister Megan, can look past them to the true self beneath, of course, looks *do* matter. Not only are they a constant subject, as the novel commences, within Laurie's family before Laurie knows about Lia, but also, Laurie and Jeff's changing looks have reversed the course of their entire lives. Duncan's point about our appearance versus our true self is much more subtle. In the scene where Laurie, loosed from her own body, regards the sleeping Lia, we can see that clearly:

She was a duplicate of myself. . . . Yet there were differences.

This girl's ears were pierced, and mine were not. Mother and I had gone through a few rounds on that issue, and she had won. "There are enough natural holes in a person's anatomy," she had said firmly. . . .

. . . There was a tiny scar on the chin that might have been nothing more than the result of scratching an insect bite, but it was a scar that I did not have.

There was a mole on the neck at a spot where I had no mole.

I continued my inspection. . . . She had perfect fingernails, the kind that had always filled me with envy. My own had a scraggly look, not exactly "bitten to the quick," but "slightly gnawed."

Small things. Unimportant. Almost unnoticeable, yet they spelled the difference between Lia Abbott and Laurie Stratton.

So it is not that looks don't matter. Not only do they matter to others—they matter because they reflect choices we have made, what has been done *by* us and *to* us. Our looks may start with what life had dealt us, but they are also about the lives we lead.

Hangin' Out with Cici
By Francine Pascal
1977

Time Outs

Getting to be thirteen turned out to be an absolute and complete bummer. I mean it. What a letdown. You wouldn't believe the years I wasted dreaming about how sensational everything was going to be once I was a teenager.

Spending time socializing with one's mother must rank up there with transcribing Haydn and laying brick as the activities your average 13-year-old is least likely to want to partake in. But Francine Pascal, best known for the *Sweet Valley High* series—you may have heard of it—manages in her most charming stand-alone novel to create the one situation wherein which bouncing around town with dear old Mom could reasonably compete with a hot date with Bruce Patman: going back in time to hang out with a mother who's, um, *very* different from the strict, easily enraged lady she knows all too well.

There's something strangely appealing about the idea of actually visiting the world your mother grew up in—especially when the idea that she had a life before you at all seems faintly humorous. The idea of witnessing the particulars of my mother's own upbringing—the sunny 1950s in Langston, Oklahoma, then as an adolescent in Queens, getting up early to take the bus and train to Bronx Science, then college years at CUNY, going on dates with my dad—seems to rank psychologically somewhere alongside visiting a fascinating, dimly lit display in a museum and watching a blurry documentary on PBS (sorry, Mom), two things I love to do but that might be taking the idea of earlier eras a little far.

But as the snapshots of my own life start to reveal an ancient palette very different from the brilliant millions-of-colors digitization of any camera-phone, Facebook-uploaded pic of me today—which is to say, as my old 1970s and 1980s haircuts start to make me look a little PBS documentary, myself—the idea of being able to breathe in the air of an earlier time, to say nothing of the air that shaped someone you thought you knew very well indeed, starts to seem all that much closer. Frankly, looking at the covers of all these books feels pretty much like going back in time to visit my own mother. Cue spooky time-travel spinny shot.

Victoria is a private-school student in New York, rebelling

as hard as she can against her school's "vomity blue blazer" and boxy pleated skirt and anything else that attempts to box her in. A humble ringleader, she modestly declines to take credit for the numerous disruptions swirling around her, even when authorities strenuously insist she take credit. Unfortunately, after a disruption involving a theater balcony, a cigarette, and a spitball directed at a teacher's head, the new principal himself requires Victoria to present herself at his office, with parental guardian at her side, to receive her just due.

For some time, Victoria and her mother have been locked in the kind of go-rounds that would bedevil a prizefighter. A typical one goes something like this:

> Now she comes stumping toward my room, saying, "You just listen to me!" She's angry and just pushes the door open without even knocking. "You're be-having like a four-year-old."
>
> And we start our usual argument. "That's the way you treat me," I say, and she tells me that's be-cause I act like one and I should realize I was wrong and accept my punishment, and it goes on that way with me saying one thing and her saying another but never really answering me. . . . I swear I'll never treat my daughter the way they treat me. I'll really be able to understand her because I'll remember how awful it was for me.

But her latest infraction changes the stakes entirely. As it happens, the principal is suggesting not only that Victoria needs to be brought into line, but that she might draw the line somewhere else entirely. And as Victoria departs for one last weekend of freedom at her cousin's birthday party—a weekend during which she is busted for, as her aunt says, "smoking a pot," only adding fuel to the ganja—she realizes her mother isn't only mad: She's about to give up on her.

But somewhere during the train ride home from Philadelphia, something strange happens. The lights go off, Victoria bumps her head, and when she wakes up, the little old lady next to her has been replaced by a young, pregnant lady, all the passengers seem to have recently picked up a child or two, and the kindly, elderly conductor is now a kindly young conductor.

You may see what's coming, but Victoria doesn't yet—quite. Walking through a slightly unfamiliar-looking Penn Station, trying to find her mother by the information booth that is strangely half the size it used to be, she decides first that they must be filming a movie, and then that New York tourism has taken an odd direction:

> You can tell they're really squares. All the women are wearing skirts and the men are dressed in baggy suits and most of them are wearing old fashioned felt hats. Not even the kids are wearing jeans. In fact, nobody is but me. It's unreal. This has got to be some kind of convention group from Missouri or someplace. Something real snappy like librarians, funeral directors, and Eagle Scouts.

She's relieved when she sees Cici, a girl her age whom she waves over, mistaking her for a friend. Cici is unperturbed, and then, after hearing her story, waits with Victoria, then finally invites her to come hang out with her in Queens until Victoria can reach her mother, whom she keeps trying to no avail. Getting on the E train, Victoria tells us, " . . . I can tell right off I'm really going to like Cici. You know how it is, sometimes you just meet someone and bang, you hit it off. Better than that, you're old friends instantly."

> Cici and I chatter away for the rest of the trip. We seem to have a million things in common. Especially problems. She tells me about how she's always getting into trouble for the littlest, most unimportant things. Just like me. Plus she hates the way she looks, too. I tell her she's crazy because she's really cute-looking, but she says her eyes are too small and close together and she thinks her knuckles are too big.

Victoria and Cici spend the afternoon together, doing wholesome activities like shoplifting and thwarting perverts in the movie theater. But throughout, Victoria is finding it harder and harder to make excuses for why her number, apparently, doesn't exist in the New York area anymore, everyone is dressed like an extra from a black-and-white movie, and in Queens, apparently everything is sold for an eighth of its usual Manhattan price.

Because the answer is . . . it's May 19, 1944! No biggie. Staring incredulously at the day's paper, Victoria is filled with despair at realizing she's truly and irrevocably screwed: "This is definitely the forties and I have no home and no family and I'm going to be stuck here forever."

But wait . . . there's more! When Cici finally manages to

drag the distraught Victoria home, she's shocked to hear a very familiar voice—and then absolutely gobsmacked to see the person that goes with it:

> Sure, she's younger and slimmer and all that. But there's no question. I know for absolutely certain that she's my grandma. And this has to mean—no! I won't let the thought come any closer! It can't be!

YES!

> Felicia! Cici! My own mother! Holy cow, I am dumb. Fantastic! I told you she looked familiar. I mean, she didn't really, but there were things about her that reminded me of someone. Not so much the features, but more like the expressions, the way she talked—I don't know what, something, maybe the look in her eyes. I just knew I knew her all along, only I thought she was a friend of somebody's or some girl I met someplace. That's what threw me. I thought she was a kid like me.
> But she's not. She's a woman. Felicia, Cici, whatever she wants to call herself, there's one thing for sure, this crazy nutty kid who isn't afraid to zonk a pervert in the shin, turn Woolworth's upside down, sneak cigarettes in a garage, and probably do a million other kooky things and maybe even some awful things like buying a science test, isn't my friend at all.
> She's my *mother*!

Hangin' Out with Cici is a wonderful way to learn all about the 1940s (where else would I have ever heard the phrase "Kilroy

Was Here"?) but it's also a great book for learning about what makes someone realize it's time to grow up. In Cici's case, it's finally being caught for a crime even she's ashamed of. But in Victoria's case, it's that, by realizing her mother is a person just like she is, she considers that she might want to start persecuting her for every conceivable crime. As she watches the young Cici scramble off a roof on her way to an ill-fated mission, she thinks:

> Watching her now reminds me how once, about two years ago, we were on a picnic with two other families in some park on Staten Island, and I don't know why, but everybody (the adults anyway) was kidding around and daring each other to do all sorts of crazy things like swinging from monkey bars and climbing trees. I remember that my mother climbed higher than anyone else, so high that I began to get a little worried. Everyone else thought it was hysterical, but it seemed kind of peculiar, even a little embarrassing to me. Now that I consider it, I guess it was kind of unfair of me to be embarrassed. After all, just because you've got children doesn't mean you're nothing but a mother. I'm hopeless when it comes to my mother. Everything about her is either embarrassing, irritating, or just plain confusing. I don't know why I can't just say she's a super climber and let it go at that.

By seeing her mother in her own place—that is, a lovely, charming girl on the verge of becoming a juvenile delinquent— Victoria is suddenly able to put herself in her grown-up mother's place, too. Suddenly, she realizes that it's not her mother who's been giving her a hard time. It's she who's been giving her mother a hard time. As the book ends, Victoria is returned back to the clog-wearing 1970s with rock-hard evidence that her mother, however shrewish she seems now, once, really and truly did know how she felt. But *Hangin' Out with Cici* isn't only really about getting to know your mother. It's also about realizing your mother, that shrew, made a choice to grow up, for a good reason—and you might want to think about it, too.

Jane-Emily
By Patricia Clapp
1969

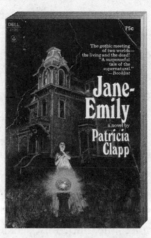

Global Terror

Any devotee of *Rebecca* or *The Turn of the Screw* (and one would hope you are already a devotee of both) will already be well prepared for *Jane-Emily*, the gothic tale of the pretty, poised Louisa and her niece Jane, and the petulant ghost, Emily, the former mistress of the house who died at the age of 12. When Louisa and Jane arrive for the summer, they find someone already in residence and unlikely to welcome them with open arms—Jane, the spoiled young lady of the house who died—in a petulant state of outrage, one imagines—two decades ago, and has no intention of letting any other girls become mistresses of the house. Angry ghosts, malevolent doubles, attempts to thwart love, rambling estates, change-of-scene summers—what's not to like?

When I read this book as a girl, I have to say I was equally taken with the idea of ghost-hood as I was with a) owning a huge, pretty, mirrored globe all to myself while being the petted, pretty child living on a beautiful estate and b) getting to own a white dress of cotton lawn with a wide blue belt. (Still am!) But upon reread, I can see the tone of the novel was actually very modern and amusing—told from the point of view of the older Louisa, it has an interesting romantic conflict in the form of a dull fiancé, Martin, and an aggravating but irresistible interloper, Adam, with whom she argues, among other things, about whether or not women deserve the right to vote. (I still growl with irritation at the smug argument that women might be too hysterical to vote wisely. Too hysterical to respond to idiot arguments without growling, maybe.)

The story is simple: Jane, naturally, seeks to spread her evil influence over both of them—not only to thwart Louisa from marrying her childhood crush, Adam, but also to take over Emily and thereby live out the childhood that's been snatched too early from her. Her evil spirit is housed in a great silvery globe on the property—although, naturally, reasonable people, like Adam, he of fear-of-hysterical-voters, are loath to believe that what's ripped Louisa's gown apart is, you know, spectral. Or that Emily's moodiness is due to a ghost's influence, when actually her parents have just died.

Luckily, though everyone adores Adam, no one takes him, or his idea that women are too emotional to deserve the vote, under serious consideration. By the time the book ends, the world may have lost one ghost—but it's added three future voters.

Down a Dark Hall
By Lois Duncan
1974

In-School Suspension

You can keep your girls of Canby Hall—if we are dibsing boarding schools. If I may, I will lay claim to the tiny class of the ominously named Blackwood School for Girls, whose intimate, supportive environment makes it all the better to channel the dead through you with, my dear. The Blackwood School—for which the tiny entering class has filled out a peculiar application that they have no idea is really meant to test how good a host they'd be for your average dearly departed genius—is a bit like a Yaddo for those in the afterlife who are peeved that they died before the advent of NEA grants and massive library bequests. While the novels, paintings, mathematical proofs, and scores the girls "produce" are most impressive, it turns out that one cannot live so intimately with an artistic genius and not go a little bit crazy. You don't say.

Chapter 8

Him She Loves?
Romanced, Rejected, Affianced, Dejected

If you've reached this far, you know I have spilled quite a bit of ink on the idea that young adult literature for girls is rife with sophisticated, subtle, and fascinating truths about the human condition. Phew. NOW WE CAN TALK ABOUT BOYS.

If you take magazines for teenage girls—or women, for that matter—as a guide, you'd have to decide that the main function of the male in the female's life is to provoke anxiety, mortification, and the exercise of a battery of stratagems worthy of Rasputin. (My old boss at a teen girl magazine was fond of saying we could run entire issues dedicated to the most-asked question of the magazine's run: *Does he like me?*) This is true in the same sense that whenever you need a cab, there aren't any—meaning, while one is enraptured, men may seem the aggravating, mysterious center of the world. Fortunately, this condition only occurs, in both cases, when you're wearing heels and under the impression you'll die if you don't get one immediately.

If you looked at the broad swath of commercial fiction, you'd find that the successful acquisition of said love interest is also the end of the story—the march into the sunset that signals you can get up, brush off the popcorn, and finally go to the bathroom. And while the comedy of errors that so often accompanies courtship is the Old Reliable of love in type, you'll actually find it far less than you'd think in the books herein.

First we have Tayari Jones's essay on *Forever*, which doesn't only focus on the book's inordinately helpful explications of the particulars of lovemaking (oh! It goes THERE, etc.), but also on how Blume's point isn't that love is grand or love is a bitch—but how we'll be able to survive the agonies of both. Then there's Paul Zindel's *My Darling, My Hamburger*, rife with agony, it's true—but also rife with an exploration of the genuine pain of love when the real world, as it annoyingly does, insists on interfering. And then we have *Happy Endings Are All Alike*, a book where lesbianism and rape, dramatic though they be, aren't the triggers for a couple's doggedly mundane breakup. Even a book like *Fifteen*, which brightly declares its boy-seeking ends right from the beginning, manages to dissect the foibles of courtship so thoroughly that, at the end of the day, it's better regarded as a cultural and psychological *précis* than an amusing narrative.

But at the end of the day, it isn't only that all these books but one end either in breakup or unspecified limbo that distinguishes them. It's that, whether in the person of *Fifteen*'s fitful Jane, unable to translate Latin, so intent she is on willing the phone to ring, or *To All My Fans, With Love, From Sylvie*'s heroine, who is under the mistaken impression that all signs of affection from men are as solemn, respectful, and loving as those she sees on the big screen, our protagonists are all given room to experience the true complexity of love at its best and at its nadir. As Margo Rabb says in her essay on Zibby Oneal's *In Summer Light*, "I'll keep rereading it, as I do every few years, to revisit that old Kate-like part of myself that tries to be mature, accepting, and to not be an idiot in love." These girls are all idiots in love, to be sure. But they remind us that, at the game of love, however old we get, we're all amateurs.

Forever

By Judy Blume

1975

The Talk

By Tayari Jones

When I was about 11 years old, my mother gave me The Talk. I am not exactly clear in my memory, but I believe that my father was in the room, too. This was their idea of being enlightened parents—having a very sane and sober discussion with their on-the-brink-of-puberty daughter about sex, although they didn't call it that. "Sexual intercourse" was the term they used and they explained it the way that you might explain the workings of a combustion engine. When they walked away, proud of themselves for being so much more open than their parents had been, I was somewhat underwhelmed. I understood how babies were made. I'd picked up a few extra bits of vocabulary like "ovary" and "spermatozoa," but I had no idea why on earth people were having this sexual intercourse in the first place.

In those fifth-grade days, I had a friend named Cookie, who was much wiser than me on every front. Much of this was due to the fact that she was the last of five children, a brood that included an older sister who had been a senior in high school when she ran away with a very famous musician for several days. (This musician, who is still quite famous, has a reputation for being litigious, so I won't mention his name here. Trust me when I say that you would know his name if I told you.) It was from this world-wise sister that Cookie had picked up *Forever*, by Judy Blume. Apparently, the juicy pages had already been dog-eared when Cookie lifted it from her sister's nightstand drawer.

The paperback was a stunner—the cover art featured a locket with a cutout depicting a complicated-looking white girl looking a little bit forlorn, a little bit wise. "*Forever* . . . A moving story of the end of innocence." When you opened the cover you saw the whole picture; there was a guy there with the locket girl. You couldn't tell if he was stroking her arm or restraining her. Around her neck was an orange scarf that seemed to be signifying something, I just wasn't sure what. "The first time, a loving time, but what about forever?" I was a little confused, but I wanted to appear as plugged in as everyone else. "Oooh," I said. With a triumphant little grin, Cookie flipped right to the page where Katherine and Michael have sex, for the first time, on the living-room floor. This time when I said "Ooh," I meant it. There are about four sex scenes in the novel, and Cookie gave me a guided tour through them all. We read the bathroom scene twice and puzzled over the logistics of woman-on-top.

This was no tidy discussion about the mechanics of sexual intercourse. In about two paragraphs flat, I fell into a world where boys named their penises "Ralph" and creamed their shorts. (*This* was what my mom and dad meant by *ejaculation*.) My parents never even mentioned the existence of a female orgasm, but there it all was, on the folded-over pages. Perhaps this is when I developed my taste for erotica. Just reading those pages gave me a tingly feeling that helped me understand the motivation behind boys and girls getting naked and putting their parts together.

I asked Cookie if I could borrow her book, not only because I wanted to read the hot pages in the privacy of my bedroom, but because I was curious about the relationship between sex and love. Until I glimpsed those pages of *Forever*, I hadn't really understood that physical intimacy could be an expression of emotional intimacy, too.

Cookie consented to let me borrow the book for one night. She was very stern about my returning it because there were other girls waiting. As an 11-year-old black girl living in Atlanta, I was completely estranged from many of the details of the story (Fondue? Water skiing? Sleepaway camp?). Still, I was given a crash course in the relationship between bodily pleasure and passionate entanglement and, of course, romantic disappointment. At the end of the novel, lover boy acts a complete ass—that's what that whole "end of innocence" tagline is all about. Several of my friends swore that they cried actual tears at the end when Katherine and Michael broke up, going on with their separate lives. I, on the other hand, was quite gratified with the no-regrets tone of those final pages. It was as though Judy Blume was promising me a world full of passion, pleasure, and romance. Sure, she seemed to say, there would be pain, but don't worry. It won't kill you.

Happy Endings Are All Alike
By Sandra Scoppettone
1978

The Price of Fault

Even though Jaret Tyler had no guilt or shame about her love affair with Peggy Danziger she knew there were plenty of people in this world who would put it down.

Sometime around the invention of email, as I was slowly drifting into cubicle death, I sent the following email to a high-school friend I hadn't spoken to in years:

H—

*What's the name of the book where there are two les-
bians and the girl gets raped under a tree? Not* My
Sweet Audrina. *There are two girls on the cover. How
are you?*

—L

The friend in question did not even bother to respond to the
perfunctory closing query. She immediately zinged back:
HAPPY ENDINGS ARE ALL ALIKE!!!!!

Such is the power of this novel, which I had borrowed from
the friend in question for months until I was forced to finally
return it, then commenced idly thinking about, roughly every
three days since. It wasn't only that there were lesbians, or rape,
or pretty girls in polo tees with shiny hair on the cover whom
I might grow up to look like. It was that, like so much of the
work of Paula Danziger or Paul Zindel, it presaged a world for
us filled with more than gym teachers hurling basketballs at us
(see Plotfinder), alive with teenagers struggling with the new
complexity of adult relationships—one in which gym teachers,
lesbian or no, weren't anywhere near the center of the drama.

I'd like to provide the nut graf for *Happy Endings Are All
Alike*, but Scoppettone's first paragraph does it so admirably it
seems a shame to mess with it:

Even though Jaret Tyler had no guilt or shame about
her love affair with Peggy Danziger she knew there
were plenty of people in this world who would put
it down. Especially in a small town like Gardener's
Point, a hundred miles from New York City. She

and Peggy didn't go around wearing banners, but there were some people who knew.

Considering the hullabaloo about teenaged sex—ANY kind of teenaged sex—nowadays, pretty much every sentence of that paragraph is mind-blowing. But remember, this is the fictional world of 1978, where parents might mention Susan Brownmiller as quickly as they asked you to set the table. Castigated by her sister, Peggy thinks resentfully to herself, "You weren't a pervert just because you loved someone of your own sex, for God's sake!" And, as the preternaturally well-adjusted Jaret puts it to said mother: "Look, I know where you're coming from, Mom, but don't let it freak you out. I'll tell you this: Whatever I did with boys I found really boring. I didn't get turned on, okay? . . . And it's got nothing to do with you and Dad. I mean, you didn't make some terrible mistake in raising me or anything. And it's not so terrible. In fact, it's pretty nice. So don't lay a guilt trip on yourself, okay?" Okay! And don't forget the napkins!

But just because Peggy and Jaret—and, nominally, their semi-informed families—are not completely up in arms about their relationship, it doesn't mean they are off the hook entirely. The ancillary characters are brought in to project the basic prejudices of their time— a narrative conceit that might seem clumsy in an adult novel but it, be-LIEVE me, provided crucial info for an 8-year-old girl.

First to hold a nasty grudge at the girls' love is Peggy's sister Claire, who is jealous not only of her sister's favor with their father but also her looks:

> She lit another cigarette, sending up a smoke screen between herself and the mirror. Again

her mind fixed on Peggy and Jaret. Both of them were attractive. Jaret might even be considered beautiful. Dammit, she was beautiful . . . by male standards, she was a knockout. And that was what really made Claire crazy. Jaret Tyler could have had any boy or man she wanted and she wanted none. Peggy, too, could have had her pick. And who did they choose? Each other. It was sick. Crazy. Enraging. Why, when they could have the cream of the crop, did they want each other?

Okay, first lesson: People think if you're good-looking, not getting with a man is a waste. Lies! Check. Scoppettone's second lesson: Not all heterosexual relationships are happy, or free of complication—but that doesn't mean married women are all oppressed. Jaret's parents are a case in point: While Kay, her mother, muses her husband is madly in love with her, she thinks with irritation how she's truly invested in his looks, even if she allows him to think it's the other way around:

> He often accused her of regarding him as nothing more than a sex object and she had a hard time denying it. "Well, kid," she often said, "I can't help it if you're a looker." "What about my mind?" he'd ask. Kay would shrug and say, "Who needs it?"
>
> Of course, she didn't really mean it. She just said it to keep Bert aware of the way women were treated. And he knew that. What he didn't know was that Kay was not overwhelmed by his mind.

Kay is an interesting character—an aggressively liberated mom who is deeply disturbed at how disturbed she is about her daughter's new relationship:

She lit a fresh cigarette. [If you're thinking of lesbians, grab a smoke.] Kay had read everything she could find on the subject of homosexuality and lesbianism and what she'd read wasn't that helpful. There were many theories as to why a person turned out to be a lesbian—environment, chromosomes, choice—and a lot of big, fat blanks. No one really seemed to know. Nevertheless, Kay couldn't help blaming herself and Bert. But why blame? Why the need to put it in those terms? She knew it was because she still had one foot in the fifties and a lesbian life-style was not what she'd had in mind for her daughter; it was not something she could fully accept as normal, no matter how liberated she might be.

Oh, what a fraud she was! Pretending to Jaret it was all fine with her, simply swell, because she wanted Jaret to like her, to think she was cool! What she really wanted to do was throw herself at her feet and beg her to see a psychiatrist so she'd get over this thing.

Equally equivocating is Peggy's friend Bianca, who reacts to the news with blasé sophistication until one day Peggy, chatting with her in the bedroom, tells her sweating friend to take off her clothes, then is shocked and appalled to realize she thinks she's hitting on her:

"Besides," said Peggy, "do you think I'm interested in all females?"

"I thought . . . I don't know," she said, somewhat ashamed.

"No, I guess you don't. I thought you understood. I mean, are you interested in every guy you see?"

This was not only a revolutionary piece of transitory logic to a third-grader, but also a good schooling in the minor injustices visited by well-meaning people on people who are different, particularly (primarily!) by their own friends. But if the emotional travails of their friends and family were the only ones in store for the girls, this would be a fairy story, not a political coming-of-age. There are deeper dangers in a character named Mid, a friend of Jaret's brother Chris and no less disturbing for being stereotypically disturbed. Musing he'd like to "knock [Jaret] on her ass" for being so good-looking and aloof, he stalks her and finds out that she and Peggy have been making love in the woods. Not realizing Peggy and Jaret's rarefied world is only agonized about their girls' predilections, not apt to disown them for them, he decides he can rape her with impunity.

The rape scene is long and awful and I APOLOGIZE. But the introduction of sex to girls, however it is rendered, is such a constant trope in the novels, it is instructive to think of how it's handled by the character—in this case, Jaret, who is shocked and destroyed, though not permanently—and by the author, whose scene is neither maudlin nor lurid, but simply chilling:

> "I hate your guts," he whispered.
>
> Why then? she wondered apathetically. His movement continued. Her head was turned to the side. Breathing became difficult. Month after month passed. Staring at the landscape, she wondered why the seasons didn't change. Where was the snow? She longed for snow, cool, white. Snow would stop the burning inside. She felt her body rock as Mid's movements quickened. Would she break apart? Explode into pieces of flesh, bone, blood, flying through the air, sticking to trees, bushes?

Was 8—or anything but 18, for that matter—too young to be exposed to this kind of thing? As horrifying as it was, I don't think so. The early exposure to injustice from someone on Jaret's side absolutely is a powerful tonic to defend against the crappy justice system the reader is going to grow into. The sheriff Jaret has to deal with after the rape is cut from the same cloth as *Are You in the House Alone*'s awful lawman, and as awful to watch as the parents who stand up for their girls are a relief:

> "What's the name of her boyfriend?"
>
> "What does that have to do with anything?" Kay asked.
>
> "Pardon?" said Foster.
>
> "Why do you want to know about a boyfriend? She was horribly beaten. It has nothing to do with a boyfriend."
>
> "Pardon, Mrs.," Foster said, "but you're out of your element here, so to speak. The girl was raped and we have to find the perpetrator. Now, please, let me do my job."
>
> "This is a crime of violence," Kay went on, "not a sexual one."
>
> Foster cackled, took a swipe at his nose with thumb and forefinger. "Well, if rape ain't sexual then I don't know what it is."
>
> "Well, I have news for you," Kay persisted, her voice rising. "It ain't sexual. It's aggressive and it's violent and it's based on hatred of women, not desire for them."

GAAAAAAAAAAAAAAAAAAAH DON'T YOU WANT TO KILL HIM! (Just wait until he gets to the part later about how it didn't matter that Jaret was raped because a) she's not a virgin and b) she's a lesbian.) So, say what you will about early exposure, but it definitely gave you your feminist talking points—of which I have personally amassed a very large collection ever since.

But—despite these handy fillips—what's wonderful about *Happy Endings Are All Alike* is how it chooses to not devolve into a paroxysm of blame. Not only is Jaret's lesbianism not Kay's fault—it's not a fault—but neither it nor the rape turns Jaret bitter against men, which is another prejudice Scoppettone uses the book to debunk. After Jaret's brother, Chris, beats up Mid, he realizes it was unnecessary:

> "Chris, you know, we never talked about what you did that day. Going after Mid like that."
>
> "What's to talk about?"
>
> "Why'd you do it?"
>
> "What d'you mean? He hurt you, I wanted to hurt him. Simple." He looked past her shoulder.
>
> "Is that the only reason?"
>
> "Sure, what else?"
>
> "I don't know." She touched his hand. "Are you angry with me? Do you hate me?"
>
> He was shocked, sat up. "Me? Hate you? No. I thought . . . I mean, wow. . . . I thought you hated me."
>
> "Why?" she asked, dumbfounded.
>
> "Well, I'm a . . . a guy."
>
> "I don't hate men, Chris."
>
> "You don't? Then how come . . . I mean, how come you're a . . ."
>
> "A lesbian? It's not such a terrible word. I'm not sure why but it definitely isn't because I hate men."
>
> "Not even after what happened?"

"No. I'm angry with him, Mid, but not all men. Not you."

"I thought for sure"—he cleared his throat—"lesbians hated men."

"Well, we don't. But what's that got to do with you going after Mid? And don't tell me it was just because he hurt me because I won't buy it."

Chris stood up, shuffled back and forth at the end of the bed. Then he said, "I thought if you saw a guy do something good, you know, kind of brave . . . well, I thought maybe you wouldn't think all guys were so bad."

"Oh, Chris." Jaret loved him more then than she ever had.

I started this review talking about how this book was brain-searing simply for its depiction of an adult romantic relationship, and I think that's true, for an 8-year-old read. But what I find so interesting as an adult is not the depiction of the romantic relationship, which, happily, seems very normal to me now, or the depiction of the rape, which, unhappily, also does, but what passes between all the family members once Jaret and Peggy come clean, and then when Jaret is assaulted. Both are huge bombs dropped on the people who love them, but instead of making the family and friends betray the girls, Scoppettone deals with the ways they feel they are—and especially why they feel they are. No family members, including Peggy and Jaret, are at fault for anything. That's a good lesson to know. But, in a novel where all of the relationships are as complex as Peggy and Jaret's love, it's nice to know that, in one author's view, family is not a fault.

Fifteen
By Beverly Cleary
1956

Prelude to a Kiss

Today I'm going to meet a boy, Jane Purdy told herself, as she walked up Blossom Street toward her
babysitting job. Today I'm going to meet a boy.

Mothers and fathers all across the world should, before re-
leasing their preteen girls on the dating market, have them
read the innocent, inspired *Fifteen*, a story whose drama rests
solely on the sweetly fraught first steps of a relationship be-

tween a wholesome girl-next-door type, Jane Purdy, and her handsome, kind, smart first boyfriend, Stan, whom she meets while he delivers doggie horsemeat to the house of a child she's babysitting for.

Fifteen, which contains no great tragedies beyond the anxiety of when and if Stan will call on various occasions, should not be mandatory in order for girls to laugh uproariously at the contrast with that hoary, rotary-phone-based wooing and whatever text-based romance they are about to click forth on, and neither is it necessary because Stan, considerate, firm, and smitten, is a good baseline for a model boyfriend. (Although he is.)

No, the book should be read simply because, without being saccharine, over-the-top, or fluffy, it takes the natural anxieties of a first relationship *seriously*, on their own alternately dreamy, moody, terrific, and terrified terms. In fact, they are the sole elements of the plot—a combination I've never seen elsewhere absent a death, pregnancy, or otherwise inconvenient act of God.

As we watch Jane and Dennis move from "first phone call" to the snapping on of Stan's identification bracelet, indicating they are now "going steady," it is as if we have been privileged to look on a Discovery-channel-type mating documentary, one in which each act, like, say, the gathering of straw for a nest, is an intrinsic and necessary part of a process that is as ageless as they are young.

When we meet Jane, she's walking home alone, moodily (there's the moody part) noting how, though she's far from the kind of girl who's off the radar entirely, she's also not the kind who triumphs socially—like Marcy, the queen bee who's waving happily at her from a convertible:

... Marcy brushed a lock of hair out of her eyes and smiled at Jane with the kind of smile a girl riding in a convertible with a popular boy on a summer day gives a girl who is walking alone. And that smile made Jane feel that everything about herself was all wrong.

The trouble with me, Jane thought ... is that I am not the cashmere-sweater type like Marcy. Marcy wore her cashmere sweaters as if they were of no importance at all. Jane had one cashmere sweater, which she took off the minute she got home from school. Marcy had many dates with the most popular boys in school and spent a lot of time with the crowd at Nibley's. Jane had an occasional date with an old family friend named George who was an inch shorter than she was and carried his money in a change purse instead of loose in his pocket and took her straight home from the movies. Marcy had her name mentioned in the gossip column of the *Woodmontonian* nearly every week. Jane had her name in the school paper when she served on the clean-up committee after the freshman tea. Marcy belonged. Jane did not.

That is, until she meets Stan, a new boy in town—and one who, she notes optimistically, does have a car, even though it's a truck that delivers horsemeat. Stan endears himself to Jane by helping her out with her young charge, who is about to dump ink on the carpet, by speaking pig latin to Jane, thereby reestablishing her role as a figure of authority—one Jane doubts herself, frequently:

Jane looked out the kitchen window in time to see him jump into a red truck with Doggie Diner— Fresh U.S. Government-inspected Horse Meat Delivered Weekly painted on its side.

Well, thought Jane. Well! I did meet a boy today! A new boy who is old enough to have a driver's license!

This endearing ability to look on the bright side, though Jane doesn't know it, actually distinguishes herself from girls like Marcy in a good way, as does her simple, unalloyed joy at being called by a boy who is nice, new, and, miraculously, interested in her:

"Uh . . . is this Jane Purdy?" asked a voice—a boy's voice.

An electric feeling flashed through Jane clear to her fingertips. The boy! It was his voice! She was sitting there thinking and wishing, and suddenly there he was, on the other end of the line. *He* was calling *her*! Jane swallowed. (Careful, Jane, don't be too eager.) "Yes, it is." Somehow she managed to keep her voice calm. To think that she and this boy she wanted so much to know were connected with each other by telephone wires strung on poles along the streets and over the trees of Woodmont! It was a miracle, a real miracle.

That last sentence may stand, simply, as the best description of the heady rush of young love in all its glory—because it's not that Jane is a narcissist, pleased to be loved, or that she's a temptress like Marcy, pleased to be in power, but that she's thrilled by a simple, unironic connection—her first one that has nothing to do with the house's old haughty cat, her slightly distracted mother and cheerily ironic father, or Gordon, who's been picked for her without her desire or volition.

But the move from first date to first kiss can't come as easily as all that. Though Stan is steady in his calm attempts to continue to know her better, she continues to doubt herself as too young, too unsophisticated, and too nervous for such a good-looking, popular boy—one who would certainly be better off with the type of girl he was meant to be with—someone like Marcy, perhaps. Because, when Jane orders a silly dish of vanilla ice cream at Nibley's, Marcy, in a sleek black skirt, orders black coffee. When they all go out to Chinatown, Marcy knows what to order, while Jane, frightened of all the new food, sticks to chow mein. And then, most horribly, when the school dance comes around, Stan doesn't ask Jane but goes instead with an adorable, sophisticated girl he knew from San Francisco ("And I suppose she has a terrible time finding anything to wear in her own size, because she is so little," Jane comments to her friend when she hears her description, finding "a certain relish in being catty herself.")

But it takes her quite a while to learn that Stan isn't interested in a girl like Marcy. First off, he thinks black coffee is bitter, and he remembers not knowing how to order Chinese food, too. On their first date, he was nervous, too, Jane remembers—having hidden his bike in the shrubbery lest she see it. He's grateful that Jane isn't ashamed of his Doggie Diner truck, and his old friend from San Francisco, whom he had promised to take to the first dance ages ago, is too short to be a good dancer. In fact, "Bitsy" is downright cruel: " 'She's not like you,' said Stan. 'She laughed at my job. She kept laughing and saying, "Imagine delivering horsemeat to dogs!" all evening. Maybe it does seem funny to some people, but I like dogs and I like my job.'"

But it's not until they have a spat over a small misunderstanding and Jane despairs of Stan ever forgiving her that she grows to have quite the same appreciation of herself:

> Jane wondered what she would do about Stan if she were some other girl. If she were the kind of girl who went to school with her hair in pin curls, she would probably telephone the disc jokey on Station KWOO and ask him to play "Love Me on Monday" to Stan from Jane. If she were intellectual like Liz, she would probably say that dancing and riding around in a model-A Ford were boring or middlebrow or something, and spend the evening writing hokkus for *Manuscript*. Or if she were the earnest type, she would write a letter to Teen Corner in the newspaper. The letter would begin, "Dear Ann Benedict, I wonder if you could help me solve a problem. Recently I met a boy . . ." If she were the cashmere sweater type, like Marcy, she would date several other boys and forget Stan.
>
> But Jane was not any of these girls. She was Jane Purdy, an ordinary girl who was no type at all. She was neither earnest nor intellectual, and she certainly wasn't the kind of girl the boys flocked around. She was just the kind of girl who liked to have a good time, who made reasonably good grades at school, and who liked a boy who had once liked her. There was nothing wrong with that. . . .

. . . Maybe if she continued to be herself, Stan would like her again. And if he didn't there was nothing she could do about it. Jane was filled with a wonderful feeling of relief. . . .

And once she makes that decision, Jane finds in fact that Stan does find it in his heart to forgive her for her small crime (lightly kissing his best friend in a Marcy-like act of *brio*), and in fact likes her all the more. Because not only does Stan appreciate Jane in all her vanilla ice-cream, chow mein, one-cashmere-sweater glory, she's the only girl who can appreciate the same ordinary things about him. Witness their first ride together in Stan's new car—not as glorious, perhaps, as the one Marcy had been chauffered around in, but one that's more her speed:

"Like it?" asked Stan.

"It's perfect," said Jane, and meant it. The car was neither a jalopy nor a hot rod. It looked plain and serviceable, exactly right for riding around Woodmont.

"I knew you'd like it," said Stan. "Some girls might think it was old and funny, but I knew you wouldn't."

"I think it's neat-looking," commented Jane.

. . . ."I—I wanted you to be the first girl to ride in it," Stan said.

"Did you really? Oh, Stan!" They drove past a girl who had been in Jane's math class and who was now walking toward the library with an armload of books.

"Hello there," called Jane. Poor girl, going to the library on such a beautiful morning!

As the book ends, Jane is riding in Stan's convertible, waving at another girl on the street—but she hasn't gotten there because she's become a Marcy. She's gotten there simply learning to like Jane. Young girls dizzy with love and dreaming of cashmere and convertibles everywhere could do worse.

My Darling, My Hamburger
By Paul Zindel
1969

Double Whopper

"It was Marie Kazinski who asked how to stop a boy if he wants to go all the way," Maggie whispered. Liz dragged her trig book along the wall files so that it clicked at every crack.

. . . "Well"—Maggie lowered her voice—"Mrs. Fanuzzi's advice was that you're supposed to suggest going to get a hamburger."

You know Maggie, and you know Liz. If you read this book, you are, obviously, Maggie. Maggie is a little dumpy and wears pleated homemade dresses and plucks her eyebrows cockeyed. She dots her i's with hearts and writes cheery, forced notes that go unanswered. Liz only reads astrology books. Liz tells Maggie her hair looks like "thin fungus," and Maggie loves her anyway, because, as Liz asserts, "it's true," and anyway, Liz has the kind of remote, galactic beauty that causes lesser planetary objects to be pulled into her orbit effortlessly, periodically setting them aflame as they burn through upon entry.

In *My Darling, My Hamburger*, the story of two young girls—one easily overwhelmed by love, the other too afraid of it to speak—and the two boys, Sean and Dennis, who cannot quite negotiate either successfully, high-school love is depicted as something that one endures, a trial by fire into adulthood, one that, if one is not careful, may leave permanent injuries.

Like most Zindel characters, Liz and Maggie are the children of parents whose indifference is matched only by either their brutishness or inability to understand their children at all. Liz is coolly built, so much so that she has no idea of the yearning that she produces in Maggie—only that, while she's fond of her friend, she's only truly bonded to Sean (who describes their union as, "Two foreign spirits trapped under skin [who] were finally able to breathe.") Sean would like to sleep with Liz, because, as he also puts it, "We love each other, don't we?" Liz is not so sure—mainly because her stepfather already thinks she has loose morals and her mother leaves statues of the Madonna in her bedroom, and this is not going to lead anyone into a positive embrace of the sexual position.

Sean has a friend named Dennis, whom they fix up with Maggie, even though they know they've been B-listed and are exactly as happy as you'd be to be paired with a loser. (Aaaaa! Why does Liz get to be so pretty and have a hot boyfriend and a LIFE and a PERSONALITY and an IDENTITY in the school, while I get fixed up with DENNIS, Sean's friend, who is always wearing A BAGGY GREEN SWEATER. I mean, why does that happen to Maggie?)

As someone who still doesn't get it that when the parking attendant says I can just pay cash and I don't need the ticket and it's all fine, he's using my $5 for beer money, I have always found the following passage a brilliant description of their power imbalance:

> "Liz, we can't go in there. We're not old enough."
>
> "They never ask for proof." Liz kept heading for the entrance.
>
> "They'll ask me!"
>
> Liz stopped and took an objective look at Maggie. She decided they probably would ask her. Quickly she opened her purse and pressed a frayed piece of paper in her hand.
>
> "What's this?"
>
> "Somebody's birth certificate. Remember, your name is Catherine Usherer tonight," Liz assured.
>
> "I can't do that!"
>
> "Why not?"
>
> Maggie could hardly find her voice. "They'll know I'm lying."
>
> "No, they won't," Liz insisted. "Unless, of course, they've already checked the real Catherine Usherer's ID."
>
> "How did you get Catherine Usherer's birth certificate?"

Liz looked at Maggie as though she had lost all patience with her. "You know Helen Bordanowitz?"

Maggie nodded.

"The way I understand it, Helen Bordanowitz used to go to Port Richmond High School, and she had the gym locker next to Catherine Usherer—whoever that is—and one day when Catherine Usherer wasn't looking, Helen Bordanowitz stole it. Understand?"

Maggie felt her heart pounding. As Liz pushed her into the crowded bar she still couldn't understand how Liz had gotten the card.

I STILL DON'T EITHER! And if I can blow some symbolic smoke rings myself, I will assert that Liz's forcing of a new identity on Maggie—the "Ushering," if you will—while being in possession of numerous ones herself is symbolic of what my friend likes to say about good girls and bad girls—namely, that they do exist, but that most of us have been both by the ends of our lives.

Because you know why the birth certificate itself is there. Liz's stepfather is going to call her "a little tramp," and she's going to decide it's not worth it to pretend she isn't one. She's going to sleep with Sean, and she's going to get pregnant. Sean is going to promise to marry her, and then his own father is going to convince him not to. And Liz is going to finally get Maggie to accompany her to her abortion—brought there by the town jerk, who, in a scene I have never forgotten, crams two hot dogs into his mouth at once while he's driving them home, then wipes his face off with his hand while looking in the rearview mirror and checking his hair.

And during the same time, what happens to Maggie? She

loses weight. She stops plucking her eyebrows cockeyed. She gets asked out by Dennis to the prom, and she has to reject him in order to go with Liz, something he won't understand until months, months later. Liz, who had based all of her hopes on the purity of love, is left with exactly the opposite. While Maggie, who was too afraid to even believe anyone liked her, winds up, like Sean, betraying Dennis, also through her own weakness. Ringing in their ears, of course, is Mrs. Fanuzzi's advice. But not because they wished they had taken it. Because it, like everything else they've been told about love up until they try it themselves, is completely and utterly beside the point.

In Summer Light
by Zibby Oneal
1985

Non-Idiots in Love
By Margo Rabb

I recently picked up an old diary I kept when I was 17, and found a page where I'd written this:

> *I feel like I just woke up from a wonderful dream. I just finished reading* In Summer Light *by Zibby Oneal—it's about Kate, a seventeen-year-old (which is partly why I wanted to read it) and about her summer, her father, her family, and falling in love*

*with a visiting graduate student, Ian, who's
twenty-five. It's one of the few books written about
someone my age which gives a teenager any bit of
credit for the ability to think, to be mature, to not
be an idiot. I related to Kate and I admired and
respected her. She was herself. Not sappy-nice, or
always perfect, but real. I fell in love with Ian also.
Nothing physical ever really happened between her
and Ian, but it all meant so much just the same.
It had so much meaning . . . they loved each other.
They didn't do anything, but it's still love.*

I reread *In Summer Light* again every few years, reveling in
this story of this rare, blurry, and intangible kind of friendship-
love that I didn't understand at seventeen, and nearly 20 years
later don't entirely understand, either.

The book is set on a Martha's Vineyard-like island in summer.
Kate is the daughter of a famous painter, and Ian has come to
catalog her father's paintings. Kate paints also, but has lost her
faith in her work, and feels crushed by the overbearing presence
of her father and his genius. Ian takes Kate's painting seriously
and encourages her, and their friendship develops into something more, which Kate realizes one day late in the summer:

Once she had asked her mother how a person
knew when she loved someone. She hadn't meant
the family kind of love, but the other kind that she
strangely imagined and sometimes thought about.
Ten years old, leaning against her mother, she'd
asked, and her mother had said, "You'll know."

And that was true, Kate thought. She knew. She
had known for quite a while. It hadn't come to her

at any one time or in any special place as she had
expected, but so slowly that she hardly recognized
its coming at all. It had been there before she gave it
a name. Like air, it had been all around her.

In so many of the books I read and movies I saw, love, especially among teenagers, was more about dithering over su-
perficial make-out sessions and mindless crushes than about
anything deep and real. I didn't want to be an idiot in love. I
wanted to be like Kate. And I wanted to understand the friendships I had that crossed over into other territory—what did
they mean? Were they real? Is it love if you never act on it, if
you never "do" anything? If it's brief and short-lived and you
never see the person again?

Alice Munro writes about the same kind of friendship-love
in her short story "Nettles":

> Love that was not usable, that knew its place. (Some
> would say not real, because it would never risk get-
> ting its neck wrung, or turning into a bad joke, or
> sadly wearing out.) Not risking a thing yet staying
> alive as a sweet trickle, an underground resource.

Literary scholars may not find much common ground between a 1985 YA novel and Alice Munro, but both beauti-
fully articulate a type of love that I've felt so keenly, but had
no words for until I saw it portrayed on the page. For Kate,
her love with Ian is a sweet trickle, an underground resource,
a source of confidence, even if it never risks getting its neck
broken or sadly wearing out.

When Ian says good-bye, there are no dramatic scenes of
lovelorn agony, but a sense of mature acceptance:

Everyone came out to see him off. Even if they had wanted to, there was no time or chance then to say more than they had already said, but there was nothing left that needed saying. "Now and here aren't all that there will ever be," he had said. There were numbers of ways that she could choose to interpret that, and Kate chose to let it stand that way, with many meanings.

At 17, I was learning that fiction was the primary way I'd understand and find meaning in life, that there were feelings I'd felt and experiences I'd had that I couldn't comprehend until I read about them in books. That some kinds of love have many meanings, and the meanings change over time, the way a book changes each time you reread it.

In Summer Light is out of print now. I want to write Oneal a letter, to tell her how much this novel meant to me at 17, and still means to me today; how I'll pass my copy on to my daughter, and I hope she'll pass it on, too. And I'll keep re-reading it, as I do every few years, to revisit that old Kate-like part of myself that tries to be mature, accepting, and to not be an idiot in love.

The Moon by Night
By Madeleine L'Engle
1963

Hit the Road, Zach

It was John's voice and he was calling for me. I supposed somewhere on the inside of my mind I realized it, but with the outside of my mind all I heard
was the constant crying of sea gulls and the incom-
ing boom of breakers.

Don't buy into the party of unity: When it comes to Madeleine L'Engle, you're either a Meg, Polly, or Vicky girl. (NO
ONE is Camilla. And whatever, Maggies—you're deliberately

being provoking.) For those of you rusty on the *trois dames* of L'Engle's works, Meg is, OF COURSE, Meg Murry, of *A Wrinkle in Time* fame, while Poly (Polyhymnia) is her redheaded daughter of the excellent *Dragons in the Waters* action. Vicky is Vicky Austin, of *Meet the Austins*, two kinds of awkward, three kinds of innocent, and strangely appealing for a 14-year-old given to frequent bouts of vigorous prayer.

I'm a Poly, of course, but I've still always had a very soft spot for *The Moon by Night*, the second in the Austin-family trilogy, for its scenic canyon views or barrage of male love interests, I couldn't tell you. (Pure jealousy, I'm sure—having never managed to escape my family's purview for more than 10 minutes on a camping trip or any other trip.) When we catch up with Vicky, she's just exited the ugly-duckling stage, where all her "sticky-out bones and unmanageable hair seem to come to some sort of agreement." (Exiting the awkward stage, as we have learned, is a narratively advantageous time to launch a novel, AS WE CAN NOW GET A LOVE INTEREST OR POSSIBLY TWO IN THE MIX. More on that soon.)

The Austin family—of the kindly physician father, the lovely stay-at-home mother, the older, supersmart brother, John, the pretty youngest daughter, Suzy, the surprise child, Rob, and Vicky in the middle—have just married off Vicky's mother's best friend to her uncle, deposited their foster daughter, Maggie, with the happy couple, and headed off on a camping trip across the country, bearing their usual Austin cheer with them:

> "When we reached the mainland we headed for a parkway and started playing the alphabet game. You know, you divide up by who's sitting on which side of the car, and you have to find the letters of the alphabet, in order, one by one, on the signs. John and

Daddy and Suzy were way ahead until they came to
Q, and then Mother and Rob and I caught up with
them and won. Then we played Animal Rummy,
and Rob saw a white horse and won that. And of
course we sang. We always do a lot of singing."

Approximately every 10 pages, to be precise. This level of
saccharine should of course be unendurable, but Vicky's innocence is the only acceptable kind. In L'Engle's world, there's no
virtue in innocence, only a testing ground for what will happen
when real choice is at stake. (Like the whole evil starfish con-
sortium in *Dragons in the Waters*! Sorry.) There are only a few
flavors of childhood in L'Engle: precocious, thoughtless, and
as-yet-unformed, all trying to contend with what they can't
understand but know they must master. In short, the Austin
family still all reads in the campground together at bedtime:
but they read *A Connecticut Yankee*.

Vicky, of course, is in the as-yet-unformed camp, every experience and piece of knowledge and opportunity to feel all the
more a meteor hurtling wildly while all around her and snug
in tight orbits:

"John [is] terrifically intelligent, but not a bit of a
grind. I mean, he just comes home from school and
sits down and gets his homework done in half the
time it takes me to do mine. He's good at sports, too,
the kind you can do with glasses on, like basketball
and track. As far as I can see he's good at just about
everything, I'm proud of him, sure, but sometimes I
feel, well, just kind of sad, because I can't ever hope
to be the kind of person John is. I don't even know
what I want to be yet."

No worries, sweets. That's why you get the trilogy! This ties in, of course, to L'Engle's vision of Christianity, one even a Spaghetti-Monster-fearing atheist might have a difficult time quarreling with, filled as it is with thoughtful analysis of one's role and an aggressive rejection of piety voiced by almost every major character. (Choice excerpt, from Vicky's uncle: "The minute anybody starts telling you what God thinks, or why he does such and such, beware.")

In fact, the whole Christianity thing is so sublimated you are mostly concentrated, like Vicky, on GETTING TO THE BOY STUFF. This occurs right after the family has settled in at one of their first campgrounds and Daddy fights off a hood because he, you know, KNOWS JUDO.

> Suzy asked, "Daddy, weren't you scared?"
>
> "I didn't like it," Daddy said, "but most hood-lums are cowards when it comes to a showdown. They're only brave when they think you're afraid of them. Now don't let this spoil our trip, and don't let it spoil Tennessee."
>
> "Are we to be frightened of our teen-agers?" Mother asked bitterly. "Has it come to that?"
>
> "Vicky and I are teen-agers," John said. "You can't blame teen-agers any more than you can Tennessee. There are dopy fringe elements in every group. I wrote a paper on it for Social Studies."

Sorry, I drifted off for a second, but is it . . . ZACH! Thank God, it's ZACHARY GRAY! Like, riding up in a big black car into the campground and Vicky's life NOW!!! Zachary of very pale skin and black hair and polo shirt and totally rich parents and bad-boy vibe! Zach, who is, in Vicky's words, "really pretty spectacular."

Because, how awesome is it that you're on a vacation and are finally pretty and your parents are nice but constantly making you sing and you kind of like it but ISN'T ANYTHING ELSE GOING TO EVER HAPPEN TO ME and the guy across the way full STROLLS UP, ASKS YOU OUT, and is a real person, filled with contradictions, enough that your family totally hates him on sight, even though he has his virtues and is not just some weird guy trying to sleep with you:

> "You've got an interesting face, Vicky," Zachary said as we walked back towards our tent. "Not pretty-pretty, but there's something more. And a darned good figure. I'd say something other than darned only I might shock little unhatched you."
>
> "I'm not so unhatched as all that."
>
> "No?"
>
> "No."
>
> "I'll bet you nothing's happened to you all your life long. Your meals have always been put in front of you and if you skin your little knee you can run crying to Mommie and Poppie and they'll kiss it and make everything all right."
>
> Well, maybe I didn't have very much experience so far. But I was on my way to getting it.

PREACH IT, SISTER! But why is Zach such an avatar of experience? Because, as we learn, he, like many of the young poets before him, suffered from rheumatic fever, leaving him with the dramatic coloring and disposition Vicky adores—and that drives her family to try to expel him like a foreign agent. ("This camping trip's a family affair, Vicky.") What's most fascinating about L'Engle is how she's able to weave the actual events of the trip with great moral quandaries to the extent that an adult can, with a stretch, almost read them as parables. You could say some delinquents throw a Coke bottle at their car, or that they, like all travelers, are beset upon by thieves on the road. They either use their station wagon to drive some Girl Scouts out of a flooded canyon, or they are Noah with an ark saving the innocents. There's a baby left in a tent with Mother, and a fallen woman who gratefully retrieves her. Vicky learns about Native Americans, a town destroyed by half the mountain, the Holocaust, and American imperialism. She sees New Mexico: "At home in Thornhill nobody is really poor, and it was awful to see the shacks and shanties and poor, foreign-looking people along the roadside. No wonder D. H. Lawrence isn't really happy in New Mexico." She sees *The Diary of Anne Frank* with Zach when the family reaches Laguna Beach. "If God lets things be unfair, if He lets things like Anne Frank happen, then I don't love Him, I hate Him!" she cries. Dude, hold on a second. YOU'RE GOING TO MEET ANOTHER GUY.

And enter Andy Ford, the moral redhead who does not want Vicky to see Zach any more than Zach wants Andy to see Vicky! Eff morality: This entire book is about two guys chasing Vicky around sunlit canyons and about dark, starry nights around the fire, and though you have to actually read about three more books to see how it resolves, I would sit through any amount of secret sermonizing to find out what happens next.

"You're a funny kid," Zach tells Vicky: "a mixture of goody-goody little Miss Prunes, and quite a gal. I look forward to knowing you in five years." Trust us, Zach, there's all this crap about dolphins and lovers and telekenesis, and it's AWESOME.

To All My Fans, With Love, From Sylvie
By Ellen Conford
1982

More than anything, Sylvie wanted to find fame...
Author of *And This Is Laura*

Ellen Conford

To All My Fans, With Love, From Sylvie

Modern Screen

AN ARCHWAY PAPERBACK PUBLISHED BY POCKET BOOKS

Riding Sidesaddle

Dear Mom,

Even though you will probably never get this, like you never got any of the other letters I wrote you because I never mailed them, I am writing anyway to tell you I am finally going to "take the plunge" and set out for Hollywood.

I've always had a soft spot for Ellen Conford, one of those authors whose works are so universally skilled and vibrant, she's prey to the solid-A-student syndrome: so dependable, readers forget she even exists. By the time our daily reading has switched to matte-finish trade paperbacks, memory has already mistakenly shelved her work in with a favorite, showier author. (My particular mis-shelf? Always to put *And This Is Laura*, her teen-psychic foray, into the Lois Duncan section.)

To All My Fans, With Love, From Sylvie—set in the 1950s, peppered with references to Sen-Sens, James Dean, and oddments spelled "Teena"—is particularly vulnerable to such unjust switcheroos, as its subject matter hits notes from favorites by several heavy hitters: After veering vaguely into Judy Blume's *Starring Sally J. Freedman as Herself* territory, we pivot momentarily off Bette Greene's *Summer of My German Soldier*, then careen for a moment into Francine Pascal's *Hangin' Out with Cici*.

But though the book bears glancing similarities to those others—a young girl obsessed with Hollywood, crappy father figures, Eisenhower-era signifiers—it's entirely its own animal: a comic quest in which a 15-year-old tries desperately to get to Hollywood before a series of foster fathers and assorted other creeps get their hands on her.

The story of 15-year-old Sylvie Krail takes place over the course of five days in which Sylvie escapes her last foster home in New York and almost makes it to Hollywood, where she's headed to become a star, the book could easily stand beside *Transamerica* in the Humorous Heartwarmers for Adults That Begin with Really Unpleasant Sexual Encounters, Actually department.

Sylvie's good looks are exactly good enough to make

Hollywood a reasonable proposition, and invite perpetual trouble. She's that strange, singularly adolescent mixture of precociously cynical and totally out to lunch, deftly avoiding being routinely pawed by her yucky "Uncle" Ted while simultaneously spending $14.99 ($3,455 in current deficit dollars) of her hard-earned $137 runaway dollars on a hatbox—must-have model's gear—in preparation for her flight:

> I figured I had about an hour and a half before they came back from church. I wished I could take a nice, cool shower, but there wasn't time. Everything had to be packed and my hatbox and suitcase had to be hidden before they got back from church.
>
> Church. That was a laugh. Uncle Ted going to church and singing the hymns and praying to God and looking all Christian and holy five minutes after trying to tuck me into bed. What if they knew what he was really like? What if Aunt Grace knew? I bet she'd drop dead right in the middle of her paint-by-numbers oil picture of the last supper.
>
> But maybe she wouldn't. Maybe she'd look straight at me and say, "Sylvie, you must be imagining things." That's what had happened the first time, when I was twelve.

So . . . bring on the screen tests! Unfortunately, Sylvie's preternatural knowledge of trademarks of the stars—"[Natalie Wood is] my ideal. We have practically identical eyebrows. The first thing I'm going to buy when I get my break in the movies is a gold slave bracelet"—does not translate into a similar knowledge of how to protect your money while on the road to

Jericho. Because somewhere around Springfield, Ohio—right after Sylvie has settled on the screen name "Venida Meredith," swiped, admirably, from a "Venida Hair Nets" ad—she too is set upon by thieves:

> I reached into my pocketbook to get a dime. I felt around, but there was so much stuff in there, I couldn't get to my wallet. I started taking things out and lining them up on the table: my compact, my lipstick, tissues, my pink scarf, the sunglasses with the white plastic frames I'd gotten at Woolworth's, my pad and pencil for letters to my mother and Judy. . . . Faster and faster I grabbed for things, and the more stuff I took out, the more frantic I got. I should have been able to get to the wallet by now. . . .

And now we come to the Extraordinarily Inopportune Moments To Have Your Wallet Stolen category. (Runner up: *Thelma and Louise?*) Delicate readers, be forewarned. Luckily, at Sal's Roadside Rest, Sylvie too finds her Good Samaritan, a certain Walter Murchison, who offers to drive her the rest of the way in his "Pontiac Chief Star Catalina." He is, luckily. . . .

> A Bible salesman! At first I felt this kind of twinge of disappointment that he wasn't a reporter, and wouldn't be doing a story about me . . . [but] what could be safer than riding with a person who was in the Bible business? Maybe I shouldn't have gotten into the car with a strange man, but if I had to get into a car with any strange man, I was certainly lucky that I had picked Walter Murchison.

This is not the first moment where, in a burst of ambition, Sylvie tosses aside all good sense. (And, unfortunately, her suitcase, which she leaves on the Greyhound and does not remember until untold towns later.)

Although Walter has the irritating habit of constantly getting single hotel rooms, he is one hell of a Bible salesman, something Sylvie has much occasion to witness as they stop off in rural area after flyover nowhere after godforsaken wasteland for Walter to unload his uplifting stock:

> "All God's work is handsome," Walter said. "But if you don't mind a little humor, Mrs. Fitch, the Good News Bible is the deluxe edition of God's work. Now, tell me the truth. Isn't this a Bible you'd be proud to have in your home? Isn't this a Bible that wouldn't be stuck on a shelf somewhere, but would deserve a place of honor right out on a table in your front room? Please look at the gold-tipped pages too, Mrs. Fitch. This isn't just the holy word of God. . . ."
>
> I forgot how hot it was. I forgot my suitcase, my three scratchy crinolines, and changing my name to something other than Venida. I kept looking from Walter to Mrs. Fitch and back to Walter again. This was like a Ping-Pong game and I couldn't figure out who was going to win.

It's around this point that a reader might look around with surprise and realize that this interaction, like all that have come before, is entirely adult—not only in constitution but in nature. There's no sassy best friend for Sylvie, no helpful older sister—not even a queen bee to make her life miserable. Her closest pals are found in her *Photoplay* magazines, and her day-to-day life is an ongoing quest to slap on enough makeup to manage to look 18 for her Hollywood arrival, the sooner to hang with Natalie on-screen—hoping events at home don't go *Splendor in the Grass.*

But it's no surprise that adults are so (oddly) central in the story—they're also oddly central in Sylvie's life—and that's the problem! If only Walter were content to exist as a sideline, a kitchen-table sage who dispensed fatherly wisdom while Sylvie went off to the movies with someone age appropriate. But instead, he's bent on muscling Sylvie out of the starring role and into a role alongside him:

> Was it just that . . . Walter was old enough to be my father and had a big Adam's apple and a bow tie and wore his belt so high that his pants were practically hitched halfway up his chest? . . . I started getting confused again. Maybe the only thing that would unconfuse me was to start concentrating on my movie career, which I hadn't thought about for what seemed a very long time.

But a savior of sorts does occur in the form of Vic, who is (appropriately enough) a lifeguard Sylvie stumbles upon in Las Vegas. Vic is a young, handsome psychiatrist-in-training who takes an interest in Sylvie, both intellectually and emotionally—although, unlike all the others, he is able to put aside the latter for the former. And if up until then Sylvie has had to suffer through adults behaving far more dismally than your average on-screen heartthrob, Vic makes up the distance immediately, providing her with shelter, sustenance, and psychological support—minus the romantic clinch.

And, as the bizarro-world romantic lead, Vic not only treats

Sylvie like a child, he makes her understand why it's okay for her to have romantic feelings—but only for someone in a very different position with Sylvie than he is. Because when Sylvie finally confesses that she wasn't most afraid of Uncle Ted, but of "myself. I was afraid—I'd let him. I wanted him to," Vic stunningly replies, "I don't think that's so unusual":

> "So you have these feelings, but what can you do about them? Now, here's Uncle Ted acting affectionate toward you, and no one else in your whole life ever has. See what I'm getting at?"
>
> "Not exactly. If I went out with boys I wouldn't feel this way about Uncle Ted?"
>
> Even in the dim, flickering light from the TV screen, I could see Vic was frowning. "I'm not sure. Maybe. I told you this was complicated. I'm just trying to figure it out from what's in my psych books. But why I said it was natural was because you always wanted somebody to love you, and Uncle Ted's acting like he loves you—or, at least, wants to make love to you. And one part of you says that's wrong, but another part of you wants it."
>
> "But that's not love!" I cried. "That's sex."
>
> "Sometimes people don't know the difference."

A lot of those other people cracking psych books are STILL trying to figure that one out. But Conford took Sylvie seriously, and she took *us* seriously enough to let us chew on that, with Walter's Sen-Sens, for a while. Because while growing up in a YA novel is one thing, Conford shows us something else we might want to think about with Sylvie: a girl who grows up just enough to realize she's still a child.

Chapter 9

Old-Fashioned Girls
They Wear Bonnets, Don't They?

Girls in White Dresses with Blue Satin Sashes

Clotted cream. Silken furs. Silk. Furs. Governesses. Starched, clean cotton. Trains, cold chicken, hot cross buns, belladonna, crimping, satin, bows, ribbons, gardens, villains, Dickon, Craven, Polly, ayahs, typewriters, Model-T's, boarding schools, shingled hair, silk stockings, thick, creamy creamy clotted creamy cream—

OH, ALL RIGHT, I'LL STOP. Those of you who stuck mainly to late-twentieth-century texts are, of course, currently feeling no pain. But all of the girls who delved into the previous era's works are, I must inform you, currently in agony.

Of all the forms of fetish pornography running rampant in society today, the deepest and most invidious must be that found in all of the stories of young orphaned girls plunked down in splendorous circumstances who proceed to go about returning all the inhabitants thereof to a state of beruffled, wool-stockinged happiness. Laura Lippman, in her essay on the works of Joan Aiken, sums up the danger signs to look out for in her neat formula, COVENS:

Clothing

Orphans, Real or De Facto

Villains

England

Nature Boys, a la Dickon

Specialized Schools—A Boarding School, a School for the Performing Arts, an Orphanage or—The Dream That I Have Yet To Find—An Orphanage Devoted to the Performing Arts.

One need only look to any Merchant-Ivory film or, God forbid, Harry Potter sequel, to see that English colonial porn is alive and well—as are its American offshoots. (Louisa May Alcott or Frances Hodgson Burnett—mutton or *marron glacé*, what's the difference if it's got a floor-length skirt of satin someplace?) Why? Well, obviously, because living a life by a crackling fire where a maid sweeps out the grate and a mysterious Indian man redecorates your room sumptuously and you are whisked away in a carriage and sent on a night train to, really, anything resembling a manor, clearly trumps any other walk of life, flush as it is with the accoutrement of great wealth without any fear of beheadings. (Works like *Cheaper by the Dozen* and *Belles on Their Toes* merely up the ante by transferring all that cozy goodness to a slightly more recent era.)

I'd like to argue that all of these texts have fascinating things to say about how society confounds and builds itself on ideas of class, ambition, empire, religion, economics, destiny, and nationhood, and in fact, they do. I'd also like to say they are vivid snapshots of history. In every case, each book is a world you would be thrilled to pluck out of its hazy black-and-white and return triumphantly to color.

However, I really just want a pair of silk stockings and an ermine-jacketed china doll.

An Old-Fashioned Girl
By Louisa May Alcott
1869

Polly Want a Slacker?

"It's time to go to the station, Tom."

"Come on, then."

"Oh, I'm not going; it's too wet. Shouldn't have a crimp left if I went out on such a day as this; and I want to look nice when Polly comes."

"You don't expect me to go and bring home a strange girl alone, do you?" And Tom looked as much alarmed as if his sister had proposed to him to escort the wild woman to Australia.

"Of course I do. It's your place to go and get her; and if you wasn't a bear, you'd like it."

I remember exactly where Louisa May Alcott's *An Old-Fashioned Girl* resided in my elementary school's quiet library, and well I should—I took it out every week. It was a hardcover edition with a clear plastic dust jacket covering a pink cover with a picture of a heart-shaped girl with round, sausage-like curls and a sweetheart neckline, and it was placed on the top right shelf in the second to last row on the right-hand side of the main fiction area, just behind a fire door and below the official children's section. In our elementary school, when you took out a book, you weren't allowed to take it home—it was only yours for the biweekly half-hour reading period, and this was probably good for my slowly disintegrating edition. Left to my own devices, I would have separated most of the crumbling signatures from their saddle-stitching in about a week.

I have your average registered bookworm's healthy regard for *Little Women*, a book I loved so much that for years I eschewed the copy of *Little Men* someone had given me as a gift, not wanting to destroy the magic of its predecessor. (I needn't have worried—my edition of *Little Women*, like many, actually contained both books, so I had read it a few dozen times. There's some sort of cognitive-behavioral lesson in there for all readers, I'm sure.)

An Old-Fashioned Girl is different, however. First and foremost, rather than forcing the reader to choose among four characters of distinctly different character (thus ushering in years of women's novels set at Harvard, and episodes of *Golden Girls* and *SATC* for the enjoyment of us all), we have only Polly, her best friend Fan, and Fan's brother, Tom. Polly is the lively country bumpkin who arrives to visit for the "season" (oh, can we BRING back social "seasons"?) with Fan. The expectation, of course, is that the family will suffer her coarse, amusing failures gracefully, slowly bringing her up to snuff as a young lady of the finest fashion.

All efforts in this regard, of course, fail. In an attempt to curl Polly's bangs, she burns them completely off. Showing a plump, pleasing white shoulder merely horrifies Tom, who's used to a rough-and-tumble girl who'd rather sled with him than promenade in fine clothes. And Polly finds that, at fine parties, she far prefers the company of the rambunctious children to the stilted ladies imitating their peers.

Her effect on the Shaw family she visits, however, is lasting and profound. "A happy soul in a healthy body," as Alcott puts it, Polly, who shuns finery, has not only the moral advantage over her hosts but also the emotional. Simply, her plain, straightforward dress, free of vanity, reflects her purity of heart and soul. On her visit, she reminds Fan of the virtues of real friendship, soothes Fan's little sister Maud's sulky passions, manages to make even the fretful Mrs. Shaw happy, bonds with Grandma Shaw and, most impressive, calms Tom down. (She is also the first person in years to show any daughterly affection for Mr. Shaw, who funds the whole operation.) In short, she shames them all and, in the best sense, reminds them of what they have in each other.

Well! All of this would be very well and give-your-Christmas-breakfast-away in the best *Little Women* tradition, but for the follow-up Alcott wrote, entitled *6 Years Later*, in which Polly returns (shades of *Vanity Fair*) from the country to the city just before the Shaws lose all their money in the crash, brings the story to its true depth by letting us get to know Polly as a woman.

I know many fans of *Little Women* find the whole Professor Bhaer situation kind of a gross-out—how can Jo, who's been scribbling with her cap on in sisterly domestic harmony for years and years with only vague inclinations toward a girlish Laurie for sexual interest, have to go live with that horrid bearded old *man*?—but in Polly's case, her love interest (Spoiler! Spoiler! It's Tom!) is a beguiling mix of manly and dandy.

I have always been sympathetic to the period of Jo's loneliness, when all her sisters marry off and she's living in a boarding house—and Polly has a similar situation, although she has to make lemonade out of far more lemony lemons. Not only is she snubbed by Tom, his girlfriend, Trix, and Fan, who have vaulted into a social circle that can no longer include Jo, but also, her job as a piano teacher keeps her ever on the verge of poverty, she is never allowed to see her brother, Jimmy, and she feels herself constantly in the position of the patronized pet, too prideful to borrow an outfit, and therefore never able to go to the party. When the Shaws lose all their money, she's able to help them with all of the cost-cutting and spirit-raising measures she's lived with her entire life, true, and there's the same satisfaction in watching her help Fan turn all her old dresses inside out to save them for the next season (Oh, seasons, seasons!) as we see with Sarah Crew inventing a warm rug and crackling fire for her bare room. But unlike in *Little Women*, the moral lessons alone are not the book's purpose. In the person of Polly, Alcott has placed not only her best arguments for the virtues of, well, virtue (I've ALWAYS felt that the girls could have at least eaten HALF of their Christmas breakfasts, and did they always have to give away all their money for presents for Marmie?) but she's placed a deep passion only hinted at in Jo, briefly. Jo is independent and willful, surely, but Polly is actually, literally independent and strong-willed—

a true adventurer, who in her youth is unafraid to make herself part of a family and change them for the better, and in her old age is courageous enough to hold out for the family she wishes to have, not the one society dictates would be most practical for her.

We're certainly happy (Spoiler! Spoiler!) when Polly and Tom have a happy ending—he goes out West to make his fortune, becomes a man, and makes himself worthy of her—but it's quite clear to us also that, whatever happened with Tom, Polly, simply by being forthcoming, open, smart, and interested in life, would have managed to craft a sequel any reader would want to take out, week after week after week.

The Wolves of Willoughby Chase

By Joan Aiken
1962

Life's a Bitch . . . and So Is the Governess

By Laura Lippman

After tea . . . the children were set to mending. The meal had consisted of bread, dry this time, and a cup of water. Sylvia had contrived to save a half of her morsel of bread for Bonnie, and she pushed it into Bonnie's hand later, as they sat working in the biggest classroom, huddled together for warmth.

This was the only time of the day they were allowed
to talk to each other a little.

. . . "We can't stay here, Sylvia."

"No, we can't," breathed Sylvia in heartfelt agreement. "But how can we possibly get away? And
where would we go?"

"I'll think of some plan," said Bonnie with invin-
cible optimism. "And you think, too, Sylvia. Think
for all you are worth."

Sylvia nodded. Then she whispered, "Hush,
Diana Brisket's looking at us," and bent her head
over the enormous rent in the satin petticoat she
was endeavoring to repair."

Whenever I visit my parents—not often enough, as they would
be the first to tell you—I always end up thinking about Maude.
Yes, that Maude. One of the many *All in the Family* spin-offs
of the 1970s, *Maude* centered on an "uncompromising, enter-
prising, anything but tranquilizing" woman from Tuckahoe,
New York. (By the way, several Internet sources claim it's "that
old compromising," which makes NO sense.) Route 404, which
winds through Maryland and Delaware, skirts Tuckahoe State
Park, so every time I come to that part of the trip—well, then
there's Maude.

And now that I've got the Maude song fizzing around in
everyone else's head—what was really so extraordinary about
this outspoken-but-privileged woman? Yes, she was mouthy,
and, yes, she had one of television's first legal abortions, but
her restless intelligence now seems wasted to me. Did Maude
work outside the home, or even volunteer? (In the home, she
had Florida to clean for her, at least until Florida got her spin-

off.) What did she do other than battle with her husband and pal around with future Golden Girl roomie Rue McClanahan?

I had a better role model closer at hand. In 1969, three years before *Maude* debuted, my mother enrolled in graduate school, intent on becoming a children's librarian. There are many, many wonderful benefits to having a mother who wants to be a children's librarian—weekly trips to the big library downtown, reading all the Newbery Award winners together, even *Gay-Neck, the Story of a Pigeon*, God help us—but the thing that stands out for me was the wonder of my mother's class project. Using knitting needles and index cards, she and a classmate created what can only be described as a non-computerized search engine. They notched the cards with a series of holes, some open at the top. The open holes corresponded to key search criteria—author, reading level, subject matter. With the help of a numeric code, you inserted the needles into the cards and lifted; the cards that fell out were the ones that matched your criteria.

I have been thinking about my mother's class project because a chance re-encounter with *The Wolves of Willoughby Chase* convinced me that it is my personal platonic ideal of children's literature, the card that would fall if I could set up a system controlling for all my favorite things in books: clothing; orphans, real or de facto; villains; England; Nature Boys, a la Dickon; Specialized Schools—a boarding school, a school for the performing arts, an orphanage or—the dream that I have yet to find—an orphanage devoted to the performing arts.

Of course, there are lots of satisfying books that score in only one or two categories. I adore Maud Hart Lovelace's happy families, thanks to the detailed descriptions of Merry Widow hats, shirtwaists, and jabots, but Deep Valley, Minnesota, is far from England. Elizabeth Enright's four-book series about the Melendy family offers only tantalizing rumors of boarding school, and only in the final book. E. Nesbit comes awfully close, especially if you're willing to consider the Psammead [CQ], a boy with a special connection to nature. (Hey, he lives in a sandpit, it's harder to get much closer to nature than that.) Noel Streatfeild's "shoe" books qualify, although she often softened her villains in the final act. Except for Mrs. Winter, mother of Dulcie in *Dancing Shoes*. Remember how she turns away, at the end, when Rachel is revealed to be the big talent in the family? Could someone please tell me why the adorable Uncle Tom is married to that woman? This has bothered me for years.

But *The Wolves of Willoughby Chase* is the gold standard, the *ne plus ultra* of the Lippman COVENS Rule. Throw in an opening that reads like the YA version of James Joyce's *The Dead* and . . . oh, excuse me, I passed out briefly from ecstasy. Here, see for yourselves:

> It was dusk, winter dusk. Snow lay white and shining over the pleated hills, and icicles hung from the forest trees. Snow lay piled on the dark road across Willoughby Wold, but from dawn men had been clearing it with brooms and shovels. There were hundreds of them at work, wrapped in sacking because of the bitter cold, and keeping together in groups for fear of the wolves, grown savage and reckless from hunger.

And—damn you, Joan Aiken—it gets better. Chapter by chapter, event by event. *Wolves* has everything. A high-spirited rich girl (Bonnie Green), her virtuous poor relation (Sylvia Green), a tragic shipwreck, an evil governess, loyal retainers, an uncannily clever and gifted goose tender, a horrible board-ing school—run by Mrs. Brisket no less, who rewards snitches with little pieces of cheese. And I'm not even going to tell you how the geese foil a dastardly crime.

Aiken, the daughter of Conrad Aiken, is a brisk tour guide. "Do try to keep up," she all but demands as the story steams along, "we have so much ground to cover." Sylvia, an orphan (O!) has left her Aunt Jane in London (E!) to go stay with cousin Bonnie, who will be de facto parentless (O!) while Lord Wil-loughby and Lady Green take a voyage intended to mend Lady Green's fragile health. Sylvia, genteel but poor, worries that her sole doll, Annabelle, will be humiliated by Bonnie's dolls for wearing only a "funny little old pelisse!" (C!) Sharing her train compartment with an odd man named Grimshaw (V!), she also frets about her aunt's very Victorian edict that she never eat in front of a stranger, difficult to do when a train ride takes almost two days. And in the middle of all these little-girl anxi-eties, she has to deal with wolves, literal ones.

. . . the train had stopped with a jerk. [Yes, his name is Mr. Grimshaw! Thank you, I'm here all week.]

"Oh! What is it? Where are we?' she exclaimed before she could stop herself.

"No need to alarm yourself, miss," said her com-panion, looking unavailingly out of the black square of window. "Wolves on the line, most likely—they often have trouble hereabouts."

"Wolves!" Sylvia stared at him in terror.

"They don't often get into the train, though," he added reassuringly. "Two years ago they managed to climb into the guard's van and eat a pig, and once they got the engine driver—another had to be sent in a relief engine—but they don't often eat a passenger, I promise you."

If Sylvia was reassured by the notion that the wolves don't OFTEN eat passengers, she is much braver than I. Yet the wolves turn out to be among the more benign forces that threaten Sylvia and Bonnie in this book. Nature can be thwarted, it turns out. People are much more trickier.

Things sour quickly at Willoughby Manor. Miss Slighcarp (V!), the new governess—and a distant relation—is about as nice as one would expect, given that her name is Miss Slighcarp. She wastes no time trying on Lady Green's clothes—including (swoon) "a rose-colored crepe with aiguillettes of diamonds on the shoulders. It did not fit her exactly." (Nice bitchy aside there from meek little Sylvia.) Mr. Grimshaw, the mysterious man from Sylvia's train, is skulking about, and no good ever came from skulking. Then news comes that the Willoughbys' ship has sunk, and the girls are packed off quickly to the "boarding school" (S!) run by Mrs. Brisket (V!). The only coddled child in the place is Mrs. Brisket's own Diana, a selfish brat, and there is a wonderful scene involving Bonnie, Diana, and some fresh eggs, in which you will cheer because someone does NOT get slapped.

A quick aside about orphans: For me, the "O" is the central letter in COVENS. Why do I love them so much? It's true, I was a latchkey kid, but my mother didn't start working until I was in junior high, so I had the best of both worlds. The simple fact is that most children's books benefit when some sort of contrivance whisks the parents offstage. It doesn't have to be death (although there are a lot of dead moms in my favorite books) or a demanding job (lots of widowers, too, throwing themselves into their work since Mom's demise). An adults-only trip or troubling surgery (*The Time Garden, Knight's Castle*) works just as well. And there's always boarding school! (*The Great Brain at the Academy, The Fog Comes in on Little Pig's Feet, Apples Every Day.*) But, of course, we don't want them to stay parent-less. That would be much too bleak.

In *Wolves*, the real orphans finally receive much-deserved succor, while the hateful Diana Brisket finds herself quite alone in the world. Yet it is Aiken's treatment of Diana, in the final act of comeuppances, that makes me love the novel even more.

The orphans, still dazed at their good fortune, sit at a table of their own, eating roast turkey and kindly averting their gaze from the pale cheeks and red eyes of Diana Brisket, who, having been in a position to bully and hector as much as she pleased, is now reduced to a state where she has not a friend to stand by her. . . . Diana has nowhere to go and is forced, willy-nilly, to stay with the orphans (where, it may be said in passing, wholesome discipline and the example of Aunt Jane's unselfish nature soon molds an improvement in her character.)

You see, there are no bad children—only bad adults. Otis Spofford, Dulcie-Pulsie in *Dancing Shoes*, even *The Bully of Barkham Street* all have their sides to the story. But grown-ups? Grown-ups can really suck. Possibly because they did not receive a timely intervention from Aunt Jane. I would add that to COVENS—No bad children, only bad grown-ups—but it would screw up an acronym that took me, literally, hours to formulate.

The Secret Garden
By Frances Hodgson Burnett
1909

Shut-in and Dig

> When Mary Lennox was sent to Misselthwaite Manor to live with her uncle everybody said she was the most disagreeable child ever seen. It was true, too.

Somewhere along the line, along with straw prams and caning rods, having a child character not even the narrator can stand went out of business. (Off the top of my head, I can only think of Ingalls Wilder's Nellie, and you know that was just the God's honest truth.) In the case of Mary Lennox, daughter of colonial India, Frances Hodgson Burnett, too, begins by insulting her yellow, priggish looks:

> She had a little thin face and a little thin body, thin light hair and a sour expression. Her hair was yellow, and her face was yellow, because she had been born in India and had always been ill in one way or another.

This is all on the *first page*, mind. Moving on to the second. Mary, whose father serves in the colonial government and is cared for only by servants because her careless, beautiful mother and her sickly, absent father cannot be bothered with her, is not only ugly but possessed of a terrible character:

> . . . By the time she was six years old she was as tyrannical and selfish a little pig as ever lived.

Okay. Ugliest, most loathsome child ever. Check! But is it possible Burnett may have established how profoundly awful Mary is at this precise moment simply to arm the young reader against becoming too terribly troubled by what's about to happen? Perhaps. Or it may be that Burnett simply loathed her to such a degree she was unable to restrain herself from killing off her mother, her father, and the entire compound with a cholera outbreak by page 4.

And . . . moving right along! We soon find Mary in the hands of Mrs. Medlock, her temporary guardian, speeding toward her next home. Mrs. Medlock is not a bad woman, but she is less interested in Mary's welfare than in the cold chicken and beef—ah, 19th-century British food porn, sigh—

they serve on the train they've taken. Mrs. Medlock is in the employ of a certain Dickensian-ish Mr. Craven, Mary's uncle by marriage after the death of his beautiful young wife. (So many beautiful young wives, so little time to kill them all off!) Mr. Craven is the kind of wealthy, damaged recluse who today might drown his grief in Percocet and unwise investments. Instead, he apparently lives in splendid isolation in his gloomy estate, Misselthwaite Manor, traveling on business as much as possible, and cared for by his servants like an exotic reptile whose diet and living area must be observed with strict discipline, despite the creature's rarely showing itself.

Misselthwaite is the kind of gloomy, old 100-room barn now made stock through a battery of media appearances (see *My Cousin Rachel*, *The Others*, *Gosford Park*, the works of Merchant Ivory in their entirety), and Mary's abrupt rustication to its gloomy corridors is the first step in toward the young girl becoming not *completely* the worst child in the world—and the first time we feel some sympathy for the poor girl.

And since Burnett—who in her age wielded literary fame something on the order of J. K. Rowling meshed with Oprah, with a little Elizabeth Taylor thrown in for marital intrigue—spends the next 300 pages emphasizing Mary's humanity, you can't fault her too much for destroying the girl's life at the outset. Before we get ahead of ourselves, however, we must see Mary's reeducation begin upon waking to her young, red-faced, *way* talkative Yorkshire servant, Martha:

> The native servants she had been used to in India were not in the least like this. They were obsequious and servile and did not presume to talk to their masters as if they were equals. They made salaams and called them "protector of the poor" and names

of that sort. Indian servants were commanded to do things, not asked. It was not the custom to say "please" and "thank you" and Mary had always slapped her Ayah in the face when she was angry. She wondered a little what this girl would do if one slapped her in the face. She was a round, rosy, good-natured-looking creature, but she had a sturdy way which made Mistress Mary wonder if she might not even slap back—if the person who slapped her was only a little girl.

It's Martha who is the first person in Mary's life to take any real interest in her (even if, at first, a good part of the interest is wondering why Mary is so completely feebleminded that she doesn't even know to tie her own shoes). It's from Martha she picks up other important notions for splendidly rich girls who are used to being waited on by ayahs, like that she might rethink not finishing her oatmeal, since all of Martha's eight brothers and sisters in a shack on the moor would eat it in about two seconds and like it, and from Martha that she learns of Martha's brother Dickon, a young roustabout who has charmed all the animals of the moor, and can talk to things like missel thrushes, whatever those are. But most important, Martha, who is not a "that's classified" sort of person, tells Mary about a very interesting garden:

> "Mr. Craven had it shut when his wife died so sudden. He won't let no one go inside. It was her garden. He locked th' door an' dug a hole and buried th' key. There's Mrs. Medlock's bell ringing—I must run."

Goddamn it, Martha, don't leave a girl hanging! But actually Martha's leaving Mary hanging saves her from an idle life of misery. Because in failing to follow her orders to spill, Martha has moved Mary from a life of idle indifference into one of curiosity, which apparently kills cats but is very good for children—as are, incidentally, the hot cross buns and milk Mary develops an appetite for from running around on the moor.

Because Mary has been put in a house of secrets. The garden is paramount, but on top of that there is the mystery of Dickon, and how a boy can talk to animals; there is the question of why Mr. Craven is so miserable and hunchbacked; there is the problem of what the hell everyone is saying, because Mary cannot understand the Yorkshire accent at *all*; and, most important, there is the issue of the wailing Mary often hears through the halls, a fretful sound she knows is more than the wind.

But *The Secret Garden*, more than anything, is about those who are locked up, and those who grow—both literally and emotionally.

This is true of persons and of nations. Mary is not the only one who, before she becomes a careful gardener, idly skims her wealth off the labor of the poor and is made sick by it. Hodgson is also writing about the wasteful, destructive nature of England—its despicable conquest of another country, its rampant profiteering, the corruption within being caused by the corruption without. England's idle rich are wealthy, but in *The Secret Garden*, their wealth only serves to oppress—even to deform, as in the case of the mysterious wailing Colin—those who possess it. Mr. Craven, Colin, and Mary are all England the colonizer—a country as piggish, tyrannical, and sickly as Mary ever was.

But this is not true of the simple people of the moor, armed with their strategic knowledge of larkspur and hot cross buns! Schooled by the simple people of the moor, by their own servants, Mary and the other inhabitants of locked-up Misselthwaite are revived.

Of course, the servants and Dickon are a little too joyously occupied with the happiness of their employers to make this a handy pamphlet for Mao, but in the case of wealthy versus healthy, colonizer versus fertilizer, they win absolutely. Because Burnett's England itself is a locked-up garden which, only tended by the wealthy and humble alike, can express the true beauty of the nation. And, left with a shovel and hot cross buns ourselves, we could all solve the problems of the world.

Cheaper by the Dozen & Belles on Their Toes

By Frank B. Gilbreth Junior & Ernestine Gilbreth Carey
1948, 1950

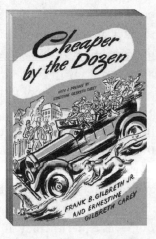

Mother Knows Best
By Laura Lippman

We made quite a sight rolling along in the car, with the top down. As we passed through cities and villages, we caused a stir equaled only by a circus parade....

...Whenever the crowds gathered at some intersection where we were stopped by traffic, the inevitable question came sooner or later.

"How do you feed all those kids, Mister?"

Dad would ponder for a minute. Then, rearing back so those on the outskirts could hear, he'd say as if he had just thought it up:

"Well, they come cheaper by the dozen, you know."

I was a reporter for 20 years, but I was never an "investigative" reporter. Although that modifier might seem redundant to civilians, it is a precise job description within a newsroom, one of the top positions, reserved for the cream. An investigative reporter needs to be dogged, capable of following extremely complicated paper trails, but also personable enough to woo sources. And in my particular workplace— The (Baltimore) *Sun*, 1989–2001—it helped to have a penis. Oh, my female colleagues did some impressive work in that timeframe, yet I can't recall one who was allowed to be a fulltime investigative reporter. But then, as our editors often helpfully explained, our newsroom was a meritocracy. It was so meretricious—um, I mean, meritorious—that it had one of the whitest newspaper staffs among metropolitan dailies, and this was in a city that was two-thirds African American. But, as ever, I digress.

To be candid, even if I lived in a world where someone might get a job based solely on the fact that she has a uterus—just speaking hypothetically here, of course—I would never have made it as an investigative reporter. I'm not thick-skinned enough. I don't enjoy making people mad at me. I left the city desk for features, then fled the newspaper for the freedom to make stuff up fulltime. So it is with some nervousness and trepidation that I take a stab at investigative journalism and announce my stunning discovery:

There were never a dozen Gilbreth children.

Or, to recast my lede in the self-important newspaper style beloved by my former employer: There were never a dozen Gilbreth children, [PUBLICATION] has learned.

To be sure, twelve children were born to Frank and Lillian Gilbreth, two industrial engineers involved in the field of motion study. But Mary, the second oldest, died from diptheria in 1912. The last of the Gilbreths, Jane, was born in 1922. Frank Gilbreth died in 1924. So there were, for precisely two years in Frank Gilbreth's life, eleven children, max. Consequently, every story in *Cheaper* that turns on a "dozen"—and there are many—is patently false. In fact, *Cheaper by the Dozen* never even mentions Mary's death, an omission made possible by the fact that it barely mentions Mary at all. Instead, her death is revealed in a footnote at the beginning of the sequel, *Belles on Their Toes*.

I feel rotten, telling you this, because I really love these books. Although, in rereading them, I realized I prefer the sequel, and not just because it drops the "dozen" charade. *Belles* is a better book than its predecessor, in part because it loses the problematic Frank Gilbreth, who may make some readers wonder where motion study ends and child abuse begins.

As depicted by two of his children—Frank Gilbreth Jr. and Ernestine Gilbreth Carey—Frank Sr. is a benevolent dictator. Actually, he's not that benevolent, although his kids appear to be crazy about him. He moves dinner discussion along by declaring that most topics are "not of general interest." He teaches touch-typing while banging a pencil on the child-typist's head hard enough to hurt. ("It's meant to hurt," he growls at the protesting daughter.) He doesn't believe in illness and his good-sport progeny almost never see doctors except when another Gilbreth is arriving. In one of the book's most memorable scenes, Gilbreth decides to use his children's tonsillectomies as the basis for a motion-study film. I confess, I find this as funny as it is appalling.

> As it turned out, Ernestine's tonsils were recessed and bigger than the doctor expected. It was a little messy to get at them, and Mr. Coggin, the movie cameraman, was sick in the waste basket.
>
> "Don't stop cranking," Dad shouted at him, "or your tonsils will be next. I'll pull them out by the roots, myself. Crank, by jingo, crank."

So, to be fair, he's kind of a dick to everyone!

Frank Gilbreth learned that he had a bad heart before his last two children were born and discussed with his wife the very real possibility that she would be widowed long before their brood had reached maturity.

> "But I don't think the doctors know what they're talking about," Dad said. [Of course not! The stupid doctors didn't even know how inefficiently they were performing surgery until Frank Gilbreth showed them his home movies of tonsillectomies.]
>
> Mother knew the answer Dad wanted.
>
> "I don't see how twelve children would be much more trouble than ten," she told him.

"Mother knew the answer Dad wanted." Am I the only one whose heart plunges a little at that sentence? At any rate, this telepathic empathy seems to have been the signature gift of Lillian Moller Gilbreth, who had a psychology degree. ("Although a graduate of the University of California, the bride is nonetheless an extremely attractive young woman," her own wedding announcement explained.) Frank Sr. first floats the "dozen" idea on their honeymoon, but she agrees readily. The single regret she voices is not insisting on hospital births until the delivery of her last child. She stays ten days. Can you blame her?

The chapters about Frank Gilbreth's death are truly moving, but *Cheaper* is ultimately more a series of set pieces than a cohesive story. There's just no larger narrative arc, which is why *Belles* is a more satisfying read. The Gilbreths were in real financial straits when their father died. Okay, they still had a full-time handyman and a place in Nantucket, but the younger children were on the verge of being dispersed to various relatives. Although she had been her husband's business partner and co-author, Lillian Gilbreth had to work hard to persuade their clients to stay with her. In turn, her oldest children—Anne, Ernestine, Martha, and Frank—took on enormous responsibilities within the household. *Belles*, like *Godfather Part II*, is that rare sequel that fulfills the original's promise. You can't understand the whole story unless you read both.

> There was a change in Mother after Dad died. A change in looks and a change in manners. Before her marriage, all Mother's decisions had been made by her parents. After the marriage, the decisions were made by Dad. . . .
>
> . . . While Dad lived, Mother was afraid of fast driving, of airplanes, of walking alone at night. When there was lightning, she went in a dark closet and held her ears. When things went wrong at dinner, she sometimes burst into tears and had to

leave the table. She made public speeches, but she dreaded them.

Now, suddenly, she wasn't afraid any more, because there was nothing to be afraid of. Now nothing could ever upset her because the thing that mattered most had been upset. None of us ever saw her weep again.

Well, I can't speak for Lillian Moller Gilbreth, but I am bawling my eyes out right now. Maybe it's hormones, which, come to think of it, are another reason women just can't do certain things.

A Little Princess
By Frances Hodgson Burnett
1905

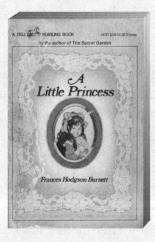

What's Mine Is Yours

Once on a dark winter's day, when the yellow fog
hung so thick and heavy in the streets of London
that the lamps were lighted and the shop windows blazed with gas as they do at night, an odd-
looking girl sat in a cab with her father and was
driven rather slowly through the big thoroughfare.

There are very few works of modern literature that successfully manage to link the possession of a large fortune to an

equally healthy moral compass—and fewer still that go ahead and make the correlation causative. Smoldering Mr. Darcy, whose just management of household wealth finally manages to earn the respect of Elizabeth Bennett (who then gets to live in that *house* . . .), is a rare standout amidst craven strivers like Becky Sharp or the hapless Hulots, who handle money about as skillfully as a greased hand negotiates an egg. It's unworthy money-grubbers who esteem Darcy for his money. Wiser personages, from his housekeeper to his dearest friend, esteem him for his money *management*.

But in the wealthy, intense bookworm Sara Crewe, author Frances Hodgson Burnett—who earlier, we determined, had a rather poisonous view of the spoils of empire—creates a character whose goodness not only equals her good fortune, but brings her fortune itself.

Sara, like *The Secret Garden*'s Mary Lennox, is a young girl brought up in colonial India, but unlike Mary, she's bright, inquisitive, and the daughter of a young, wealthy officer who adores her completely. (Her mother has been dead for many years.) As the novel commences, he's bringing her to London to enroll her in a fancy girls' school run by the odious, aptly named Miss Minchin, about whom we could write several essays alone. You will forgive me for turning immediately to the wardrobe her father provides Mary for her scholarly debut:

> There were velvet dresses trimmed with costly furs,
> and lace dresses, and embroidered ones, and hats
> with great, soft ostrich feathers, and ermine coats
> and muffs, and boxes of tiny gloves and handker-
> chiefs and silk stockings in such abundant supplies
> that the polite young women behind the counters

whispered to each other that the odd little girl with the big, solemn eyes must be at least some foreign princess—perhaps the little daughter of an Indian rajah.

Sigh . . . anyway. At the school, Sara is distinguished from the other well-to-do girls not only by trouncing whatever finery they have with her epic wardrobe, private playroom, and French maid, but also by subtler characteristics—her strange, compelling looks, her love of books, her ability to speak French, her warm, empathetic nature, and most of all, by her strong sense of fancy, which is regarded at turns as charming, immature, eccentric, and, to her likable, slightly thick friend Ermengarde, simply miraculous:

> "Yes," Sara answered. " . . . When I play I make up stories and tell them to myself. . . ."
> . . . Emengarde stopped short, staring, and quite losing her breath.
> "You make up stories!" she gasped. "Can you do that—as well as speak French? *Can* you?"
> Sara looked at her in simple surprise.
> "Why, anyone can make up things," she said. . . . Have you never pretended things?"
> "No," said Ermengarde. "Never. I—tell me about it."

Sara's ability to tell stories doesn't only prove a powerful attraction to the other girls in the school, who love to gather around to hear her make things up by the fire. (That crackling, India-financed grate!) Her creative mind also encourages her

to ruminate on her own circumstances, after which she concludes that much of her good nature may result only from private financing:

> Sara was praised for her quickness at her lessons, for
> her good manners, for her amiability to her fellow-
> pupils, for her generosity if she gave sixpence to a
> beggar out of her full little purse; the simplest thing
> she did was treated as if it were a virtue, and if she
> had not had a disposition and a clever little brain,
> she might have been a very self-satisfied young
> person. But the clever little brain told her a great
> many sensible and true things about herself and her
> circumstances, and now and then she talked these
> things over to Ermengarde as time went on:
>
> "Things happen to people by accident," she used
> to say. "A lot of nice accidents happened to me. It
> just happened that I always liked lessons and books,
> and could remember things when I learned them.
> It just happened that I was born with a father who
> was beautiful and nice and clever, and could give
> me anything I liked. Perhaps I have not really a
> good temper at all, but if you have everything you
> want and everyone is kind to you, how can you help
> but be good-tempered? I don't know"—looking
> quite serious—"how I shall ever find out whether I
> am really a nice child or a horrid one. Perhaps I'm
> a hideous child, and no one will ever know, just be-
> cause I never have any trials."

Was that a *dare*? Poor child, let me introduce you to the whole
"knock wood" thing! Sara will need that imagination, and the

ability to be rather dispassionate, in just a moment. Unfortunately, smack in the midst of her lavish birthday party, where among her gifts there were "lace collars and silk stockings and handkerchiefs; there was a jewel-case containing a necklace and tiara which looked quite as if they were made of real diamond; there was a long sealskin and muff; there were ball dresses and walking dresses and visiting dresses; there were hats and tea-gowns and fans. . . ." Where was I? Ah, yes. The terrible news, which is that not only is Captain Crewe dead of brain fever in the jungle, but that his entire fortune is gone, invested in a friend's diamond-mine venture that's gone smash.

Shockingly enough, this does not go over well with Miss Minchin:

"Where is Sara Crewe?"

Miss Amelia was bewildered.

"Sara!" she stammered. "Why, she's with the children in your room, of course."

"Has she a black frock in her sumptuous wardrobe?"—in bitter irony.

"A black frock?" Miss Amelia stammered again. "A *black* one?"

"She has frocks of every other color. Has she a black one?"

Miss Amelia began to turn pale.

"No—ye-es!" she said. "But it is too short for her. She has only the black velvet, and she has outgrown it."

"Go ahead and tell her to take off that preposterous pink silk gauze, and put the black one on, whether it is too short or not. She has done with finery!"

Then Miss Amelia began to wring her fat hands and cry.

"Oh, sister!" she sniffed. "Oh, sister! What can have happened?"

Miss Minchin wasted no words.

"Captain Crewe is dead," she said. "He has died without a penny. That spoiled, pampered, fanciful child is left a pauper on my hands."

So the same girl who, only weeks earlier, befriended the downtrodden housemaid Becky by telling her, " . . . We are just the same—I am only a little girl like you. It's just an accident that I am not you, and you are not me!" now finds that that is unfortunately this case. While Miss Minchin does not quite reduce Sara to Becky's level of wretchedness ("Becky is the scullery-maid. Scullery-maids—er—are not little girls."), she puts Sara to work immediately, banishing her to live in the attic along with Becky, where she too listens to rats scurry by night and by day, then heads off to tutor the children in French, runs horrible errands, and generally is plagued by anyone with the authority to plague her.

Fortunately, Sara finds that her ability to imagine, which once gave her the ability to be compassionate to people like Becky, now gives her the ability to muddle through her own troubles. Her bare quarters, she laughs bitterly to herself, are the ideal environment for flights of whimsy: "It's a good place to imagine in."

"You see," she said, "there could be a thick, soft blue Indian rug on the floor; and in that corner there could be a soft little sofa, with cushions to curl up on; and just over it could be a shelf full of books so that one could reach them easily; and there could be a fur rug before the fire, and hangings on the wall to cover up the whitewash, and pictures. They would have to be little ones, but they could be beautiful; and there could be a lamp with a deep rose-colored shade; and a table in the middle, with things to have tea with; and a little fat copper kettle singing on the hob; and the bed could be quite different. It could be made soft and covered with a lovely silk coverlet. It could be beautiful. And perhaps we could coax the sparrows until we made such friends with them that they would come and peck at the window and ask to be let in."

Some of Sara's imaginings try to give dignity and drama to the squalor—like the routine she makes up to pretend she and Becky are prisoners in the Bastille, or the notion that, tromping through the mud to pick up meat for the cook, she's in fact a soldier. But the one that endures is a fancy she's brought from her salad days—that she's a *princess*. Not the kind who lives among riches in a tower, but rather, the kind who labors quietly in disguise, brought down by some evil force, until she's revealed to be the true heir to the throne and ascends to her rightful place.

That sounds like a good way to go! In addition to giving her something to look forward to, knowing she's secretly a princess allows Sara to stand all of the abuse heaped on her by Miss Minchin and the other household help, who seem determined to grind her face in her fall from wealth as much as they can.

In fact, her imagination comes to mean life or death—

because for the one brief moment, confiding in her doll, Emily, she drops her charade, she loses her faith in her future entirely:

> "I can't bear this," said the poor child, trembling. "I know I shall die. I'm cold; I'm wet; I'm starving to death. I've walked a thousand miles today, and they have done nothing but scold me from morning until night. And because I could not find that last thing the cook sent me for, they would not give me any supper. Some men laughed at me because my old shoes made me slip down in the mud. I'm covered with mud now. And they laughed. Do you hear?"
>
> "You are nothing but a doll!" she cried; "nothing but a doll-doll-doll! You care for nothing. You are stuffed with sawdust. You never had a heart. Nothing could make you feel. You are a *doll*!"

But in a stroke of luck, a man from India, very wealthy, and very ill, moves in next door, and Sara is swept up in another tide of "supposing" about the mysterious gentleman that distracts her entirely from her rough circumstances. In one of my favorite scenes in literature, Sara trudges through the winter night, aching with hunger, and finds fourpence. Though she's starving herself, she stands by the princess code:

> "Suppose I had dry clothes on," she thought. "Suppose I had good shoes and a long thick coat and merino stockings and a whole umbrella. And suppose—suppose—just when I was near a baker's where they sold hot buns, I should find sixpence— which belonged to nobody. Suppose, if I did, I

should go into the shop and buy six of the hottest buns and eat them all without stopping."

. . . It was actually a piece of silver—a tiny piece trodden upon by many feet, but still with spirit enough left to shine a little. Not quite a sixpence, but the next thing to it—a four-penny piece.

. . . And then if you believe me, she looked straight at the shop directly facing her. And it was a baker's shop, and a cheerful, stout, motherly woman with rosy cheeks was putting into the window a tray of delicious newly baked hot buns, fresh from the oven—large, plump shiny buns, with currants in them.

Sigh! Okay:

"If I'm a princess," she was saying—"if I'm a princess—when they were poor and driven from their thrones—they always shared—with the populace—if they met one poorer and hungrier than themselves. They always shared. Buns are a penny each. If it had been sixpence I could have eaten six. . . ."

". . . See," she said, putting the bun in the ragged lap, "this is nice and hot. Eat it, and you will not feel so hungry."

The child started and stared up at her, as if such sudden, amazing good luck almost frightened her; then she snatched up the bun and began to cram it into her mouth with great wolfish bites.

"Oh, my! Oh, my!" Sara heard her say hoarsely, in wild delight. "*Oh, my!*"

Sara took out three more buns and put them down.

The sound in the hoarse, ravenous voice was awful.

"She is hungrier than I am," she said to herself. "She's starving." But her hand trembled when she put down the fourth bun. "I'm not starving," she said—and she put down the fifth.

This small act—as readers know—changes the course of that girl's life entirely. But it hasn't wrought the titanic change because Sara has been *good*. Giving away the buns IS good, of course, but Sara has only been able to do it for two reasons. First, her imagination has allowed her spirits up, which keep her heart open to others. Second, her imagination allows her to envision the circumstances of others—to feel them so strongly that she knows, even though she is wild with hunger, that the girl is starving.

I've always disliked the title of this book, because it seems to evoke a girl swathed in cloying, mincing pink, as far from the intense, intelligent Sara as one can be. Princesses in fairy tales are saved from drudgery because of something "princess-y" in their essential natures that is revealed as their birthright, but Sara acting like a polite princess changes little in those who would seek to destroy her. (Obviously, it completely enrages Miss Minchin beyond belief.)

And that's because being a princess is really only a vehicle for Sara. Although Miss Minchin thinks she puts on airs, Sara is not of the belief that she's inherently better than anyone else. Even if she was, what matters is that she's just able to *imagine* better than anyone else—which, in turn, makes her a better person. When a rat skitters out into her attic room, she doesn't kill it—she understands it: "I dare say it is rather hard to be a rat," she mused. "Nobody likes you. People jump and run away and scream out, 'Oh, a horrid rat!' I shouldn't like people to scream and jump and say, 'Oh, a horrid Sara!'"

That rat becomes her friend. Her imagination gives her power over others as well—not only to keep Miss Minchin at bay, but to find other friends—ones who, as in the ancient fairy tale, eventually restore her to her rightful place, all her diamond mines intact. But despite those diamonds, and despite the title, Burnett isn't arguing that holding a glass slipper to our hearts is the way to save ourselves. If we can learn anything from Sara, we should know it's this: Telling stories is.

All-of-a-Kind Family

By Sydney Taylor
1951

The L.E.S. Pinafore

There may be no better housecleaning scheme in all of literature than that found in an early scene in this series, the wonderful story of Ella, Charlotte, Sarah, Henny, and Gertie, five Jewish (what else?) girls growing up on New York's Lower East Side at the turn of the century. Okay, so here is Mama's method. To make sure the girls dust the entire front room, she places buttons for the girls to find in all the hard-to-find spots. When they find all the buttons, they have finished the room.

But wait! you ask. What about how once the girls find one

button (say, on a table leg) they might leave the rest of the table undusted? Well! You will be very happy to hear, as I was, that Mama is crafty, and in time, periodically places a few buttons on one item, or none, or a penny, to prevent just such an eventuality.

Phew. And now, we come to yet another deliriously fetishized vision of household labor, one in which young Gertie, given a gift of her choosing, pipes up, "I want a little washboard and a little tub so I can wash my dolly's clothes." (Well, I do, too.) Taylor hews to the Dickensian model of providing pretty much one event per chapter, preferably something illustration worthy, which means you can successfully call up the entire text by simply listing the chapter titles. (The Library Lady, Dusting is Fun, Rainy Day Surprise, Who Cares if t's Bedtime?, The Sabbath, Papa's Birthday, Purim Play, Sarah in Trouble, Mama Has Her Hands Full, Fourth of July, Family Outing, Succos, A New Charlie.) You're welcome.

Chapter 10

Panty Lines
I Can't Believe They Let Us Read This

Playing Hide-the-Library

You did it under covers, in the dead of night, hiding, hoping no one would walk in on you. You snuck off to do it, you did it when no one was home, you talked about doing it with your friends, laughing hysterically—and sometimes you even talked about the best parts of doing it at sleepovers, when it was the big elephant in the room. You knew there was nothing wrong with it, yet you felt vaguely dirty about it—like you'd be embarrassed if your parents knew you did it—and thinking about it now, you still feel slightly embarrassed about doing it, even though you know almost *everyone* does it. You—what's that?

No, I am talking about *reading dirty books*, you ninny. But I'm glad you brought that up—since you almost certainly learned about *that* by doing it, too.

In general I'm against book banning, but in the case of filthy literature, I'm all for it. How else would we find out which are the best ones? I think it's possible the *CW* generation might go so far as to set aside their disbelief at the outlandish idea of iceboxes, Walkmans, and corded phones to stand agog at the fact that, once, it was impossible to learn about coitus simply by turning on the TV. (Or the computer. Or *car radio*.)

No, those who needed to know what went where and how and when had to either have careless parents or very careful friends, the kind who could sneak a copy of *The Joy of Sex* off the nightstand and replace it before it was missed, or who could tuck a copy of *Wifey* between *Tuck Everlasting* and *Sounder* and slide it past the librarian for a supremely unwholesome threesome. And even more daring girls, the kind who knew about works like *The Group*, *The Secret Garden*, *Scruples*, *The Carpetbaggers*, *Kinflicks*, *The Thorn Birds*, even *The Godfather*—forget about it. Armed with a pen and the ability to dog-ear, they wrote their own ticket, ruling the playground, the lunchroom—let's face it, the world.

But, as we soon learned, many of these books (inexplicably) didn't require much sneaking at all. Take the works of V. C. Andrews, forty times as filthy as that toilet seat your mother was always warning you about. (Or, as Andrews might put it, "Filthier by thousandfold!") Alongside fat chocolate bars and gum, they hid in plain sight at the head of the grocery aisle, their spooky black covers with alabaster faces staring out like a ghost story by way of *Sweet Valley High*. ("Oh, honey. Well, only if you promise to finish *The Red Pony*.")

Or take the works of Norma Klein, which often just featured a moody-looking girl on the cover, perhaps one in the throes of the same crush as the ones on those other innocent paperbacks, or worried about a divorce or whatever—but certainly not posing *nude* for a Columbia professor, sleeping with her science teacher, or engaging in a lengthy flirtation with a senior citizen.

And don't even get me started on Jean M. Auel. *The Clan of the Cave Bear* and *Broud*? *Valley of the Horses* and the longest, hottest loss of virginity on record? *The Mammoth Hunters*, of the swaying pachyderms and other protuberant objects? Those three may have managed to sneak their way onto some *reading lists* seeking fictional works on the Paleolithic period. (Dinosaur bones!)

But my personal hiding-in-plain-site filth is *Jaws*. Who knew the word *pudenda* appeared in the first pages of *Jaws*? (Well, now you.) Who remembers that there's other splashes than the shark's, like the married woman shifting on a vinyl seat, worried she's so wet she'll drip through her dress before her lover shows up? (Hey, *I* didn't write it—talk to Peter J. Benchley!)

I often feel bad about *Forever*, the relatively tame love story that became the lightning rod for outlawed info for the underaged. Those mothers were onto *Forever*, that's for sure—for a while it was harder to get ahold of than *The Joy of Sex*. But on the other hand, I'm grateful. That classic playground Samizdat was sacrificed at the altar to all the reads we *did* get away with.

So. *Jaws*. Your kids will thank me later.

My Sweet Audrina
By V. C. Andrews
1988

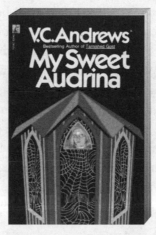

A Tale of Two Sisters

> There was something strange about the house where
> I grew up.

For those of you unfamiliar with V. C. Andrews's oeuvre (and pity you, poor souls!), she can best be described as the occultress of the way-too-familiar family, which, in her world, is a cloying blind, a knot of secrets in which the sensual spills over into the actionable in fairly short order. Instead of pedestrian pancake slicing, in an Andrews creation breasts jiggle ominously, bottoms are spanked until they are duly red, and flat chests produce buds that grow into full, swollen breasts against which men of all ages are helpless, especially if they are genetically linked to the breasts in question.

The Andrews heroine with whom most of you are likely familiar, is, of course, Cathy of *Flowers in the Attic*'s Dollenganger clan, a sister so unfortunate as to be locked up with her brother long enough to imprint herself on his prepubescent psyche, thus ruining him for other women forever. On a purely Best-in-Waiting-Room level, I have always favored Heaven of the Casteel clan, pure "hill trash" whose violet eyes and teeny waist propel her firmly out of Appalachia. But Audrina, the 9-year-old with a Swiss-cheese memory, ("prismlike"?) "chameleon" hair and, uh, violet eyes, always seemed the youthful template for these creations, a standalone whose story could be taken as a long exercise in how to write a 400-page book in which 90 percent of the events occur in one house.

When we meet Audrina Whitefern Adare, she is a lonely child living in the shadow of her older sister, who has died in apparently horrendous but unknown circumstances. With her in the huge, rambling mausoleum referenced above is her papa, a rakish tycoon, her mother, the beautiful Lucky, her dour aunt Ellsbeth, and Ellsbeth's daughter, Vera, a venomous slattern who is BAD NEWS BEARS for all involved.

Audrina is tortured by the fact that she has no memories of any of her childhood, and cannot keep track of time, finding that months have passed when she thinks only a week has gone by. Vera, of course, gives her hell about this, and also about the fact that Audrina is the great favorite of the household, while

Vera's own mother can barely tolerate her, to say nothing of the uncle and aunt upon whom they both depend. Audrina is also somewhat rattled by the fact that her father is given to locking her in her dead sister's room and making her rock in her dead sister's chair, apparently to access some special "gift," although Audrina only sees visions of being horribly ravished and left for dead under a "golden raintree," which sounds kind of like some eco-friendly detergent but is apparently not.

Into this mix soon come Audrina's love interest, Arden—yup, he's named "Arden"—as well as Arden's mother, Billie, a legless former skating champion who is shockingly beautiful with skin like porcelain. (In Andrews-land, all are preternaturally beautiful until you find their secret flaw: for Audrina, the aforementioned memory loss; Vera, bones so fragile they break if she falls; Lucky, a heart condition; and Sylvia, Audrina's retarded little sister, who is the cause of Lucky's dying in childbirth. Even Arden—so dedicated to Audrina he acquires a symbolic name to keep it at the top of your mind!—will turn out to be not what he seems.)

But in between finding out the grand mystery at the center of the novel, there's a lot of positively filthy stuff to keep you alert. Here's Papa castigating Lucky for her behavior at a dinner party he forces her to have in her sixth month of pregnancy: "You flirted, Lucietta. Flirted and in your condition, too. You cuddled so close to the teenage piano player on the bench you seemed blended into one person. You jiggled! Your nipples could be seen."

Gotta love that passive! This is followed, of course, by a whipping in bed Audrina sees through the keyhole, which she eventually decides is the cause of Sylvia's condition. Alongside the memory of her sister's rape, the following scene in which

Vera describes losing her virginity completes Audrina's sexual education:

> "I have seen a naked man, Audrina, a real one, not just a picture or an illustration. He is so hairy. You'd never suspect just how hairy by looking at him fully clothed. His hair travels from his chest down past his navel and runs into a point and keeps going and getting bushier until—"
>
> "Stop! I don't want to hear more."
>
> "But I want you to hear more. I want you to know what you're missing. It's wonderful to have all those nine inches stabbing into me. Did you hear me, Audrina? I measured it . . . almost nine inches, and it's swollen and hard."

Jesus *Christ*, this book was dirty! But in Andrews, the passages about sex are meted out with a strange primness, as in the scene where Arden's mother Billie winds up in bed with Papa:

> "They were in their underclothes, Arden's legless mother and my father, playing intimately with each other."

Jeez, you'd think by the time you socked the legless lady in bed with the dad, you could rock out with something more indelicate than "playing intimately with each other." (Maybe like "great gun cocked and aimed . . . ," another Vera contribution.) It still, however, breaks up the myriad scenes in which characters simply hurl backstory at each other like so many brickbats:

"Ellsbeth," shrieked Momma after some insult about the house she loved, "the problem with you is you're so damn jealous our father loved me better. You sit there and say ugly things about the house because you wish to God it belonged to you. Just as you cry your heart out each night, sleeping alone in your bed, or lying there restless and awake, jealous again because I always got what you wanted—when you could have had what I have if you'd kept your damned big mouth shut!"

"And you certainly know when to open your big mouth, Lucietta!" barked my aunt. "All your life wandering through this mausoleum and gushing about its beauty. Of course our father left this house to you and not to me. You made me want to vomit you were so sweet. You set out to rob me of everything I wanted. Even when my boyfriends came to call on me, you were there smiling and flirting. You even flirted with our father, flattering him so much you made me seem cold and indifferent. But I did all the work around here, and I still do! You prepare meals and you think that's enough. Well, it's not enough! I do everything else. I'm sick and tired of being everybody's slave! And if that's not enough, you're teaching your daughter your tricks!"

Well! There'll be a quiz on all this tomorrow. But rather than spoil all this for you, I'll simply defend Andrews's use of the purple—as well as our enthrallment to it—by saying that, as over the top as she was about it, Andrews depicted the internal experience of pubescence for girls with stunning precision: the dangerous, teeming sexuality implied in the smallest touch, and the knowledge that you are flying blind in a world where everyone knows more about who you've been and who you're becoming than you.

Whatever! You know you were just going to reread it for all the "swollen breast buds" parts, anyway.

The Clan of the Cave Bear

By Jean M. Auel
1980

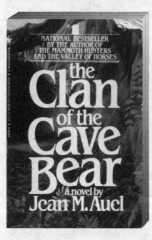

Ayla Kicks Ass

By Cecily von Zeigesar

When I was 11 or 12 I tore through *The Clan of the Cave Bear* by Jean M. Auel in a matter of hours. The book was full of information I hadn't found in any other book—information about the relationship between men and women in particular. Nudge, nudge.

Fundamentally, *The Clan of the Cave Bear* is a coming-of-age story, about a young girl, Ayla, who loses her family after an earthquake. Wandering lost and alone and nearly dead from starvation, Ayla is eventually found and adopted by cavemen from the Clan of the Cave Bear. She soon learns to talk like them, with grunts and hand motions. She learns to behave like them, sticking to her adoptive family's hearth and helping them with their work, the work of survival. She becomes a medicine woman, taught by her adoptive mother. She learns to hunt with a sling by watching the older men teach the younger boys. And, at the age of 11or 12 (the clan do not count past 10), the same age I was when I first encountered the book, she gives birth.

Of course the part when Ayla gets pregnant in the first place is what I thought I remembered most about the book. At that age I hadn't read any books with sex scenes or even allusions to sex in them. Nothing could have been more exciting than caveman sex! It was raw and naked and dirty and fast, and I couldn't believe I was reading it.

I've been reading a lot of boring books lately, so when I decided to reread *The Clan of the Cave Bear*, I was eager for the caveman-sex part. I even hid the cover of the book from passersby on the subway, worried that they'd know just how juicy the book was because I'd be blushing while I was reading it. I glanced at my neighbors constantly to see if they were reading ahead. Had they come upon any exciting words, like "throbbing organ," yet?

The thing was, I never found that juicy sex scene. The disturbing passage below is the one I remembered reading when I was a girl:

> She was nearly unconscious when he threw her over on her face, feverishly ripped her wrap aside, and spread her legs. With one hard thrust, he penetrated deeply. She screamed with pain. It added to his plea-

sure. He lunged again, drawing forth another painful cry, then again, and again. The intensity of his excitement urged him on, rising quickly to unbearable peaks. With a last hard drive that extracted a final agonized scream, he ejected his built-up heat.

It's a rape scene. Ayla is nearly killed. Even my 11-year-old self must have recognized that she wasn't exactly consenting and she certainly wasn't having any fun. Disappointed—in my young self, in my memory of what I had thought was a fun, at-the-beach sort of book—I read on. And even the second time around I found I could not put the book down. Not because of the sex, but because of the way it shows a young girl figuring her shit out. In particular, Ayla figures out shit about not taking shit from guys. And I started to think that maybe, just maybe, the book was so memorable to me because it's *empowering*.

Sure the book is about hairy bigheaded grunting cavemen in the early days of man, but the lessons still apply. The cave women bow and shuffle and serve the men. The cave women prepare the food but aren't allowed to hunt. They're isolated during their monthly "curse." Cavemen were allowed to beat cave women when they did not do as they were told, and even when they gave the cavemen dirty looks. And cavemen were allowed to relieve their "urges" whenever they felt like it with whomever they wanted, not just with their mates. Little boys even stuck it inside little girls just for fun, and the author goes into detail about how most little girls' hymens were broken during this sort of horseplay. *Hello?*

Ayla refuses to take it. She tries very hard to fit in and act like a good cave woman is supposed to, but she just can't. She speaks her mind. She becomes a better hunter than any of the men, and she makes herself indispensable to the clan by becoming the best medicine woman they ever had. She never mates (that's "getting married" to us evolved persons). In the end, when the jerk who raped her, the father of her son, gives her the death curse and boots her out of the clan, she tells him to go rip himself a new one. And then she's off, on her own, and I, the reader, am left at the end of the book with the feeling that she's only just getting started.

As a girl I always shied away from books that taught obvious lessons, thinking them too preachy and unsubtle. It's something I'm very careful of in my writing, too. There's nothing worse than a book that shoves a message down its reader's throat. Even the word *empowering* makes me cringe. But I have to give my younger self credit. I may have been in it for the sex, but I came out of it feeling like a natural woman.

Wifey

By Judy Blume
1978

JUDY BLUME's
Wifey
An Adult Novel

THE NATIONAL BESTSELLER
OF A VERY NICE HOUSEWIFE WITH
A VERY DIRTY MIND
OVER 3 MILLION COPIES SOLD!

Rejecting the Norm

Sandy sat up in bed and looked at the clock. Damn!

Can someone please explain this five-course multiple-orgasm thing to me? I am not a tyro at the buffet table—but I still would like someone to iterate the exact circumstances under which one would be able to claim one had enjoyed "Breakfast, lunch, dinner, and a snack." The source of the question in question is one Sandy Schaedal, a housewife in Plainfield, New Jersey, flush in the middle of late-1960s Jewish suburbia, wherein which the children of hardworking, Depression-era parents are suddenly experiencing all that club memberships, trips to the Bahamas, open marriages, and browned chicken from Elegant but Easy cookbooks can add to the quota of human happiness.

When we encounter Sandy, she's just recovered from a serious bout of classic debilitating housewife hysteria, and is at the end of her rope with her husband, Norm, the upright, uptight owner of a chain of dry-cleaning stores. Norm is the kind of tidy husband who asks Sandy to keep track of his dog's "sticks" and "wees," likes his (browned) chicken on Wednesdays and his sex on Saturdays, and chooses to retire to his side of their twin beds every night, joined only by one headboard:

> One bed for Norman, with cool, crisp sheets, preferably changed twice a week, not that he didn't want fresh ones daily . . . and one bed for Sandy, where, once a week, on Saturday nights, if she didn't have her period, they did it. A Jewish nymphomaniac. They fucked in her bed, then Norman went to the bathroom to wash his hands and penis, making Sandy feel dirty and ashamed. He'd climb into his own bed then, into his clean, cool sheets, and he'd fall asleep in seconds, never any tossing, turning, sighing. Never any need to cuddle, or laugh quietly with her. Three to five minutes from start to finish. She knew. She's watched the digital bedside clock often enough. Three to five minutes. Then he'd say, "Very nice, did you get your dessert?"
>
> "Yes, thank you, dessert was fine."
>
> . . . She's learned to come in minutes, seconds if she had to, and she almost always made it twice. No problem there. She almost always got her

main course and her dessert. But usually it was a
TV dinner and Oreo when she craved scampi and
mousse au chocolat.

Conjured up like some priapic avatar of her most unseemly
desires, Sandy has of late been haunted by an odd type of
ghost, who conforms to his kind only in that he, too, sports a
white sheet (hospital variety). Briefly, there is a man who drives
up on her lawn with a motorcycle wearing a Stars-and-Stripes
helmet who masturbates on the lawn, then departs with a wave.
(Norm's comment after the first incident: "The motorcycle: Did
it leave ridges in the lawn?")

Naturally, this cannot stand, but Sandy's life simply as the
mother of two children, Jen and Bucky, who are now away at
camp, has left room for the kind of whole rampant for over-
examination, both mental and physical, that needs to find its
outlet somewhere—which it has, in a raging itch that's taken
over her nether regions. Asked by her brother-in-law, a gyne-
cologist (no comment), about whether or not it might be psy-
chosomatic, she replies, "I don't think I can discuss it with you,
Gordon. . . . I don't think I could discuss the subject at all."

Except, of course, with the reader:

My sex life? Oh, you mean my sex life. Yes. Well.
Let's see. Ummmm, if you want to judge it strictly
on the basis of orgasms it's fine. Terrific. That is,
I masturbate like crazy, Gordon. You wouldn't
believe how I masturbate. God, I'm always at it.
Driving here, for instance, this morning . . . Driving,
get that, in traffic, no less . . . Not, not the Cadillac,
Norm took that to work. The Buick . . . driving the
Buick . . . I hear this song on the radio . . . from my

youth, Gordy, like when I was seventeen or something . . . Blue velvet, bluer than velvet was the night.
. . . It reminds me of Shep . . . and I get this feeling in
my cunt . . . this really hot feeling . . . and just a little
rubbing with one hand . . . just a little tickle, tickle
on the outside on my clothes . . . just one-two-three
and that's enough . . . I'm coming and I don't even
want to come yet because it feels so good . . . I want
it to last. And guess what, Gordy? I never itch after
I come that way. I itch only after Norman. So, you
see, it must have something to do with him. Maybe
I am allergic to his semen . . . maybe I'm allergic to
his cock . . . maybe I'm allergic to him!

But Sandy isn't only chafing (literally) at Norm but also
her good-housewife place in the late–1960s culture as a
whole, which is erupting into all kinds of nasty itchings and
burnings, both racial and sexual. Unbeknownst to Norm, a
stalwart member of the Young Republicans, Sandy has actually voted for Kennedy, for whom she sits shiveh, to Norm's
consternation, tossing sheets over the mirrors in the house.
("Jesus Christ, now you're going Orthodox?") When, at the
urging of her traditionally good-looking, well-adjusted sister,
Myra, the couple joins the area's exclusive Club, Norman
immediately joins the grievance committee and kills on the
tennis court while Sandy struggles through golf lessons, idly
fantasizing about Roger, the club's golf pro and only black face
on the scene, noting that the only part of the lesson she enjoys
is when he stands behind her and wraps his arms around her
to show her how to hold the club.

She also has very little in common with Myra's friends,
who radiate health and wealth in equal proportions, in con-

trast with her sickly, uncoordinated, secretly sex-craving self. At one of Myra's parties, meeting her tennis-playing buddies, Sandy gets embroiled in a conversation about moving from increasingly black Plainfield to willfully white Watchung:

> Sandy thought she might like Funky, with a bandana tied around her head, loaded down with Indian jewelry, best, until they got into a discussion about Plainfield.
>
> "Plainfield, my God!" Funky said. "I thought Plainfield was all black."
>
> "Not quite."
>
> "You mean not yet! If I were you, I'd get out while the going's good and move up to the Hills. . . . In Watchung you could send them to public school. We have only two black families in town and both are professional."
>
> "It's really not a racial thing," Brown said, joining them. "It's more of a socioeconomic thing, don't you think?"
>
> "Yes and no," Funky said. "Yes, in the sense that professional ones tend to think more like us and want what's best for their children. No, in the sense that they're still different no matter how hard you try to pretend they're not. I mean, put one in this room, right now, and suddenly we'd all clam up." She took a cheese puff from the tray offered by Elena, the black maid. "Thank you."

Sandy is no social revolutionary, but she's also not particularly invested in her own upward mobility—and therefore not invested in keeping others down. She's not about to join the

Black Panthers—her sense of injustice is far more internal, a mordant irony that she only expresses to herself. (Remembering how the one time Norman tried to give her oral sex he had to gargle with Listerine for a half hour, she quips to herself, "That's why I douche with vinegar . . . cunt vinaigrette . . . to make it more appetizing . . . you know, like browned chicken.") However, in the days where feminism ("Women's libbers," to Norm. "Dykes who want to be on top.") is located only in encounter groups in a Manhattan that may as well be 2000 miles instead of 20 minutes away, Sandy has only her fantasies to rebel with—until they slide, as it were, very easily into reality.

Her first affair is with her brother-in-law, Gordy, and occurs at one of Myra's blowout parties, when Sandy goes into a room to rest and finds herself assailed by a very drunk Gordy, who is endearingly straightforward: "I've always wanted you, Sandy . . . always loved your little ass . . . your cunt . . . every time I examine you I want it . . . want to kiss it . . . to fill it. . . ." Her second is with Shep, the boy she didn't marry because her mother never thought he'd go anywhere. "You can't eat handsome!" Actually, Mother, you can, Sandy thinks, remembering:

> Still, she dreamed of Shep. She dreamed of kissing him there and over midwinter vacation had a sudden urge to take him in her mouth. What was she going to do about these disgusting thoughts? Decent people, normal people, didn't do those things . . . didn't even think about them. Shep was perverted. But she let him do that to her. Just once. And oh, it was so good. Like nothing she had ever experienced. She came over and over, as he licked and kissed and buried his face in her. Until she

cried, "Stop . . . please stop . . . I can't take any
more. . . ."

. . . And then he kissed her face and she tasted
herself on him. And she liked it.

Sandy's fantasies—and subsequent affairs—aren't because
she's a nymphomaniac, but rather because she's trying to resolve the two things about Norm she can't reconcile: his liking
for the rigid class code of the Club, and his liking for an equally
rigid sex life, where his irritation with Sandy's needs, his inability to give love, leaves her, appropriately enough, irritated
("Norman, do you love me?" "I'm here, aren't I?"). Gordy,
sister-in-law fucker though he may be, is not a pervert—he's
just as depressed with the code of the Club as Sandy is. ("You
know something, Sandy, I hate this fucking house, this stupid
party.") And though Sandy would like to convince herself that
she would have had a very different life with Shep, she finally
has to admit that it would have entailed the same things as her
life with Norm—the Club, kids, car pools—and their same
deadening effects.

The flap copy calls Sandy "a very nice housewife with a very
dirty mind," but in fact she's neither. Sandy, cosseted by a life
of leisure that's become a straightjacket, buffeted by fucking on
the brain, is very, very normal. "So where did things go wrong,
Norm?" she thinks, lying in bed. "So what happened? Comfortable. Safe. We had our babies. We made a life together. But
now I'm sick. . . . And I'm so fucking scared! . . . Oh mother,
dammit! Why did you bring me up to think this is what I
wanted? And now that I know it's not, what I am I supposed
to do about it?"

It would have been very easy to make Norm the enemy
here, and, truthfully, the husband who rants about women's

libbers—who tells Sandy she doesn't know how good she has it, then responds to her entreaty that she could get a job with, "Your first duty is to make a home for me and the kids. After that, you want a little part-time job, it's fine with me"—is grounds for massive enragement.

But after Sandy gets gonorrhea and has to tell Norman about her affairs, she finds a cache of letters written from an ex-girlfriend in the attic:

> She had a sudden desire to call Brenda, to ask her what Norman had really been like way back then. Because she could see now that there must have been another Norman. A Norman who dreamed of becoming a biologist . . . of saving the world. A Norman who loved intensely. Could that Norman still be locked inside the Norman she knew, just as another Sandy was inside her, struggling to get out?

You bet your ass! In fact, America of 1970 is a nation of Norms, struggling to reconcile their golf shoes with riots in Newark. At age 8, I'd never noticed the epigraph to the book, which is a quote from *Good Times* by Peter Joseph. "In terms of affluence," it reads, "America in the 60s reached a stage that other societies can only dream of." It's no surprise that the mystery masturbator wears a Stars-and-Stripes helmet. *Wifey* isn't a novel of raunch—it's a novel about two Americas, the old 1950s model and the long-haired 1970s edition that suddenly need to resolve Sandy's greatest complaint: "Paying isn't caring, Norman."

But caring is caring, and that's what Norman and Sandy find out they both do. Shattered by Sandy's betrayal, Norm doesn't throw her out but instead makes a surprising offer:

"We could get a double bed. I know you've always wanted one." (He also agrees to try oral sex after being told by Sandy, "I think you have to develop a taste for it, Norm, like lobster.") Surprisingly, Sandy hasn't gone mad on her bed in a room of yellow wallpaper. She's made several beds, and she's lain in every single one. God Bless America!

The Clan of the Cave Bear
By Jean M. Auel
1980

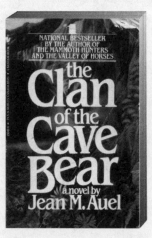

Do the Wild Thing

The naked child ran out of the hide-covered lean-to toward the rocky beach at the bend in the small river. It didn't occur to her to look back.

Somewhere around my 80th reading of *By the Shores of Silver Lake*, I halted on a scene that, after waxing rhapsodic on sparkling glass panes wrapped in brown paper and a clean-smelling, yellow pine floor freshly scoured with sand, lingered inordinately on the matter of the new straw ticking for Ma and

Pa's bed. The cause of the halt was the revelation that, though it was placed behind a curtain, the bed was crowded in the room with not only the coal stove freshly covered with blacking and the brindle bulldog, Jack, but three daughters all blessed with perfect hearing, crackling on their own straw ticking. By this point in the scene, Ma had sunk, sighing with pleasure, into her new bed and was pronouncing it divine. "Mom," I asked (my mom was good about stuff like this). "MOM. Do you think they had sex that night?"

"Oh, absolutely!" my mother said. (Told you she was good about stuff like this.)

It's unsurprising that a series that engages so profoundly with the sensual in the ordinary life—butter thickly clotting, fish violently flopping, cotton palpably stiffening—might at some point arouse in the young reader the revelation that its characters were probably clotting, flopping, and stiffening along with their visual accoutrement, but obviously, Wilder was unable, for numerous reasons, moral and cultural, to really follow through on this. And that's where authors like Jean M. Auel come in.

The Clan of the Cave Bear, the first of the "Earth's Children" quartet, is the story of Ayla, a 4-year-old *Homo sapiens* girl who, after a dreadful earthquake, loses her family and almost dies, until she is rescued by the Neanderthal medicine woman, Iza, one of the Clan of the Cave Bear. On a line-by-line, chapter-by-chapter view, *The Clan of the Cave Bear* is the pinnacle of dawn-of-mankind porn—leather thongs, bison, chewed roots, cozy fires over the hearth—with a riot of detailed explication that makes the simple butter-churning passages of Wilder look like a phone book. (When you launch with a taxonomy of the different fibers used to absorb baby shit, you win by default immediately.) However, on a large scale, *The Clan of the Cave*

Bear is much more: a novel of a dying breed set up against a new one, but, more important, how gender relations lie at the heart of this changing world.

And Ayla, a gangly, blond, sky-eyed child stuck with the wrong race, is the avatar for all this tumult. Auel immediately makes us aware of the lowly position of women in the clan: Iza has to kneel before Brun, the leader—as all women do when approaching a man—to plead her case for keeping the girl. While thinking it over, he ruminates, "But medicine woman or not, she's just a woman. What difference will it make if she's upset?" which pretty much sums up the position of women in the clan, who walk softly and carry sticks to dig roots while the men carry big spears and can beat them, have sex with them or treat them equally, as they choose.

Auel's position on all this is not to condemn entirely, as she explains that the Neanderthals' lack of capacity for change, which allows them to retain the memory of the entire race in one person, is also how nature has decided to let them survive. Men hunt because they've always hunted, women know roots because they always have, and it's awesome because you don't have to reinvent the wheel—which in fact hasn't been invented at all—every time a new generation is born.

But Ayla upsets this whole apple cart. Apparently, the Others—the clan's name for the *Homo sapiens* new on the scene—are different. The Mog-Ur, the great spiritual leader and Iza's brother, eventually recalls how an Other man that lived with them once was different—he liked to talk to men and women, and had great respect for the medicine woman, on par with that for the men. First off, Ayla, mauled by a cave lion, has the totem of that powerful beast, which makes the tribe worry that she can't have children, since "they would fight off the impregnating essence" of a man with a weaker totem. (Plan T!) She quickly surpasses Mog-Ur in simple math when he decides to explain numbers one day. She sees the men playing with slingshots and learns to hunt, a crime punishable by death in the clan.

And, over and over again, because she has been lucky for the Clan, she is forgiven these crimes and they are incorporated into their lives—to the head-splitting rage of the tribe leader's son, Broud.

BROUD! Omigod, BROUD! There's just no way anyone good is named Broud. Spoiled, swaggering, petulant and, you know, proud, braggart Broud has hated Ayla ever since she stole his thunder at his first hunt ceremony by being given the cave lion totem. The more of a man's rights she is given, the more enraged Broud is—especially as the elders of the clan respect her increasing worth to the tribe as both a hunter and skilled medicine woman as much as or more than they respect him.

And here's where the sex comes in! I don't have to tell you all the sexual stuff in *The Clan of the Cave Bear* is kind of horribs, since Auel, in this first work, hasn't quite yet realized she can have fun with the sex stuff, too, as she did in the epic all *Homo sapiens* 20-page sex scene where Ayla loses her "virginity" (more on that in a sec) to Jondular in *Valley of the Horses* or all the fur-covered rutting and breast-baring happening in *The Mammoth Hunters*, where Ayla is torn between Jondular and Ranec, a kind of Paleolithic Obama with ties to both Africa and Asia, insofar as those land-masses were happening. And the ladies with red-tinged feet, who are high slatterns of the temple. ANYWAY!

Most horribly, and most pertinently, Ayla is brought low just as she's reached the crest of her status in the tribe and her sexual development:

The Woman Who Hunts earned the full title during the winter that began her tenth year. Iza felt a private satisfaction and a small sense of relief when she noticed the changes in the girl that heralded the onset of menarche. Ayla's spreading hips and the two bumps swelling her chest, changing the contours of her child's straight body, assured the medicine woman that her unusual daughter was not doomed to a life in permanent childhood after all. Swelling nipples and a light sprinkling of pubic and underarm hair were followed by Ayla's first menstrual flow; the first time the spirit of her totem battled with another.

Ayla understood now that it was unlikely she would ever give birth; her totem was too strong. . . .

Not so fast, Ayla. Unfortunately, babies are not actually made by the battling of random tribe totems, but you're going to figure that out anyway, because you're *Homo sapiens* and your brain is capable of intuitive leaps based on observable data, but anyway. Broud? You were saying?

He looked around, then down at the woman sitting at his feet, waiting with unruffled composure for him to get on with his rebuke and be on his way. She's worse than ever since she became a Woman, he thought. . . . What can I make her do? . . . Wait, she's a woman now, isn't she? There's something I can make her do.

Broud gave her a signal, and Ayla's eyes flew open. It was unexpected. Iza told her men only wanted that from women they considered attractive; she knew Broud thought she was ugly. . . . He signaled her again, imperiously, to assume the position so he could relieve his needs, the position for sexual intercourse . . .

Ayla knew what was expected . . . Many young girls of the Clan were pierced by pubescent boys who lingered in the limbo of not-yet-men, before their first kill; and occasionally a man, beguiled by a young coquette pleased himself with a not-quite-ripe female . . . Within a society that indulged in sex as naturally as they breathed, Ayla was still a virgin.

The young woman felt awkward; she knew she must comply, but she was flustered and Broud was enjoying it. He was glad he had thought of it; he had finally broken down her defenses. It excited him to see her so confused and bewildered, and aroused him . . .

Broud got impatient, pushed her down, and moved aside his wrap exposing his organ, thick and throbbing . . . She's so ugly, she should be honored, no other man would have her, he thought angrily, grabbing at his wrap to move it out of the way as his need grew. . . .

But as Broud closed in on her, something snapped. She couldn't do it! She just couldn't. Her reason left her. It didn't matter that she was supposed to obey him. She scrambled to her feet and started to run. Broud was too quick for her. He grabbed her, pushed her down, and punched her in the face, cutting her lip with his hard fist. He was beginning to enjoy this. Too many times had he restrained himself when he wanted to beat her, but there was no one to stop him here. And he had justifiable reason—she was disobeying him, actively disobeying him . . .

She was nearly unconscious when he threw her over on her face, feverishly ripped her wrap aside, and spread her legs. With one hard thrust, he penetrated deeply. She screamed with pain. It added to his pleasure. He lunged again, drawing forth another painful cry, then again, and again. The intensity of his excitement urged him on, rising quickly to unbearable peaks. With a last hard drive that extracted a final agonized scream, he ejected his built up heat.

Well! Smell you, Nancy Drew! That is where dawn-of-mankind porn slips right into PORN, I guess—which is probably a good 85 percent of why THIS STUFF IS COMPLETELY ADDICTING. (You don't really get any kinkier than human/Neanderthal sex.) But I do think you can differentiate the books from other fur-wrap rippers by the fact that *The Clan of the Cave Bear* is not only about some overheated welter where both the earth and the beings upon it rumble with ecstasy and agony and split on a regular basis. On a fundamental level, it's about sex not for sex's sake but for how it interacts with our lives—how Ayla suffers to keep the baby that results from Broud's raping her and her status as hunter and medicine woman, and how, in the next few novels, she strives to find a partner not only of her own kind, but of her own *kind*—an equal partner that appreciates Ayla the species and Ayla the woman. As the novel ends, Brun berates Broud for having brought chaos and dishonor to the clan by his treatment of Ayla: "She was a woman, and she had more courage than you, Broud, more determination, more self-control. She was more man than you are. Ayla should have been the son of my mate." Doesn't quite have the ring of "Like a fish needs a bicycle," but a good dawn-of-mankind start nonetheless.

Flowers in the Attic
By V. C. Andrews
1979

He Ain't Sexy, He's My Brother

Truly, when I was very young, way back in the fifties, I believed all of life would be like one long and perfect summer day. After all, it *did* start out that way.

About a decade ago, bouncing around a bookstore with my best friend, I ascertained with increasing horror that she had somehow managed to plow through the field of YA literature from the 19th through the 20th centuries without seeding any

V. C. Andrews. "You have to read this!" I said, shaking *Flowers in the Attic* at her frantically, disturbing the other Eileen Fisher-clad patrons. "Uh-huh," she said, turning over some Alan Shapiro to read the back. "No, really!" I pressed. It is a testament to her forbearance that, after she passed on buying the book and I insisted on buying it FOR her, she suffered me enough to open it and read the first page. At which point she immediately ceased to respond to all communications until she had reached the last one.

What is it that makes V. C. Andrews, and particularly *Flowers in the Attic*, so compelling? The story of Cathy Dollenganger, nee Foxworth, and her siblings, Chris, Cory, and Carrie, *Flowers in the Attic* is the compelling story of a family's betrayal and heartbreak, love and revenge, apparently. (See above.) More precisely, it is the story of a blond, Dresden-doll family torn apart after the death of a father—and a mother who sacrifices her own children to get a massive inheritance she finds she loves more than her own flesh and blood.

WHY do I not have a successful career as a flap-copy writer? Anyway, when we meet the Dollenganger clan, they are in the waning days of their picture-perfect life. Cathy, at 12, is an aspiring ballerina, while Chris, her older brother, is a brainy know-it-all who delights in tormenting her. (More on that later.) The young twins, Carrie and Cory, are not that interesting. (They are twins, etc.) And the parents, Christopher and Corrine, are possessed of a shattering beauty as well as an icky, overarching sensuality:

> Our father was perfect. He stood six feet two, weighed 180 pounds, and his hair was thick and flaxen blond, and waved just enough to be per-

fect; his eyes were cerulean blue and sparkled with laughter. . . .

Yada yada yada, await the yick:

> His booming greeting rang out as soon as he put down his suitcase and briefcase. "Come greet me with kisses if you love me!"
> Somewhere near the front door, my brother and I would be hiding, and after he'd called out his greeting, we'd dash out from behind a chair or the sofa to crash into his wide open arms, which seized us up at once and held us close, and he warmed our lips with his kisses. . . .
> . . . Love was a word lavished about in our home. "Do you love me?—For I most certainly love you; did you miss me?—Are you glad I'm home?—Did you think about me when I was gone? Every night? Did you toss and turn and wish I were behind you, holding you close? For if you didn't, Corrine, I might want to die."

BEST argument for fathers having to work such long hours in a coal mine is that they come home and start drinking in front of the TV immediately, EVER. But Corrine, the mother—Cathy's model for womanity—is no better. Without any employment other than maintaining her beauty, she shows Cathy precisely how a woman grooms herself to maintain a husband's interest:

> On Fridays, Momma spent half the day in the beauty parlour having her hair shampooed and set

and her fingernails polished, and then she'd come home to take a long bath in perfumed-oil water. I'd perch in her dressing-room, and watch her emerge in a filmy negligee. She'd sit at her dressing-table to meticulously apply make-up. And I, so eager to learn, drank in everything she did to turn herself from just a pretty woman into a creature so ravishingly beautiful she didn't look real. The most amazing part of this was our father thought she DIDN'T wear make-up! He believed she was naturally a striking beauty.

Lying whore betrayer! Seriously, she is. You'll see. Because, after her husband's untimely death, she is shortly going to lock her children in the attic of her parents' estate—" . . . My parents are rich! Not middle-class rich, or upper-class rich! but very, very rich! Filthy, unbelievably, sinfully rich!" Wait, what are they?—in order to wile her way back into her father's good graces, which she fell out of after marrying her half-uncle and presumably bearing their Devil's Issue. (I hate it when that happens!)

As Corrine brings the children to the enormous, grim estate, her stated plan to her four charges is as follows: They'll hang out for a few days until she prepares her father to meet them. Then they'll charm him with their blond perfection, he'll write them into the will, and everyone will be happy and blond. Or, she'll just charm him and he'll die, which is the preferred plan.

What they haven't banked on is the grandmother who greets them:

Her nose was an eagle's beak, her shoulders were wide, and her mouth was like a thin, crooked knife slash. Her dress, a grey taffeta, had a diamond brooch at the throat on a high, severe neckline. Nothing about her appeared soft or yielding; even her bosom looked like twin hills of concrete.

Not only does this modern Miss Minchin have a bad attitude, she seems to have a bad view of the children: namely, that they are Devil's spawn. As she leads them through a long list of do's and don'ts that includes always brushing one's teeth, never opening the blinds, and staring at the Bible to try to absorb the "purity of the Lord and his ways," the children begin to cotton on to the fact that something is amiss: "Eight: if I ever catch boys and girls using the bathroom at the same time, I will quite relentlessly, and without mercy, peel the skin from your backs."

Okay first, who WANTS to use the bathroom with someone at the same time—to say nothing of using it with a BOY? But the senior Mrs. Foxworth will not be put off:

"They're only children," Momma flared back with unusual fire. "Mother, you haven't changed one bit, have you? You still have a nasty, suspicious mind! Christopher and Cathy are innocent!"

"Innocent?" she snapped back, her mean look so sharp it could cut and draw blood. "That is exactly what your father and I always presumed about you and your half-uncle!"

Finding out you're your own first cousin . . . I HATE it when that happens!

And thus begins a long series of days that stretch from two or three into, I don't know, FOUR YEARS, during which the

children subsist on a daily diet of cold bacon, toast, jelly sandwiches, warm milk, and fried chicken; are almost forced to eat
mice; make a paper garden in the attic, and slowly grow thin
and spindly along with the flowers they have placed in the wan
sun. Corrine's response to this treatment is to continue to buy
them more games and expensive clothing, and assure them
that the father is about to die, and they are going to lose their
investment if they rush things now: "Just have patience. Be understanding! And what fun you lose now, I'll make up to you
later, a thousandfold!"

This is all very well, except for how being locked alone in a
room for four years, cast as the de facto parents of the twins,
Cathy and Chris begin to have a shaky sense of their own roles
as well:

> Now the twins ran to me with their small cuts and
> bruises, and the splinters garnered from the rotten
> wood in the attic. I carefully plucked them out with
> tweezers. Chris would apply the antiseptic, and the
> adhesive plaster they both loved. An injured small
> finger was enough to demand cuddly-baby thing,
> and lullabies sung as I tucked them into bed, and
> kissed their faces, and tickled where laughter had
> to be freed. Their thin little arms wrapped tightly
> around my neck. I was loved, very loved, and
> needed.

I have always wondered if Andrews's continued use of the
passive voice is what creates such an urgent air of mystery
around her characters, as if whatever agents of activity afoot,
unspecified, might not belong to the agents in question but to
the grim finger of fate. And they are completely without any

control over their circumstances—not over the grandfather who won't die, the grandmother who won't stop beating them, or the mother who is showing up increasingly less often.

Worst of all, however, is the problem arising that no one can control—Chris and Cathy's burgeoning sexuality:

> I was coming alive, feeling things I hadn't felt before. Strange achings, longings. Wanting something, and not knowing what it was that woke me up at night, pulsating, throbbing, excited, and knowing a man was there with me, doing something I wanted him to complete, and he never did . . . he never did. . . .

Tell me about it, sister. But Cathy, who is the only child cynical enough to see that her mother has no intention of ever letting them out ("It was my way to turn over all that glittered and look for the tarnish") is unable to see her brother (sorry) coming:

> We were not always modest in the bedroom, nor were we always fully dressed. . . . None of us cared very much who saw what.
> We should have cared.
> We should have been careful. . . .
> . . . "It would help if you weren't so near, so un-available."

Okay, Cathy. Just, whatever you do, don't sleep with your brother. Don't sleep with your bro—

> He yelled out something like, "You're mine, Cathy! Mine! You'll always be mine! No matter who comes

into your future, you'll always belong to me! I'll make you mine . . . tonight . . . now!

I had the strong dancer's legs, he had the biceps and greater weight . . . and he had much more determination than I to use something hot, swollen and demanding, so much that it stole reasoning and sanity from him.

And I loved him. I wanted what he wanted—if he wanted it that much, right or wrong.

Somehow we wound up on that old mattress—that filthy, smelly stained mattress that must have known lovers long before this night. And that is where he took me, and forced in that swollen, rigid male sex part of him that had to be satisfied. It drove into my tight and resisting flesh which tore and bled.

I can confirm how impossible it is to attempt to maintain the reader's interest without lapsing into narrative Red-Bulls-like incest, beatings, poison, and disgusting lies. (My character had to be content with doing a lot of cleaning.) But the stifling scenes depicted in *Flowers in the Attic*—and all of Andrews— take soap opera to a new level. Cathy tells Chris:

Chris, soap opera people are like us—they seldom go outdoors. And when they do, we only hear about it, never see it. They loll about in living-rooms, bed-rooms, sit in the kitchens and sip coffee or stand up and drink Martinis—but never, never go outside before our eyes. And whenever something good happens, whenever they think they're finally going to be happy, some catastrophe comes along to dash their hopes.

But if a soap opera is opera in drag, V. C. Andrews is a drag queen, holding a scented hanky to her heaving bosom, standing in front of an Elvis preacher at a Las Vegas chapel on New Year's Eve. No one ever turns—they spin around with their legs flashing through a thin negligee. There's face cupping and bosom clutching extraordinaire. Fists bleed. Bodies swell. Odors are left, things are returned tenfold! Innocent, Beave-like protestations—"I didn't mean to rape you, I swear to God!" "I just couldn't believe this fantastic tale of something he called 'nocturnal emissions!'— exist alongside cloying, tooclose informations, glances at cleavage, sighs like, "Let me have all those swelling curves that men desire." If there were ever a book meant to be read aloud by Blanche Devereaux, this is it. Andrews writes like a non-native speaker who has done time in a jail where they only show 1960s sitcoms and *One Life to Live*, and my small heart aches and blood runs from many small paper cuts as I read her, beating my small fists on the pages.

Domestic Arrangements

By Norma Klein
1981

Girls on Film

You will forgive me for looking forward, on the day of my 14th birthday, to a battery of mildly unorthodox events. First, there was the old artist who was going to ask me to model nude, compliment me grumpily, then decline to do away with my virginity. There was the awkward boyfriend whom I'd play tennis with who would not. There was the film I might be asked to star in, in which I'd model nude, an act which would be met without comment by my peers, and then there were the parental affairs I'd observe without too much comment either, letting my elders work out their sex roles just as I was working out mine. There were the gallery openings and Upper West Side apartments stuffed with books and African masks I'd visit, and there were the bagels and lox and Chock Full O' Nuts coffee I'd consume while either participating in and/or listening to energetic debates about art, feminism, death, God, sex, the government, and whether or not my boyfriend at the time could sleep over. (He could.) Perhaps when I hit my twenties, I'd even bear the child of one of my two genial lovers, then name him Bruno. Life would be, in short, something like *Manhattan*—but with Mariel Hemingway in the starring role.

I did, in fact, do one or two of those things that year, mainly because I already had (viz: eat bagels and lox, visit apartments stuffed with books) but my life stubbornly refused to produce the remainder, if it did at all, until I was well of age. By then, of course, some of the offers had lost some of their appeal. (The request to model nude, in particular, proceeds past its sell-by date somewhere around the time you turn 17.) But I was only confused, not bereft. I hadn't expected all those things because I was a preternatural sophisticate chomping at the bit, being denied my rightful place in the boho parade. I'd just expected them because I'd read too much Norma Klein.

Cultural gatekeepers appalled at the sex-ready, credit-card-armed avatars of youth culture today should simply instruct their DVRs to continue recording episodes of *Gossip Girl* if they want to keep body and soul together, because opening any Norma Klein novel might actually put them out of commission forever. While it's easy to scapegoat the over-the-top depictions of youth today for, you know, whatever, Klein's characters are far harder to pin down as the enemy. Simply put, they're nice, smart, appealing kids, and they're interested in the idea of sex not only for its own sake, but also to get a sense of how it should fit into a monogamous, loving relationship. It's kind of hard to fault them for that. (Though many would try.) There's only one problem. In the midst of all this philosophical sexual rumination, the darn kids keep *having* it.

Domestic Arrangements' Tatiana Engleberg, who lives with her long-legged soap-actress mom and documentary-director dad, is one of my favorite Klein characters. She's not explicitly sophisticated—in fact, she's mildly giggly and innocent, to the irritation of her older sister, Deel—but she still manages to have innocent, unremarkable sex in the first few pages of the novel ("Then we studied a bit and then we fucked and then we went to sleep"), to the great consternation of her father and to the mild delight of her mother, who seems to welcome her daughter's sexual awakening at the same time she's decided to break out of her own tired marital bubble.

In the course of the novel, Tatiana also manages to star in a film (nude!), get put on the cover of *People* magazine, carry on a relationship with her increasingly jealous boyfriend, Joshua, witness the dalliances of both of her parents, then lie in the arms of a naked gay man whom she finds hot, kissing, while on a jaunt to L.A. It's not hard to imagine what any director would do today with such explosive material—and it seems certain that the notions of *scandal* and *intrigue* would enter the picture. But what's most remarkable about *Domestic Arrangements* is not only how ordinary Tatiana is, but how free the world around her is of any of the notions we take for granted today—irony, image control, the selling of sexuality. (A director takes her to a tennis court to see how she jiggles around, then patiently explains, "If you're a movie star, you're going to be the subject of a lot of men's fantasies.") It might seem strange to long for a time when a pervy director could perve without being pervy rather than long for, say, a time when we all just talked to each other across the room for a few months, then asked our parents if we could got married. But that's why what Klein does is revolutionary. Not only does she write the go-to manual for love and sex. She manages, like whoever that dude is who wrote the Bible, to make it innocent again.

LIZZIE SKURNICK is the columnist for Jezebel.com's *Fine Lines* and the author of ten teen books in the Sweet Valley High, Love Stories, and Alias series. Her literary blog, *Old Hag*, is a Forbes Best of the Web pick. She's on the board of the National Book Critics Circle and has written on books and culture extensively for the *New York Times Book Review*, *Times Sunday Styles*, the *LA Times*, NPR.org, *The Washington Post*, and many other publications.

Lizzie Skurnick